# ENVISIONING EDEN

# New Directions in Anthropology

General Editor: **Jacqueline Waldren**, *Research Associate at the Institute of Social and Cultural Anthropology and International Gender Studies, Oxford University and Director, Deia Archaeological Museum and research Centre, Mallorca.*

Twentieth-century migration, modernization, technology, tourism, and global communication have had dynamic effects on group identities, social values and conceptions of space, place, and politics. This series features new and innovative ethnographic studies concerned with these processes of change.

For a full volume listing of the series, see pages 225 to 226.

# ENVISIONING EDEN

## *Mobilizing Imaginaries in Tourism and Beyond*

Noel B. Salazar

**Berghahn Books**
New York • Oxford

First published in 2010 by

*Berghahn Books*

www.berghahnbooks.com

©2010, 2013 Noel B. Salazar
First paperback edition published in 2013

**Library of Congress Cataloging-in-Publication Data**

Salazar, Noel B., 1973-
    Envisioning eden : mobilizing imaginaries in tourism and beyond / Noel B. Salazar.
        p. cm. — (New directions in anthropology ; v. 31)
    Includes bibliographical references and index.
    ISBN 978-1-84545-760-0 (hbk.)--ISBN 978-0-85745-903-9 (pbk.)
    1. Culture and tourism—Case studies. 2. Tourism—Indonesia—Yogyakarta
3. Tourism—Tanzania—Arusha. I. Title.
    G156.5.H47S35 2010
    338.4'791--dc22

                                                                            2010023976

**British Library Cataloguing in Publication Data**

A catalogue record for this book is available from the British Library

Printed in the United States on acid-free paper.

ISBN: 978-0-85745-903-9 Paperback   ISBN: 978-0-85745-924-4 Retail Ebook

*Nothing is built upon rock, for all is built upon sand,*
*but let each man build as if sand were rock...*
*Jorge Luis Borges*

To all those who guide

# CONTENTS

# FIGURES

❧

## Maps

## Figures

# FOREWORD
# CIRCULATING CULTURE

My first ethnological research in Indonesia was conducted among the Toba Batak, an ethnic group located in the highlands of North Sumatra. I lived in a village community and subsequently extended my work among the Batak to those who had migrated to the coastal city of Medan, to Jakarta and Bandung on the island of Java, and even to Batak settlements in Denpasar, Bali. My objective was to study how Batak culture and identity had changed in different localities and settings.

In the 1980s, I shifted my research focus to the study of tourism in Bali and elsewhere, but I retained my interest in Indonesian and especially Toba Batak identity and cultural change. On one trip to Bali, I stopped off in Jakarta to visit with two of my former students, Koentjaraningrat and Parsudi Suparlan, both of whom were now professors in the anthropology department of the University of Indonesia. I met with anthropology majors and graduate students on social occasions and took the opportunity to interview them informally about issues of identity and particularly about their own experiences living among so many different ethnic groups in Jakarta, the capital and foremost urban centre of Indonesia. My thought was that these young, sophisticated intellectuals would not only have fresh insights but would represent one of the most modern segments of Indonesian society.

They were forthcoming in telling me personal stories of their experiences, and I avidly took field notes, but soon their responses seemed, somehow, hauntingly familiar. I finally realized that they were repeating to me my own analysis of Indonesian identity that I had previously published in venues such as the *American Anthropologist* and in a monograph of the British Association of Social Anthropologists. I learned that my work had been assigned reading in university anthropology classes taught by my former Indonesian students, now professors. There were, of course, individual variations and some adhered to my views more closely than others did, but the basic pattern of my analysis of ethnicity was evident.

Well, I thought, possibly they are just being polite and reserved, following deeply rooted Javanese practice, and are consciously telling me what they thought I wanted to hear. Further inquiry, however, revealed that my writings had become internalized and that they often used Indonesian translations of my own language. My publications had helped to shape their understandings of their own experiences of ethnicity. I felt that they were not dissembling but that they truly believed what they were telling me. After all, how one experiences ethnicity in an urban setting—with others from many different ethnic backgrounds who speak not only standard Indonesian but also mutually unintelligible ethnic languages and have varied ethnic customs—is often inchoate, or not consciously articulated, so that an interpretation in writing, taught by their instructors at the university, based on the research of a high-status foreign scholar takes on a degree of credibility and authority that is hard to resist. There are in Indonesia over three hundred different ethnolinguistic groups, spread over a three-thousand-mile-long archipelago, and how one practices ethnicity has to be balanced against the official government position stressing a single Indonesian identity. The national government's principle is unity in diversity, but how ethnicity is handled in Indonesia is complex, politically loaded, often felt as a struggle and is frequently contested. Possibly the students welcomed an authoritative perspective that served to settle what had been problematic.

What a predicament! I thought I was gathering new ethnological field data but actually the students were repeating myself to me. My writings were used to interpret their experiences, which were then fed back to me as fresh ethnographic information. That early encounter in Jakarta, however, was not the only time this has happened.

Noel Salazar, in his stunning book *Envisioning Eden,* writes that 'Pak Hardi, the Yogyakarta chairperson of HPI (Indonesian Tourist Guide Association), has a Bachelor's degree in anthropology from Gadjah Mada University. When I was in Tanzania, I received a message from him, proudly telling me he is now using Bruner's *Culture on Tour: Ethnographies of Travel* (2005) in his classes'. Thus, the chair of the Yogyakarta tour guide association is using my book to teach prospective tour guides about tourism. If in the future I were to study tour guides in Central Java, it is entirely possible that they would present the substance of my own writings back to me, or at least they might interpret their experiences of tourism in light of my work. So where is the dividing line between raw data in the field and our own scholarly anthropological research reports? In the past, we anthropologists made a firm distinction between those in the field, the natives, the source of the data and our ethnographic analysis and theorizing, but for at least three decades this distinction has been called into question and is increasingly losing its standing in our globalizing world. Culture is circulating, and the subject and the object are merging.

I have elsewhere illustrated how these processes work on the cultural level, and how blurred the binary opposition is between ethnography and tourism (Bruner 2005: 198–201). In Bali in the 1970s, a cultural performance called the 'frog dance' was invented for tourist consumption. The dance drama was a purely commercial production, an innovation, and had no 'authentic' counterpart located elsewhere in Balinese culture. In the 1980s, however, that frog dance began to be performed at Balinese weddings so that what had emerged in tourism had entered Balinese ritual performance. Sometime in the future, an ethnographer studying life-cycle rituals in Bali who is unaware of how the frog dance developed might well describe it as a 'traditional' part of Balinese wedding ceremonies. Similarly, the *kecak* or monkey dance created by the German painter Walter Spies in the 1930s was performed for Ronald Reagan on his 1986 presidential visit to Bali. It was presented as emblematic of Bali even though it was not part of indigenous Balinese ritual, but was a new dance drama invented a half-century ago by a German artist working with Balinese dancers.

To switch culture areas, in East Africa, at the Kichwa Tembo camp on the Masai Mara game reserve, the tourists attend what is called the *Out Of Africa Sundowner* performance. The phrase 'Out of Africa' is familiar to Americans as it is the title of the 1985 Hollywood movie starring Robert Redford and Meryl Streep, based upon Isak Dinesen's 1938 book about life in colonial Kenya. At the event, Maasai warriors circle the performance space, singing and dancing among the tourists who are standing or sitting on folding chairs. The camp employees then sing the Kenyan song *Jambo Bwana,* which welcomes the tourists to Kenya and contains the phrase *Hakuna Matata,* which means 'no worries, no problems', a familiar phrase to an American audience as it is the theme song, written by Elton John, of the 1994 animated Disney film, *The Lion King.* The hotel employees at the Sundowner follow by singing *Kum Ba Yah,* a song originating in Africa but popular in America as a spiritual, folk, protest and gospel song.

What has happened here? *Hakuna Matata* and *Kum Ba Yah* are understood in American pop culture as associated with Africa and blackness, so that American understandings are re-presented to American tourists in Africa by Africans at a Maasai dance performance. Anthropologists know well that transnational influences are widespread, that culture flows around the globe and that global images of African tribesmen are shown to foreign tourists. This is not news. What is news, however, is that Americans who have travelled far to experience African culture are instead presented with American cultural content that is essentially an American image of black Africa. The tourists accept this presentation as it is familiar and well known, and hence feels authentic (Bruner 2005: 83–87).

Finally, we may turn to *Envisioning Eden,* a study of tour guides in Yogyakarta, Indonesia, and Arusha, Tanzania. As local tour guides are the primary agents who explain the local peoples and sites along the tourist itinerary, a key research question becomes: how do guides acquire the information that they tell to the tourists? The 'common sense' answer would be that the tour guides, embedded as they are in the indigenous milieu and setting, would explain the local to the tourists based upon their own knowledge and experience. The foreign tourists in turn, naïve as they are about the destination culture, would learn based upon the tour guide tellings as well as their own observations. This picture is too simplistic, as Salazar shows. In the first place there are no naïve tourists as they all have some familiarity with the places they are to visit, their pre-tour understandings, which they acquire from the tour brochures and multiple other sources before they leave for their journey. The predicament of the tour guides is that they must become aware of the tourist preunderstandings or worldview if they are to communicate with them. They must be able to see their own culture through the eyes of the tourist. In my experience in Indonesia and Africa, the best tour guides have an easy familiarity with Western culture with the consequence that they can more readily explain the destination culture in terms that will be understood by the tourist. Salazar shows us how these processes work in great detail and presents the remarkable ethnographic finding that the tourists and the tour guides share the same global imaginaries and master narratives. How does this happen?

Salazar writes, 'Most guides . . . learn about tourist imaginaries ... (through) foreign televised documentaries (National Geographic, Discovery Channel and History Channel), guidebooks (Periplus, Insight Guides, Lonely Planet, Le Routard and The Rough Guide), newspapers and magazines. ... in-flight and travel magazines (often received from tourists).'. These are, of course, exactly the sources that shape the tourist imaginaries and preunderstandings. Similar sources are used by schools teaching tour guiding, so that the guides are indoctrinated 'with foreign interpretations of their own natural and cultural heritage'. It is indeed a globalized world.

One wonders if these foreign-based interpretations, which so permeate tour guide dialogue, have also moved beyond the tourism sphere to influence how local peoples view their own culture. In Bali, foreign fascination with the *barong* and trance dances led the Balinese to enhance the importance of the barong in their own cultural practices. Tourism imaginaries do circulate locally and become part of how indigenous people interpret their own culture to themselves. In 1998, I taught a tourism seminar at the Chinese University of Hong Kong and I required that my students conduct tourism research and present a paper at end of semester. Tourism is big business in Hong Kong—in 2005 there were 28 million visitor arrivals—and the Hong Kong Tourist Board is the designated government agency to devise advertising campaigns to promote tourism. My students reported that materials created by the Tourist Board to enhance foreign tourism were used by Hong Kong residents to explain their own culture, not only to foreigners but also to themselves.

Of course, culture does not circulate in a closed system, an endlessly repetitious loop, for there is change and innovation. We anthropologists know that every replication is a transformation, for as Geertz has famously said, copying originates. Performance is constitutive. However, the master narratives about well-known tourist destinations have shown a remarkable continuity over the years. Tourist Egypt is the land of the pyramids and the pharaohs focused on the very ancient past, to the neglect of Egyptian historical and cultural development over the last few thousand years. I was one of a group of scholars who examined tourism imaginaries of the Maasai and other East African pastoralists—those proud and noble warriors—and we found a remarkable stability over the past century. The image of Bali, the island paradise, the land of beauty and mysticism, has been essentially unchanged in its main themes at least since the 1920s, when tourism promotion began in earnest by Dutch companies. Worldwide, new elements have been added to global imaginaries, such as the recent concern with the environment, the preservation of indigenous cultures and eco-tourism, but old narratives are still the mainstay of tourism imaginaries, which suppress as much as they reveal. They focus on those particular aspects of culture and time periods that resonate most deeply in Western culture.

I found this book so evocative and so full of insights and new perspectives that I could continue with my free associations and reflections, but I will stop here to allow the readers to experience the adventure of reading *Envisioning Eden* on their own.

**Edward M. Bruner**
Professor Emeritus
University of Illinois at Urbana-Champaign

# PREFACE

❦

Everything is connected, everything changes, pay attention
—Jane Hirshfield (poet; 1953– )

From 5 to 8 May 2002, the American Association for Thoracic Surgery organized its 82nd Annual Meeting at the Washington Convention Center in Washington, DC. Not that I was present or am particularly interested in this medical specialty, but while conducting ethnographic fieldwork in Africa on an entirely different subject, I was reminded about this conference almost every day. Joseph, my Tanzanian research assistant, had bought one of the meeting bags—made in China—on the second-hand clothing market in Tengeru village. Because the black-coloured sack is made of solid canvas and has a top zipper closure and a frontal flap, it provides ideal protection against the fine reddish dust that is so common in the Arusha region. One day, after having finished a lengthy interview with a senior safari guide, Joseph and I were relaxing with a coffee on the terrace of Stiggbucks Coffee, a local copycat version of Starbucks. I was daydreaming about the lovely time I spent in Indonesia the year before, recalling the equally tasty cappuccino at Debucks Coffee in Yogyakarta. Joseph used my mental absence to order his own thoughts and suddenly remembered he had something for me. He opened his classy bag and, after rummaging through it, pulled out a VCD of the Discovery Channel documentary *Natural Born Winners*. I was dumbfounded when I noticed that the cover of the illegal copy was not in English but Indonesian. 'I thought this might interest you', Joseph confided in a stage whisper with a radiant smile.

This anecdote about Joseph's bag and its contents reinforces the common impression (especially among people in affluent countries, institutions and positions) that we live in an era of constant flux, with people, goods and ideas flowing in every direction across the planet. Anthropologists—the academic clan to which I belong—are, with the exception of impersonators of Indiana Jones, no longer spending time among allegedly lost 'tribes' in remote jungles. Instead, we earn our intellectual stripes by investigating the global reach of broad issues such as migration and diaspora; cosmopolitanism and transnationalism; markets, factory labour and commodity chains; grassroots organizing, environmentalism and human rights; and information and communication technologies, media and public culture. Yet, our surprise and wonder at the speed, intensity and extent of global mobilities and interconnections has the danger of overlooking those people, places and things that are immobile or disconnected, be it temporarily or permanently. No, not everything is connected, and not everything changes, so we had better pay attention to what is happening around us.

A deceivingly simple question triggered the research on which this book is based: why is a Belgian nonprofit association inviting a select group of Indonesian and Tanzanian tour guides jointly to Europe for a crash course in intercultural communication? In March 2002—shortly before the meeting of the American Association for Thoracic Surgery in Washington—I was in Belgium, finishing a master's degree in Cultures and Development Studies. Knowing my fascination for travel and tourism, one of my fellow students invited me to an event of the NGO for which she was working. Under the name 'dialogue trip', they had invited five Indonesian and five Tanzanian tour guides for a one-month visit to Western Europe. During this period, the group underwent an intense two-week experience as international tourists—a kind of role-reversal exercise—and they participated in an interactive course on professional guiding and intercultural communication, while staying with guest families. I attended some of the activities and kept an eye on the rest of the journey through the guides' online diary (a precursor to modern-day blogs).

My initial reflections upon this remarkable event resulted in many questions. While I clearly saw the benefits of giving tourism workers from developing countries a travel and training experience in Europe, the encounter between Indonesians and Tanzanians intrigued me. Not only did the guides come from dissimilar sociocultural backgrounds, they were working in quite distinct types of tourism, respectively cultural tourism and wildlife tourism. What did they themselves get out of this experience and what did they think about being brought together with such 'exotic' colleagues? Unfortunately, the guides had returned to their countries before I had a chance to talk to them. Little did I know that my pursuit for answers would involve an extensive personal voyage, literally transporting me around the globe—from Europe to the United States, and from Indonesia to Tanzania and beyond—and leading to a completely new set of issues. As I discovered along the way, this was not a straightforward story about development cooperation, tourism or cross-cultural exchange, but a complicated case of transnational networking and cosmopolitan mobility, reconfirming the enduring power of the human imagination and revealing the manifold ways in which discourses and practices of local-to-global processes intersect, overlap and clash.

Even though globalization—a scarcely structured assembly of multifaceted processes that operate simultaneously in diverse realms across the globe—is a popular concept among academics, activists and policy-makers, the human mechanics behind it are poorly understood. How does globalization work and who are the globalization workers? In what directions do people, objects and ideas move across the planet, how and why do they circulate, and what does this tell us, more generally, about the current human condition? Concrete attentiveness to human agency, to the social practices and cultural negotiations of everyday life, gives us insight not only into how people mediate, oppose, contest and reformulate processes of global mobility, but also into how they, often unconsciously, replicate and reinforce them. Such analyses gain even more weight when they are embedded in larger historical and material contexts, describing the institutions and power relations through which globalization as well as localization (or local differentiation) are made possible. This book aims precisely to apply such a holistic approach. An ambitious agenda, so it seems, but not an impossible one.

## Travel Mobilities

When I set out to conduct ethnographic research on tour guiding in Yogyakarta, Indonesia, and Arusha, Tanzania, I was mainly interested in studying the interplay between global(ized) tourismscapes and local service providers in two destinations, or, more broadly, in researching the intricate ways in which processes of globalization and localization interconnect and collide with one another. Only when I was invited to speak at a plenary session of the European Association of Social Anthropologists biennial meeting in Ljubljana, Slovenia, I began to conceptualize my findings in terms of (im)mobility. The enthusiastic comments by Dame Marilyn Strathern and Ulf Hannerz, who were among the EASA audience, stimulated me to fine-tune my theorizing along these lines. The constructive feedback I received after the invited lectures I gave at the University of Leuven, the University of California at Berkeley and the University Paris 1 Panthéon-Sorbonne inspired me even more. It is a happy coincidence that this book is published as part of a Berghahn book series entitled 'New Directions in Anthropology' (implying movement too). It is not difficult to see that international tourism, which is both constituted by and constitutive of globalization, includes huge movements of people (tourists as well as tourism workers), capital (investments and tourist dollars), technologies of travel and the circulation of closely related tourism media and imaginaries. In tourism studies, paradoxically, the tendency has been to see places in developing countries (and, by consequence, their inhabitants) defined by immobility, and international travel as something that happens in a sort of nonplace between home and destination. Even though some authors hint at the mobility of locals living and working in tourist settings, others seem to silently reinforce the false binary between the ephemeral roles of mobile tourists (or researchers, for that matter) and place-bound locals. This, of course, tells us more about the positionality of the scholars themselves than about the reality on the ground.

The core of tourism consists of people's movements that have helped tear down certain borders, but these processes and practices have erected new boundaries too. While tourism marketers and imagineers represent the world as borderless, in reality travel for leisure is heavily regulated and monitored on local, national, regional and global levels. This affects tourists as well as tourism workers, a fact corroborated by this study on local tour guiding. Even if the development of the guiding profession and tour-guide policies in Indonesia and Tanzania are at different levels, the parallels are striking. In both countries, there is increasing control, an ongoing process that is steered internationally, legalized nationally and implemented locally (although the latter is the weakest element in the chain). The multiple inequalities entrenched in international tourism between tourists, tourism intermediaries and locals serve as a reminder that boundaries do not exist naturally but are made in social practices. Divisions can occur along lines of social class, gender, age, ethnicity, race and nationality. Destinations of travel try to maintain, or increase, a distinctive local identity while at the same time undergoing homogenizing global influences. It is noteworthy that anthropology does not play a neutral role in the tourism business of maximizing differences over similarity. Tourism marketers borrow from traditional ethnology an ontological and essentialist vision of exotic cultures, conceived as static entities with clearly defined characteristics. Ideas of old-style colonial anthropology—objectifying, reifying, homogenizing and naturalizing peoples—are widely used by tourismified communities, staking their claims of identity and cultural belonging on strong notions of place and locality. Ironically, this is happening at a time when anthropologists themselves prefer more constructivist approaches, taking it for granted that cultures and societies are not passive, bounded and homogeneous entities.

Scholars from a variety of disciplines have come up with possible reasons why people desire to travel. This book illustrates how historically laden fantasies are at the roots of many physical as well as imagined journeys to unknown destinations. Empowered by mass-mediated master narratives, such imaginaries have become global. They are sent, circulated, transferred, received, accumulated, converted and stored around the world. Studying the (im)mobility of these imaginaries offers a novel way to grasp the ongoing transformations of globalization. During my fieldwork, I gathered ample evidence that the daily lives and practices of people in Yogyakarta and Arusha are shaped by any number of imaginative as well as real links to other worlds near and far. Innumerable border crossings, physical or virtual, are generating ever-thickening webs of interconnectivity that help people not only to envision the world at large, but also to become aware of how localities such as Yogyakarta and Arusha are positioned within the transnational nexus of places. Increasingly, people are beginning to imagine the possible lives that might be available 'out there' because widely circulating imaginaries are convincing them that life is 'better' in those other places.

It is important to stress from the outset that it was never my aim to compare Yogyakarta and Arusha in a direct manner. Rather, I wanted to illustrate ethnographically how similar global processes are operating in two very different tourism destinations. However, while conducting fieldwork, every now and then something would link my two sites, illustrating the remarkable transnational circulation of people, objects and ideas. Joseph's VCD, mentioned earlier on, is only one example. In Arusha, I met a PhD student in anthropology from the University of Wisconsin who was conducting research in Tanzania but who had, the year before, accompanied her husband when he was doing fieldwork in Indonesia. I also came across tour leaders and international tour guides who had worked in both Arusha and Yogyakarta. An Australian lawyer working for the UN International Criminal Tribunal for Rwanda in Arusha had previously operated as a tour leader in Indonesia. The most incredible connection was directly related to my research. When I joined a group of European tourists on a cultural tour in Arusha, one of them came up to me and enthusiastically greeted me. 'What are you doing here? I thought you were doing research on tourism in Indonesia!' I did not immediately recognize the woman. Apparently, I had observed a tour in Yogyakarta the year before in which she had participated as a tourist too. This served as a humble reminder that not only anthropologists engage in multisited activities these days. Informants can be more mobile than fieldworkers are and their border-crossing wanderings increasingly set our ethnographic course.

The start of my fieldwork in East Africa coincided with the seventh World Social Forum in Nairobi, Kenya. Because my spouse works in the NGO sector and our plane was landing in Nairobi, attending the forum was an opportunity not to be missed. There were around 25,000 participants, representing 1,400 organizations from 110 countries. What we had imagined to be an informative global happening turned out to be a commercialized fair of social movements and international NGOs vying for attention and power. The utopias and promises of a better world that were sold on the forum grounds were far removed from the harsh reality just outside the stadium where the activities took place. The participating activists and idealists were reminded of this in a rather shameful way when dwellers from the nearby Kibera slum stormed the gates to protest against the meeting, criticizing the high price of entry and the soaring cost of food sold around the premises. I saw this rather sad event as a reconfirmation that processes of globalization are exceedingly differentiated and uneven, that they are as much about people as anything else is, and that powerful imaginaries are (mis)used outside tourism too.

## Fieldwork Facts

I carried out fieldwork over a period of 25 months, 14 months of which I was in Indonesia (July–August 2003, January–December 2006) and 11 months in Tanzania (June–August 2004, January–August 2007). In Indonesia, the research mainly took place in the Javanese Special Province of Yogyakarta (see Map 1), in Tanzania in the northern Arusha Region (see Map 2). Ethnographic data collection is somewhat an art of the possible, where one always has to keep an eye out for new opportunities. The methodology I used, distinctively (though not uniquely) anthropological, involved mixed methods. The advantage of relying on various kinds of data is that it allows you to crosscheck information by comparing sources (data triangulation). I started collecting data long before I embarked on my fieldwork. I systematically kept track of information appearing on the World Wide Web and other media sources concerning Yogyakarta and Arusha and I had regular virtual exchanges with local contacts in both places.

Although I had been to Southeast Asia as a tourist and visited East Africa for work, it was only by being there for longer periods that I started perceiving the many similarities Yogyakarta and Arusha share. Both are quickly expanding and modernizing medium-sized cities, offering an excellent quality of life compared to the rest of the country. As such, they draw people from far and wide (even from beyond the country's borders), leading to ethnically mixed populations. Being centres of higher learning, with universities and professional schools, the cities attract young people and stimulate a vibrant youth culture. There is also a similar linguistic situation, with trade languages (Indonesian and Swahili) as the main means of communication, combined with a dominant local language (Javanese and Maa). Both cities breed a cosmopolitan atmosphere, marked by sizable expatriate communities (businesspeople, missionaries, students, volunteers, etc.) and a whole infrastructure (an international airport, international schools, multinational corporations, and transnational hotel, restaurant and shopping chains). Related to this, Yogyakarta and Arusha are tourism hotspots, mainly because of their location. As a result, many locals try to make a (partial) living from tourism-related business.

A major part of the fieldwork consisted of extensive observation. As a participant, I joined tourists on twenty-eight tours in central Java and twenty-four trips in northern Tanzania. This was not as enjoyable as it would seem, because I visited the same sights repeatedly, but had to remain sharp-eyed and -eared. After a while, I became so accustomed to the common guiding narratives and practices that I could easily have started taking tourists around myself (some local guides actually suspected that was my main final aim). I discuss most of these data in chapters 4 and 6. The tours I joined lasted from a minimum of one hour to one week. Because the reproduction of entire guiding narratives would take up far too much space here, I instead present multiple small snippets that illustrate theoretical points, and I provide enough background information to place the fragments in their wider context of occurrence. As an observer, I spent countless hours socializing with local tour guides and informally talking to them. These different types of observation led to hundreds of pages of field notes. The second-most important source of data are interviews. I conducted and recorded in-depth interviews with guides (26, 30) and semistructured interviews with people involved in guide training (6, 7), local tour operators (5, 15) and tourism authorities at local, national and regional levels (11, 13). The numbers in parentheses indicate how many people I interviewed in Indonesia and Tanzania respectively. In Yogyakarta, I selected guides from the member list given to me by the Indonesian Tourist Guide Association (HPI), and most interviews were conducted in Indonesian. In

Arusha, the easiest way to contact tour guides was through local tour operators, and the interviews were predominantly in English.

Almost all the interviewed guides agreed to fill in a questionnaire that collected basic demographic information and data on education, guiding, tour preparation and information resources, travel experience, hobbies and the use of new information and communication technologies. My local assistants carried out additional short, structured street interviews with locals (35, 23). We transcribed all interviews shortly after conducting them. In order to protect the anonymity of the people who participated in this research through interviews or observation, I have changed all information that could possibly identify them (e.g., by using pseudonyms). Exceptions to this rule are statements made by official functionaries in their public roles. In addition to observations and interviews, I collected various types of secondary data: newspaper and magazine articles, online publications, official documents (e.g., tourism laws and regulations), tour guiding syllabi and all kinds of tourism-related brochures, pamphlets and other promotional materials. In Indonesia, I gathered supplementary data from tourists through a short questionnaire on tour guiding; in Tanzania, I obtained the same information talking to tourists during safaris. In all instances of data collection, I identified myself as a foreign researcher or anthropologist and, if appropriate, I showed the official accreditation provided by the Indonesian Institute of Sciences (LIPI) and the Tanzanian Commission for Science and Technology (COSTECH).

I did extensive background literature research at various libraries: the University of Pennsylvania and the University of California at Berkeley in the United States; Gadjah Mada University, Sanata Dharma University and the Stuppa Indonesia Foundation for Tourism Research and Development in Indonesia; the University of Dar es Salaam, the Economic and Social Research Foundation, Research on Poverty Alleviation and the Professional Tour Guide School in Tanzania; and the University of Leuven in Belgium. In addition, I consulted the Indonesian collections of the Australian National University and the National Library of Australia in Canberra and the National University of Singapore, and the African collections of the Africa Museum in Belgium. Tapping into various literatures—on anthropology and ethnography, globalization and mobility, tourism and travel, Indonesia and Tanzania—might have been time consuming, but it allowed me to make theoretical and conceptual connections I never would have made otherwise.

My spouse accompanied me intellectually throughout the research and physically on the two longer stays abroad. She was of tremendous help with many practicalities (housing, paperwork, etc.). In addition, she acted as an extra source of information (e.g., during the earthquake in Yogyakarta), and the networks she developed through her own professional activities facilitated my access to key informants in unexpected ways (e.g., contact with the expatriate communities in Arusha). Without her, I would never have known, for instance, that the Arusha monthly women's book club was reading and discussing novels such as *The White*

*Maasai*—a book (turned into a movie) whose popularity draws on the same class of romantic ideas about East Africa that prevail in tourism imaginaries as well.

To date, my research assistants and some of my contacts keep me informed about what is happening in Yogyakarta and Arusha through e-mail and short text messages (SMS). These information and communication technologies also came in handy during my fieldwork. Without a cell phone, it would have been impossible to (re)schedule meetings and I would have obtained much less information, and not instantaneously. In fact, I did not possess a cell phone before starting my fieldwork. It was one of my first purchases in Indonesia because I quickly realized that exchanging messages (rather than actually phoning) was one of the most prevalent ways of communication. This was even truer for Tanzania, where landlines are rare but cell phones are common. It was through SMS that a fellow anthropologist informed me about bribery at the Prambanan temple complex minutes after it happened and that a Tanzanian driver-guide on his way to a national park told me about a robbery in which a colleague of his had been attacked.

As a final point, a note on language. Research on international tourism often involves complex linguistic situations, and this is especially so when focusing on tour guides who are themselves multilingual. I studied Indonesian informally and through an intensive language course in Yogyakarta. I took elementary and intermediate Swahili at the University of Pennsylvania and received private tutoring while in Arusha. Due to my multicultural European background, I am also fluent in Dutch, French, Spanish, German and Italian. Proficiency in these languages was of great value when observing the interactions between tourists and guides and when interviewing people (and it gave me the much-admired status of an experienced cosmopolitan). This book contains words or phrases in several of these foreign languages. When not clear from the context, I will mark the languages as follows: I = Indonesian (national language of Indonesia), J = Javanese (language spoken by the Javanese, the dominant ethnic group on Java), S = Swahili (national language of Tanzania) and M = Maa (language spoken by the Maasai, the dominant ethnic group in many parts of the Arusha Region). Other languages will be indicated. All translations are my own. In order to increase intelligibility, I made minor corrections to the English used by nonnative speakers.

This is neither a travel ethnography nor, strictly speaking, an ethnography about travel. Instead, I invite you on a mental journey that explores some interesting theoretical and methodological horizons. There are no special requirements to participate, only an open mind. As your tour guide, I will take you along well-trodden paths and landscapes as well as less-known trails and viewpoints. In order not to get lost, we will need to revisit some places—a déjà vu can be reassuring now and then. To arrive to the most exciting sites, the highlights of the trip, we will unavoidably have to pass through some more mundane backgrounds. Please remember that not everything is connected (and not everything changes).

# ACKNOWLEDGMENTS

The writing of this book was made possible thanks to the generosity and kindness of many people, tour guides and others, who opened their homes for me and who shared their ideas. In Indonesia, I affectionately remember the hospitality of Martina Slamet Riyadi and her family; the intellectual assistance of James Spillane, Mie Cornoedus, Hendrie Kusworo, Muhammad Baiquni and Wiendu Nuryanti; the practical help of Hardi Wahyono, Pak Murteja and Pak Santoso, Vita Ferida, Yusup Sudadi, Agnes Priyanti and Christian Awuy; and the good company of Eric, Koen, Yvonne and Petrus, Dhani, Shirin, Wina and Ari, Daniel and Diah, Junaidi, Rina, Ruli, the 'jilbab trio' (especially Tyas) and the entire ViaVia team. In Tanzania, special thanks go to the people of Centre House for their hospitality; Vedasto and Victor Izoba, Horace Nassary, Willy Lyimo, Mustafa Akunaay, Mary Lwoga, Barbara Cole, Thomas Holden, Mary Rijnberg and Liz McKee for disclosing the local tourism scene; Francis Lyimo and the late Chachage Seithy Chachage for their academic contributions; Aaron and Anton, Dominiek and Kristin, Dirk and Inneke, Axel and Leen, Jo and Judith, the Canadian medical volunteers from the University of Western Ontario and the staff of the ViaVia for ensuring continuous social activities. Without the advice of Rita Daneels the research undertaken for this book would have been completely different. Nelden and Joseph Djakababa and Asumpta Ngonyani were perfect hosts in Jakarta and Dar es Salaam respectively. My local assistants deserve credit for helping me throughout the fieldwork: Robert Suharyanto, Erlis Saputra and Sazkia Noor Anggraini in Yogyakarta, and Samwel Rwahura and Joseph Ole Sanguyan in Arusha.

Gadjah Mada University in Indonesia and the University of Dar es Salaam in Tanzania acted as the local institutional sponsors, while the Indonesian Institute of Sciences (LIPI Research Permit No. 8093/SU/KS/2005) and the Tanzanian Commission for Science and Technology (COSTECH Research Permit No. 2007–16-NA-2006–171) gave me the necessary research clearance. Finding funding for multi-sited ethnographic research was a challenging undertaking. The University of Pennsylvania repeatedly expressed its belief in my project through a four-year William Penn Fellowship and two one-year Fellowships from the School of Arts and Sciences. Funding for the actual fieldwork came in the form of two Field Research Grants from the Department of Anthropology and a Research Improvement Grant (and Supplement) from the National Science Foundation (Awards No. BCS-0514129 and BCS-0608991). A Marie Curie International Reintegration Grant of the Seventh European Community Framework Programme (Grant Agreement No. PIRG03-GA-2008–230892) and a Fellowship of the Research Foundation—Flanders (FWO PDO No. 1.2.210.09. N) made it possible to finalize this manuscript.

At Penn's Department of Anthropology, Sandra Barnes, Peggy Sanday and Greg Urban steered my research in the good direction. Without their constructive feedback, this piece of writing would have been much less sophisticated. Deborah Thomas, Kathleen Hall and other faculty provided additional guidance. Steve Feierman, Paul Kaiser and the African Studies Center deserve credit for familiarizing me with East Africa, while Asif Agha and Stanton Wortham sharpened my curiosity in linguistic anthropology. Many of my peers were instrumental in shaping my theoretical thinking. Vida Bajc from the Department of Sociology stimulated my interest in researching tourism. In my own department, archaeologist Benjamin Porter did the same. Brian Daniels provided detailed comments on various drafts of this text. Nelson Graburn and his multidisciplinary Tourism Studies Working Group at the University of California at Berkeley made me feel at home in the Bay Area and, much to my surprise, in Singapore as well.

Jacqueline Waldren from the University of Oxford was quickly convinced that this manuscript would be a valuable addition to her 'New Directions in Anthropology' series. She, publisher Marion Berghahn and the dedicated staff at Berghahn Books skilfully guided me throughout the production process. Thanks to Pascal Vermeersch for his professional advice on the cover of the book, to Steven Demeyer for allowing me to use one of his photographs and to all my other friends for keeping me 'sane' throughout the writing process. My gratitude goes to my parents and other relatives, who supported me from a distance. Last, but far from least, I want to acknowledge my spouse, Monica Espinoza. Without her unconditional help and continuous feedback, I would never have been able to finish this ambitious project successfully. She, together with Keila Luna and Eva Yani, our two cute daughters, are the ones who 'keep me going'.

Noel B. Salazar
Brussels, Summer 2010

# Abbreviations

APEC — Asia-Pacific Economic Cooperation
ASEAN — Association of Southeast Asian Nations
ASITA — Association of Indonesian Tour and Travel Agencies
BAPARDA — Badan Pariwisata Daerah (Provincial Tourism Office; Yogyakarta)
CTP — Cultural Tourism Programme (Tanzania)
EAC — East African Community
HPI — Himpunan Pramuwisata Indonesia (Indonesian Tourist Guide Association)
IDR — Indonesian Rupiah
ILO — International Labour Organization
NCAA — Ngorongoro Conservation Area Authority
PAPTA — Paguyuban Pemandu Wisata Nusantara (Archipelagic Association of Guides)
SADC — Southern African Development Community
TANAPA — Tanzania National Parks
TATO — Tanzania Association of Tour Operators
TTB — Tanzania Tourist Board
TTGA — Tanzania Tour Guides Association
TZS — Tanzanian Shilling
UNDP — United Nations Development Programme
UNEP — United Nations Environment Programme
UNESCO — United Nations Educational, Scientific and Cultural Organization
UNWTO — United Nations World Tourism Organization
WFTGA — World Federation of Tourist Guide Associations
WTTC — World Travel and Tourism Council

MAP 1 • *Map of Indonesia, Showing the Special Province of Yogyakarta*
(Adapted from Wikipedia)

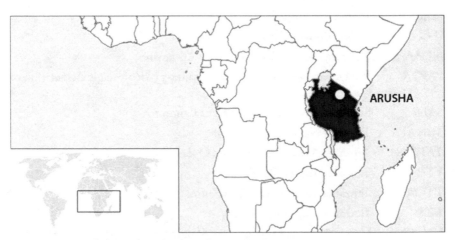

MAP 2 • *Map of Tanzania, Showing the Arusha Region*
(Adapted from Wikipedia)

# 1
# PREPARING A ROADMAP

The notion of globalization functions as an omnipotent metaphor, evoking images of a world in continuous motion, with people, cultures, goods, money, businesses, diseases, media, images and ideas flowing in every direction across the planet.[1] The phenomena and processes that we think of as global refer implicitly or directly to border-crossing mobilities (cf. Urry 2007).[2] The scholarly literature is replete with concepts and metaphors attempting to clarify altered or intensified spatial and temporal realities, including the experience of large-scale movements: deterritorialization and scapes; time–space compression; the network society and its space of flows; cosmopolitanism, and the possibility of leading bifocal and multifocal lives in several locations simultaneously through transnational migration. Some scholars have named this trend the 'mobility turn' in the social sciences, challenging their colleagues to change the objects of inquiry and the methodologies for research (Hannam, Sheller and Urry 2006). It is no coincidence that many of these academics developed their mobility framework while studying tourism, the business of travel for leisure, which is characterized by huge movements of people (tourists as well as tourism workers), capital (investments and tourist dollars), technologies of travel and the circulation of closely related tourism media and imaginaries (Sheller and Urry 2004). This book equally uses tourism as an analytical entry to examine issues of corporeal and imaginative human mobility with a global reach. However, before delving into the crux of the subject matter, it is essential to delineate the broader theoretical field within which this study engages and to refine the conceptual tools needed to approach and analyze the problems under investigation.

## Travel Warnings

If you reject the food, ignore the customs, fear the religion and
avoid the people, you might better stay at home.
–James Mitchener (writer; 1907–1997)

While doing fieldwork at the Buddhist shrine of Borobudur, near Yogyakarta, I heard the story of Philip Beale. After having finished a study on Papua New Guinean traditional canoes in 1982, this young Englishman switched roles from researcher to tourist and explored neighbouring Indonesia. When he arrived on the island of Java, he visited Borobudur. There, he came across a 1,200-year-old carved stone relief of a vessel with outriggers like the wings of a bird. Beale was convinced this was the kind of boat daring Asian seafarers had used, even centuries before Borobudur was erected, to sail across the Indian Ocean to East Africa. This journey formed part of the ancient Cinnamon Route, which brought spices from the Indonesian archipelago to East Africa and then onto Egypt and Europe. Beale pulled together a team of experts to build a replica vessel and, in 2003, successfully made the crossing—aptly calling his project the Borobudur Ship Expedition.

Archaeological and historical research has shown that, after 600 BCE, an expansive Indian Ocean trading system developed (LaBianca and Scham 2004). This oceanic commercial enterprise was bounded on the east by the Indonesian archipelago and the lands surrounding the South China Sea, on the north by the coasts of southern India and Sri Lanka, on the northwest by the Persian Gulf and southern Arabia and on the west by the East African coasts, with Zanzibar as a stepping stone to sail further south and even around the Cape of Good Hope (Rofé 1980). Asian merchants brought to Africa many spices and the living shoots of banana and coconut trees, rice plants and various types of yams. They returned with ivory and rhinoceros horn, tortoise shells, animal skins and African slaves. Their perilous round-trip journeys took up to three years to complete. Although sailors from the Indonesian archipelago were among the earliest Asians to reach and settle on the East African coast, there is little material evidence left of this historical cultural exchange, apart from striking similarities between Indonesian and East African musical instruments (xylophones, musical bows and slit iron bells), board games and traditional canoes (Jones 1971).[3] The 2004 Indian Ocean tsunami served as a vivid reminder of the interconnectedness of the Indian Ocean region (and both Indonesia and Tanzania were hit).

The encounter I witnessed in Belgium between Indonesian and Tanzanian tour guides in 2002 (see Preface) is thus far from being a pioneering one, but inscribes itself in a long and rich history of human mobility and cultural contact. Clearly, globalization—'the intensification of global interconnectedness, suggesting a world full of movement and mixture, contact and linkages and persistent cultural interaction and exchange' (Inda and Rosaldo 2007: 4)—is not a wholly new phenomenon (cf. Featherstone 2006; Mintz 1998). Some might raise objections because the ancient Indian Ocean trading system or the Cinnamon Route never covered the entire globe, but very few present-day processes labelled as 'global' actually do (Cooper 2001). A major difference is that it does not take months and monsoons anymore to get from Indonesia to Tanzania (or anywhere else) and back. For many people, the ever-increasing speed, intensity and extent of globalizing processes is accelerating the experience of time and reducing the significance of distance, what Harvey calls 'time-space compression' (1989: 240). However, archaeological and historical records show not only that humankind has always been characterized by mobility but also that certain groups were actually more physically mobile in the past than they are now (e.g., nomadic pastoralist groups such as the Maasai).

A second caveat is that human mobility is spread very unevenly within societies and across the planet. The world may be full of mobilities and complex interconnections, but there are also huge numbers of people whose experience is marginal to or excluded from these movements and links. Processes of globalization are patently structured and regulated, such that while certain groups are permitted to travel and cross borders, others are not. For the very processes that produce movement and global linkages also promote immobility, exclusion and disconnection (Tsing 2005; Cunningham and Heyman 2004). Some people argue that 'the West continues to travel to its peripheries for pleasure, whereas the reverse migration is still, by and large, rooted in the labour requirements dictated by the North' (Gogia 2006: 373–74). However, this ethnography illustrates that the transnational movements of people are much more complex than a simple binary opposition between rich northern tourists and poor southern migrants.

Global mobility is clearly more than a mere metaphor; it is materially grounded. As any human mobility scholar knows, to assess the extent or nature of movement, or, indeed, even 'observe' it sometimes, you have to spend time studying things that stand still: the borders, institutions and territories of nation-states, and the (imagined) sedentary 'home' cultures of those that do not move. In other words, motion is always framed within a material and institutional infrastructure, and the circulation of people is constantly limited or promoted by economic coercions, political guarantees and sociocultural imaginaries. The incessant mobility that is often seen these days as characteristic of contemporary life is only one part of the story. Globalization processes have been overtheorized in terms of social openness while they remain undertheorized in terms of social closure. Human mobility has certainly increased worldwide, but attempts to control and restrict movement are just as characteristic of the era in which we live (Cresswell 2006). Moreover, the vast majority of people never moves to another place to settle—migrants, for instance, comprise a mere 3 per cent of the global population. This presents a serious criticism to the overgeneralized mobility discourse, which assumes 'without any research to support it that the whole world is on the move, or at least that never have so many people, things and so on been moving across international borders' (Friedman 2002: 33). In sum, border-crossing mobilities as a form of human experience are still the exception rather than the norm. Even migrants, who are depicted as icons of movement, 'do not really spend that much time "moving" in the sense assumed by the notion of "mobility"' (Hage 2005: 463).

Research on international travel shows that mobilities and borders are not antithetical. Modern passports, issued by the traveller's country of origin, and visas, issued by the destination country, did not come into widespread use until the First World War, and there would be no cosmopolitan travellers if there were no (national) boundaries to cross in the first place. An increasing concern with networks and movement, especially in the context of thinking about globalization and cosmopolitanism (largely theorized in terms of transborder travel), has stimulated theorizing on the changing nature of boundaries. State borders, for example, are not singular and unitary, but are designed to encourage various kinds of mobility (business travellers, tourists, migrant workers and students) and discourage others (illegal migrants and refugees). At transnational borders, one group's mobility seems to be facilitated at the expense of the other. The post-9/11 securitization era is full of examples showing how globalization dynamics produce significant forms of immobility for the political regulation of persons. This has led some scholars to conceive of globalization as consisting of systemic processes of closure and containment (Cunningham and Heyman 2004). Consideration of these themes breaks with theoretical tendencies that celebrate unbounded movement and instead focuses academic inquiry on the political-economic processes by which people are bounded, emplaced and allowed or forced to move. I follow this line of analysis by researching the mechanisms of tourism to developing countries that reinforce the imagined binary between mobile tourists and immobile locals.[4]

## No Routes without Roots

> Dwelling was understood to be the local ground of collective life,
> travel a supplement; roots always precede routes.
> —James Clifford (1997: 3)

While studies of mobility can provide an innovative way to understand the multiple transformations that accompany globalization, they also seem to imply profound methodological and conceptual challenges for anthropology as a discipline (Gupta and Ferguson 1997; Tsing 2000). Clifford (1997) argued over a decade ago that ethnography needs to leave behind its preoccupation with discovering the 'roots' of sociocultural forms and instead trace the 'routes' that (re)produce them. This kind of thinking is further elaborated in Latour's (2005) actor-network theory, which transforms the social into a circulation. Some scholars, however, have conflated the excitement of so-called postlocal approaches in anthropology and that of new developments in the world 'out there', weakening the case for each. With the current hype over flux and change, anthropologists risk forgetting their own disciplinary origins. The idea and study of mobility has a deep genealogy in the discipline. It is already present in the late nineteenth- and early twentieth-century notions of (transcultural) diffusion, while French structuralists only developed it more fully in their thinking on exchange.

Anthropologists have known about cultural mobilities, movements infused with complex webs of meaning, long before the current vocabulary became fashionable, but most did not acknowledge this as it was not the focus of the discipline (Trouillot 2003). From Malinowski's pioneering fieldwork onward, the notion of ethnographers as itinerant and going somewhere, as practicing mobility, has been reinforced and reproduced, as has been the notion of 'being there' in a fixed place, even if only for a short period of time (hereby reasserting the implicit connection between culture and place). This continuing emphasis on place risks overlooking the constructed nature of all fieldwork and ethnographic fields, particularly in research projects where participants are highly mobile. Clearly, the interest in issues of mobility is not new to the discipline and 'old' anthropology can help us formulate answers to exciting contemporary questions (Salazar 2010a). I would argue that one of the great advantages of the researcher mobility of ethnographers is that we not only circulate geographically, moving between home and field, but also socially, moving up and down social hierarchies in our association with people often quite dissimilar from ourselves. It is in these encounters of difference that we are faced most palpably with boundaries—immobilities of others (often when 'studying down') and of ourselves (often when 'studying up'). Such boundaries can be tangibly real or purely imagined. It is to the power of the human imagination that I turn next.

## A World of Imaginaries

> He that travels in theory has no inconveniences; he has shade and sunshine at his disposal, and wherever he alights finds tables of plenty and looks of gaiety. These ideas are indulged till the day of departure arrives, the chaise is called, and the progress of happiness begins. A few miles teach him the fallacies of imagination. The road is dusty, the air is sultry, the horses are sluggish, and the postilion brutal. He longs for the time of dinner that he may eat and rest. The inn is crowded, his orders are neglected, and nothing remains but that he devour in haste what the cook has spoiled, and drive on in quest of better entertainment. He finds at night a more commodious house, but the best is always worse than he expected.
> –Dr. Samuel Johnson (writer; 1709–1784)

We live in imagined (but not imaginary) worlds, using our personal imagination as well as collective imaginaries to represent our lifeworld and attribute meaning to it. Many of our daily activities—reading novels, playing games, watching movies, telling stories, daydreaming, planning a vacation, etc.—involve imagining or entering into the imaginings of others. The vernacular or unofficial imaginations people rely on, from the most spectacular fantasies to the most mundane reveries, are usually not expressed in theoretical terms but in images, stories and legends (long-standing objects of anthropological inquiry). They may take a variety of forms—oral, written, pictorial, symbolic or graphic—and include both linguistic and nonlinguistic ways of producing meaning.

Imaginaries, as representational assemblages that mediate the identifications with Self and Other, are 'complex systems of presumption—patterns of forgetfulness and attentiveness—that enter subjective experience as the expectation that things will make sense generally (i.e., in terms not wholly idiosyncratic)' (Vogler 2002: 625). Gaonkar defines them as 'first-person subjectivities that build upon implicit understandings that underlie and make possible common practices' (2002: 4). Although culturally shaped imaginaries influence collective behaviour, they are neither an acknowledged part of public discourse nor coterminous with implicit or covert culture (Thoden van Velzen 1995). They are imaginary in a double sense: 'They exist by virtue of representation or implicit understandings, even when they acquire immense institutional force; and they are the means by which individuals understand their identities and their place in the world' (Gaonkar 2002: 4). Paradoxically, human imagination helps produce our sense of reality. The imaginary can thus be conceived as a mental, individual and social process that produces the reality that simultaneously produces it (Figure 1).

Scholars from a wide array of disciplines have given attention to the imagination and the existing literature is vast.[5] As I will show in the case of international

FIGURE 1 • *Imagining Ethnographic Fieldwork ... or Volunteering Abroad?*

tourism to developing countries, the analysis of imaginaries offers a powerful deconstruction device of ideological, political and sociocultural stereotypes and clichés. At the same time, I want to stress that imaginations are unspoken schemas of interpretation, rather than explicit ideologies. While they are alienating when they take on an institutional(ized) life of their own (e.g., in religion or politics), in the end the agents who imagine are individuals, not societies. A given group of tourists, for example, can participate in shared practices and can be exposed to discourses and symbols that evoke conflicting meanings, but tourists' subjectivities are not completely expressed by collective imaginaries and have to be understood in their particularity.

The notion of the imagination draws, among others, on Lacan's (1977) mirror phase in human development, when a child sees its own reflection as Other. This confused identification permits the appropriation of certain critical and valuable aspects of the Other as an essential part of the self. Not surprisingly, many imaginaries are structured by dichotomies—sometimes difficult to discern in practice—that construct the world in often paradigmatically linked binominals: nature–culture, here–there, male–female, inside–outside and local–global (cf. Durand 1999). An individual's propensity to produce imaginations is the primary fact; economy and politics provide triggering mechanisms, assisting in bringing idiosyncratic images together in socially acceptable formulas, but remaining secondary facts when studying the sociocultural production of fantasy (Thoden van Velzen 1985: 108).

Acknowledging the importance of learned cultural understandings but not conceiving culture as a fixed entity to be held in common by a geographically bounded or self-identified group, I distinguish between more widely shared imaginaries (both within and between cultures) and personal imaginations. International tourists, for example, may share some imaginaries with each other, but be fractured with respect to other cultural understandings, which can be shared among people who have had the same formative experiences despite living in different parts of the world and not having a common identity (e.g., tour guides). I will pay particular attention to how personal imaginations interact with and are influenced by institutionally grounded imaginaries implying power, hierarchy and hegemony. I will also discuss the multiple links between tourism and imaginaries of cosmopolitan mobility, focusing on the overlapping but conflicting ways in which cosmopolitan aspirations drive tourists, culture brokers and locals alike.

## Going against the Flow

Is a railroad local or global? Neither. It is local at all points … Yet it is global …
There are continuous paths that lead from the local to the global, from the

7

circumstantial to the universal, from the contingent to the necessary,
only so long as the branch lines have been paid for.
—Bruno Latour (1993: 117)

Critics have pointed out that much anthropological writing invokes vague notions of the global or globalization, rather than empirically analyzing them.[6] The result are ethnographies situated within an imagined, if not imaginary, global context or studies of globalized processes that lack thick description, the texture of lives lived and identities constructed (Comaroff and Comaroff 2003). While calls for localization and attention to lived experience have become common in anthropologies of globalization, too often the act of imagining is detached from the specific forms, times and places through which people project their possible lives. Weiss warns us that 'the analytical coupling of the imagination to processes of globalization has often obscured the ways that imaginative acts are in fact materially grounded in social activities' (2002: 93). By presenting ethnographic data from Yogyakarta and Arusha, this book affirms that lived worlds, distinctly situated as they may be on this globalized planet, are increasingly constructed through fantasies and fabrications that must first be imagined in order to be realized. The focus on the mobilizing force of imaginaries in tourism and beyond substantiates Weiss's (2002) argument that many of the tangible links through which a global order of relationships is concretized are dependent upon the dissemination of imaginative forms.

It matters which metaphors we—scholars and lay people alike—use to think phenomena and processes with. The global space is often thought of as the 'flow' of people, objects and ideas across national borders and geographic regions. Although such an image is visually striking, the actual processes at work are more complex. The fashionable imagery of flows is badly chosen if we want to describe how people, objects and ideas move around the world. Global forces are evidently not neutral but always subject to economic privileges and political agendas. While flows may span the globe, they do not necessarily cover it. Furthermore, if flow itself always involves making terrain, there can be no territorial distinctions between the global transcending of place and the local making of places. Tsing reminds us that flow is 'movement stimulated through political and economic channels' and urges scholars to pay attention to 'the missed encounters, clashes, misfires, and confusions that are as much part of global linkages as simple "flow"' (2000: 338). In a similar vein, Ferguson argues 'the "global" does not "flow," thereby connecting and watering contiguous spaces; it hops instead, efficiently connecting the enclaved points in the network while excluding (with equal efficiency) the spaces that lie between the points' (2006: 47).

The popularity of metaphors of global processes in general draws from their evocation of multiple causes, agendas and historical layers of imagery. After all, 'the global' is a concept-metaphor, 'a space of theoretical abstraction and processes, experiences and connections in the world, important not only to social scientists but now part of most people's imagined and experienced worlds' (Moore 2004: 71). Because not only academics use these images, any ethnography of globalization should investigate how subjects live in relation to these grounding tropes. Anthropology as a discipline is being strongly moved to consider the discordant representations, displaced imaginaries and cultural contestations of our globalized world. What are the contours of power, agency and subjectivity in imaginaries of global mobility and the intersecting social categories those fantasies both reify and dissolve? This book demonstrates that people can develop creative ways of imagining the world and its local-to-global connections, drawing on powerful cosmopolitan and other imaginaries that ethnographers had better not ignore.

As I will illustrate, imaginaries do not float around spontaneously and independently; rather, they 'travel' in space and time through well-established circular conduits. These channels include documentaries and fictional film; art and museum exhibitions and fairs; trade cards, video games and animation; photographs, slides, video and postcards; travelogues, blogs and other websites; guidebooks and tourism brochures; coffee-table books and magazines; literature; advertising; official documents; news coverage; quasi-scientific media and academic productions. How these products and productions influence a broad public is an ambiguous question that merits grounded ethnographic research on reception and consumption rather than mere ideological critique. Images, discourses and ideas have certain points of origin—in tourism many of them are marked by distinctly Western genealogies—but are now incessantly moving in global 'rounds', not strictly circular, reaching new horizons and periodically feeding back to their places of departure. The older the imaginaries and the longer they have been circulating, the harder it becomes to trace where they originated. Circulation is different from flow because in its articulation between the ideological and the material, it requires some sort of 'material and institutional infrastructure of movement' (Tsing 2000: 338). Imaginaries, for instance, circulate unevenly, not freely; their circulation is shaped by processes that delimit and restrict movement (Cunningham and Heyman 2004; Ferguson 2006). In order to understand how circulation works, we not only need to study what is circulating but also the sociocultural structures and mechanisms that make that circulation possible or impossible.

Like mobility, also the concept of circulation has a deep genealogy in anthropology. Malinowski's pioneering fieldwork pointed to the complexity of the circular movements of the Melanesian Kula ceremonial exchange, which ensured the movement of valued objects and thus social relations throughout the Trobriand Islands. The circulation concept is used, above all, in economic and linguistic anthropology and in migration studies (e.g., Agha 2006; Kearney 1986; Haugerud, Stone and Little 2000). Another important influence in the anthropological theorizing of circulation is actor-network theory, which views texts, people and artefacts as mutually constituting entities. According to Latour

(2005), the most useful contribution of actor-network theory has been to trans-form the social into a circulation, from what was only a surface, a territory, or a province of reality. Because we never 'see' social relations or things, the idea is that ethnography should only aim to document the circulation of network-tracing tokens, statements and skills.

Circulation is often conceived as a process that simply transmits meanings, rather than as a constitutive act in itself. However, circulation is 'a cultural pro-cess with its own forms of abstraction, evaluation, and constraint, which are created by the interactions between specific types of circulating forms and the interpretive communities built around them' (Lee and LiPuma 2002: 192). In this view, culture both produces circulation and is a product of it. The force and impact of any global interconnection (capital, ideas, images, goods, styles, services and disease) depends on its circulation, thereby creating volume and va-riety. At the same time, circulation mediates the local and the global (Mazzarella 2004). There is a widespread assumption that the global circulation of ideas is increasing cultural homogeneity. Yet, as Appadurai (1996: 7) suggested over a decade ago, global ideas circulating through various media also spark resistance, selectivity and agency, creating vernacular (or glocal) forms of globalization. We should thus always treat the global as 'a project that is humanly mediated' (Inda and Rosaldo 2007: 38n9) and examine more closely how translocal ideas and discourses change and remain the same while they circulate around the globe. This ethnography aims to do precisely that.

## Revisiting the Local

What needs to be addressed ... is precisely the production of locality, that is, the social machines that create and recreate the identities and differences that are understood as the local. The differences of locality are neither preexisting nor natural but rather effects of a regime of production. Globality similarly should not be understood in terms of cultural, political, or economic homogenization. Globalization, like localization, should be understood instead as a regime of the production of identity and difference, or really of homogenization and heterogen-ization. The better framework, then, to designate the distinction between the global and the local might refer to different networks of flows and obstacles in which the local moment or perspective gives priority to the reterritorializing barriers or bound-aries and the global moment privileges the mobility of deterritorializing flows.
—Michael Hardt and Antonio Negri (2000: 45)

Localities, however defined, have been conceived of as articulations with, effects of or dynamic responses and resistances to moving global forces (Comaroff and Comaroff 2001; Burawoy 2000). Although the local is at the centre of the anthro-pology of globalization, the concept requires ethnographic rethinking (Lewellen

2002: 201; Sassen 2000). Multilocal production processes and assemblages have become the rule, and locating historically or geographically fixed centres and peripheries is getting ever more difficult (Kearney 2004). Disentangling the complex local-to-global nexus through ethnographic fieldwork has become the heart of anthropological analysis (Lewellen 2002: 185–231). Some, however, are of the opinion that anthropology's current concepts and models may be 'inadequate for understanding the interconnections, processes and aspirations of local–global relations, non-isomorphic patterns of change, and flows that coalesce and diverge along constantly changing lines of fracture' (Moore 2004: 86).

Undeniably, the local is constructed in contradictory ways; it is always already the social and historical product of movement, interaction and exchange. The histories through which localities emerge are eventually subject to the dynamics of globalization, especially the neoliberal market. Sometimes it even seems that the most global(ized) localities are also the most ardently 'local' (Rees and Smart 2001: 4). However, the local that is imagined is always already global; it has no origin or starting point (Moore 2004: 83). In other words, 'there is nothing mere about the local' (Appadurai 1996: 18). Under globalizing conditions, the local has to be continuously constructed and invented, but it remains crucial and meaningful to everyday life. The fierce local (and national) power struggle over globally circulating tourism imaginaries seeking to redefine peoples and places re-affirms that the social construction of place is still partly a process of local mean-ing-making, territorial specificity, juridical control and economic development, however complexly articulated localities become in transnational economic, po-litical and cultural movements. The multiple conflicts of interest between local tourism stakeholders remind us that the local should not be seen as a constant and steady space in relation to globalization (Bruner 2005: 231–52).

While much of the literature on the local-global nexus finds local factors criti-cal of the diversity of globalization processes, few authors notice that the local itself has multiple faces when it is globalizing.[7] The local interacts with global processes not in a unified way, but in multiple ways (Rodman 1992). As I will show throughout this book, tourism research provides a welcome antidote against too much stress on 'deterritorialization', detaching production, consumption, identities and communities from the local (Kearney 1995: 552–53). Despite the increased importance of deterritorialized relations in global social life, these are only viable insofar as spatial fixity and concrete places continue to provide loca-tions through which such global processes can circulate. For tourism, locality and the characteristics of place are of increased relevance. Why would people care to choose different travel destinations if sights would all be the same? In other words, the growing circulation of people, capital and information also stimulates localization or territorialization.[8]

The neologism 'glocalization' (Robertson 1992, 1995) has been proposed to capture the highly individual ways the global and local can be mediated.[9] Globalization always takes place in some locality, while at the same time localities, as particular places, are produced in discourses of globalization (Salazar 2005, 2006c). Glocalization—the patterned conjunctions that shape localities and by means of which they shape themselves—is a first approximation that suggests equal attention to globalization and localization (local differentiation) existing in a complex, two-way traffic. It is a fitting term for the intertwined processes whereby new boundaries are created between local and global orders, and both the global order and the local gain strength. Although the notion itself is relatively uncommon in anthropology, glocalization is a standard theme in nearly all ethnographic writing about globalization (Salazar 2008b).[10]

FIGURE 2 • *Copycat Glocalization in Arusha and Yogyakarta*

It is not difficult to see that cities such as Yogyakarta in Indonesia and Arusha in Tanzania are important crossroads in the circulation of people (businesspeople, volunteers, tourists and migrants), capital (trade and remittances), objects (food and drinks, clothing and consumer goods) and images and ideas (popular culture media and the Internet). One can encounter bits and pieces from all over the world. A short stroll through the city centres leaves one inundated by indexical markers to distant elsewheres. Shops, restaurants, vehicles and so forth are named after faraway places or personalities that stir the imagination. People watch Latin-American sitcoms and Hollywood and Bollywood films, and on the radio they hear music coming from every corner of the planet. Youngsters indulge in appropriating foreign-sounding names and fitting identities, not only in virtual environments such as the hugely fashionable Facebook and other virtual social networks, but also among friends.

Glocalization becomes tangible, for instance, when Starbucks—a global brand image in the world of coffee consumption—inspires local entrepreneurs to start copycat coffee houses such as Debucks or Stiggbucks. Arusha also hosts a McMoody's, while in Yogyakarta Kentucky Fried Chicken and McDonald's operate next to Kentukku Fried Chicken (*kentukku* (J), you should buy) and McPitik (*pitik* (J), chicken)—literally 'telescoping global and local to make a blend' (Tulloch 1991: 134) (Figure 2).[11] While the glocalization concept provides us with an attention-grabbing analytical perspective to study the intertwining of globalization and localization (and the in-between levels of regionalization and nationalization), it does not provide us with a decisive theory explaining the human mechanics behind these processes. This is one of the shortcomings this book aims to address.

## Point of Departure

> Looking obliquely at the edges of things, where they come together
> with other things, can tell you as much about them, often, as can
> looking at them directly, intently, and straight on.
> –Clifford Geertz (2001: 12)

Historically laden imaginaries are at the roots of many physical and imagined travels to unknown destinations, be it in the context of tourism (Amirou 1995) or migration (Pajo 2007). It is in acknowledging the role of the imagination in mobility that possibly one of the most exciting opportunities for an anthropology of global and transnational processes is located (Wilding 2007). During my fieldwork, I gathered ample evidence that the lives and practices of people in Yogyakarta and Arusha are shaped by any number of imaginative as well as real links to 'Other' worlds near and far. Being exposed to media, goods and ideologies never before available, people are dreaming 'the signs and styles of a global order, while facing ever narrower means by which to satisfy them' (Weiss 2002: 8). Local tour guides, having privileged contact with foreigners and easier access to foreign resources through tourism, are clearly frontrunners in this process (Salazar 2005).

In 2008, the United Nations World Tourism Organization reported over 900 million international arrivals worldwide, with revenues surpassing US$850 billion (UNWTO 2008).[12] The WTO's (2001) *Tourism 2020 Vision* forecasts that international arrivals will reach nearly 1.6 billion by the year 2020 (of which 1.2 billion will be intraregional and 378 million will be long-haul travelling), almost doubling the current earnings to US$1,550 billion. With an infrastructure valued in excess of US$3 trillion, the ensemble of tourism service industries can be viewed as one of the most significant contributors to the global economy (with gains being spread very unevenly across the globe).[13] Undoubtedly, tourism has become a phenomenon of global importance, acting as an engine of economic growth and as a sociocultural force. It can be considered simultaneously a global product and a producer of global processes and phenomena. Tourism is a cause of global transformations because it induces the worldwide circulation of people, ideas, images and capital. As an effect, it results from an increasing global interconnectedness of economic, technological and sociocultural transformations. Tourism thus seems an ideal analytical entry into the admittedly vast and complex research field of globalization studies.[14]

Tourism is an excellent subject area to study mobility and the intertwining of local to global processes (Hall 2005), although by no means the only one—others include popular culture (music, film, spectator sports, fashion, food and drinks) and new information and communication technologies. Destinations worldwide are adapting themselves to the homogenizing trends of the global travel and tourism system while at the same time trying to commoditize their local (and national) distinctiveness. The tensions between the two become visible where international tourists meet local manufacturers, retailers and service providers in the (re)production and sale of glocalized tourism goods and services (Salazar 2005, 2006c; Yamashita 2003). Whereas in its original micromarketing meaning, glocalization referred to tailoring global products to particular local circumstances (Tulloch 1991: 134), in the case of tourism service providers it involves tailoring local(ized) products (representations and enactments of natural and cultural heritage) to changing global audiences (international tourists coming from various parts of the world and with different preferences). This happens by repackaging already glocal peoples and places as 'local'; 'overt glocalization does not sell in a global market that trades on the romance of difference, so the "g" in glocal must remain silent' (Thornton 2000: 84).

Stories, images and desires, running the gamut from essentialized, mythologized and exoticized imaginaries of the Other to more realistic frames of reference, function as the motor setting the tourism machinery in motion. The global tourism system disembeds images and ideas of destinations from their original context, making them available through their transformation, legitimization, institutionalization and distribution. Through this continuous circulation, which is 'a constitutive activity of representations' (Crang 2006: 48), tourism fantasies help in (re)creating peoples and places.[15] Such imaginaries are easily reembedded in new contexts by a process that constantly alters both the imaginaries and the contexts, building on local referents to establish their meaning and value. Where do such tourism imaginaries come from, how and why are they circulated across the globe, what material impact do they have on people's lives, and what do they tell us, more generally, about processes of globalization and localization?

In this book, I want to unravel some of the mechanisms that turn tourism into an icon of both the global and the local. I do this by tracing the historical and semiotic makings of tourism imaginaries, while keeping the very material effects of these processes in view. Currently fashionable metaphors like flow, flux, mobility, and movement hint at instability and uncertainty, but tourism sells meaning and experience by creating essentialized representations of peoples and places in an exoticizing and static frame—the liminal space of the 'exotic elsewhere'. Because a great deal of existing research focuses on the production and consumption of tourism imaginaries, I want to concentrate on the human mechanics of their circulation, especially by those people who are far removed from the original production sources. Who are the tourism workers circulating tourism imaginaries and appropriating them? How do they replicate, sustain and contest tourism fantasies in their own narratives and practices? How are images and ideas of tourism transformed by the process of their circulation?

Destinations of travel are the physical and mental landscapes where a multitude of imaginaries meet and, occasionally, clash. Tourism, especially in developing countries, shapes frameworks for cultural interaction and influence against a broader background of cultural dissimilarity and the imaginative possibilities this creates (e.g., to build up cosmopolitan capital). With accelerating mobility and intensifying connectivity, both tourists and tourism workers are transformed in conjunction with the movements of the world economy and are positioned as simultaneously local and global. Local intermediaries play an instrumental role in glocalizing tourism. Ong remarks that 'while anthropologists have talked about the imaginaries and cultural landscapes emerging out of transnational "flows", less attention has been paid to the actors and agents who are part of these movements and who must manage the cross-currents of cultural winds' (1999: 93). Others have noted the lack of

> any analysis concerning the many human actors operating in the concrete locations from which these flows originate—engaged in constructing them in the first place while linked into complex collaborative human activities at the same time—but also

the many others situated in yet other locations who pass them on, process, deconstruct and ultimately re-ground them into their own locations according to their particular needs and responsibilities. (Kennedy 2007: 274)

What anthropology offers that is often missing in other disciplines is a concrete attentiveness to how people mediate and react to processes of globalization (Graeber 2002: 1222–23; Moore 2004: 72; Lewellen 2002: 30, 36). At the same time, ethnographies of those actors playing a pivotal role in 'making globalization happen' are still relatively rare. Feldman believes a fuller understanding of global power requires that 'anthropologists ask how specific people located in "macrosystems" ... also mediate those same processes' (2005: 222). He uses the example of diplomats, and one could make a similar case for corporate managers, bankers or policy-makers. I would argue that equally important, and probably more suited to anthropology's traditional methods (Holmes and Marcus 2004), are studies of the 'mechanics of glocalization', those skilled technicians labouring hard to keep global processes operating properly while making sure these processes are localized so that they become more easily acceptable.

I focus on local tour guides because they are key agents in (re)producing circulating tourism imaginaries of peoples and places. They are certainly not the only players in this process, but their role (and the role of tourism workers in general) has received relatively little attention in traditional anthropologies of tourism that focus on the essentialized categories of 'hosts' and 'guests' (Smith 1989, 1977; Smith and Brent 2001). I argue that the specific everyday practices and discourses of different and heterogeneous groups—tourists, intermediaries and locals—together shape and translate global tourism imaginaries into a series of complex and different performances, thereby shaping cultural and natural heritage and creating opportunities for figurative cosmopolitan mobility or 'cosmobility'. Debates over global circulations and forces do not necessarily shed light on the abilities of people to act in an intensely interconnected world. However, viewed from a perspective that always keeps individuals within a globalized world in the foreground (Rapport 2006), we can observe an enormous amount of institutional structure in constant play, swept along by circulating capital, both financial and symbolic, in multiple directions.

## *The Way to Follow*

If we are always arriving and departing, it is also true that we are eternally anchored. One's destination is never a place but rather a new way of looking at things.
–Henry Miller (writer; 1891–1980)

Conducting an ethnographic study of the circulation of imaginaries seems as daunting as it is exciting. What are the analytical tools to be used and which concepts enable critical analysis and open new understandings? How does one deal with different units of analysis and various kinds of subjects? How can one consider all levels of agency and institutional powers? Many of the theoretical anxieties I encountered while thinking about my research were translated into methodological concerns during the fieldwork. I was relieved to find my worries reflected in a significant body of scholarship.[16] The fundamental methodological challenge that studies of circulation and mobility pose to anthropology is one of scale. How well can we anthropologists, with our traditional ethnographic field-work methods, encompass increasingly wider and complex contexts of analysis? Rethinking the condition of the local in current planetary conditions invites us to rethink what scale means and does not mean. Scale is not the same as size; it has to do with the presence or absence, and relative efficacy, of overarching institu-tions, not geographic or demographic extent. Glocalization invites us to rethink ethnography's 'conventional scale', treating the local as a space contained or en-compassed by larger spaces. The main ethnographic advantage of rethinking the local is the possibility of reclaiming some of the questions that the conventions of scale ordinarily preclude (Strathern 1995).

Glocal ethnography, as I call it, simultaneously focuses on the macroprocesses through which the world is becoming increasingly, albeit unevenly, intercon-nected and on the way subjects mediate these processes.[17] I define glocal eth-nography as a fieldwork methodology to describe and interpret the complex connections, disconnections and reconnections of local-to-global phenomena and processes. This is achieved by firmly embedding and historically situating the in-depth study of a particular sociocultural group, organization or setting within a larger (and, ultimately, global) context. This happens figuratively by putting the *G* of global in front of the concept local: G-local (encompassing the scales that lie in between the global and the local). The stress is on the local, but that local is embedded in and dependent on larger contexts. Anthropologists certainly have a comparative advantage in studying glocalization, focusing at once on the large-scale processes (circulation of subjects and objects and the architecture of social relations) through which the world is interconnected and on how subjects shape and are shaped by these processes in culturally specific ways—'the native's point of view' (Geertz 1983: 55–70).

Glocal ethnographies incorporate the two major ways to address the conun-drum of scale. First, they scale vertically ('scale up') by providing close-grained studies of how a single locale or group of people is connected locally, nationally, regionally and globally. Traditional fieldwork, however, may be just the begin-ning if the goal is deep system awareness. Instead of cherishing a fetishistic obses-sion with participant observation, therefore, we need to reinforce this technique with other methods. Gupta and Ferguson, for instance, call for bringing in a multitude of 'other forms of representation' besides fieldwork: 'archival research, the analysis of public discourse, interviewing, journalism, fiction, or statistical representations of collectivities' (1997: 38). Vertical scaling can also include a multitemporal (longitudinal or historical) dimension (Comaroff and Comaroff 1992). The presence of these new types of material 'may require, and also provide openings for, new skills of composition and synthesis' (Hannerz 2003: 35).

The second strategy included in glocal ethnography is to scale horizontally ('scale out'), by including more than one locale in the analysis. For many ethnographers, the global is an emergent dimension for exploring the connections among sites or people. This latitudinal approach is better known in anthropology as 'multisited ethnography' (Marcus 1998).[18] Multilocal or multisited research might actually not be an adequate description as many places are somehow linked or networked to each other—what Hannerz calls a 'network of localities' or 'several fields in one' (2003: 21). A single site within a complex society may be conceptualized as a multiple one, whereas multiple localities can be seen as 'a single geographically discontinuous site' (Hage 2005: 463). Hannerz therefore advocates 'translocal' research (2003: 21), clarifying the nature of relations between localities. While the analytical entity is translocal or glocal, the fieldwork is multilocal, because the ethnographer is always somewhere. Merry, on the other hand, proposes a 'deterritorialized ethnography' (2000: 130), not restricted to predefined sites but following patterns of circulation.

Burawoy defines the agenda of global ethnography—what I thus call 'glocal ethnography'—as a way to 'replace abstract globalization with a grounded globalization that tries to understand not only the experience of globalization but also how that experience is produced in specific localities and how that productive process is a contested and thus a political accomplishment' (2001: 157–58). When processes of globalization and localization are investigated empirically, they dissolve into complex webs of social relations, which are in constant change and mutually influence each other. The advantage of scaling up or scaling out is that both techniques have the potential of opening up new theoretical vistas (Strathern 1991). Naturally, the more complex the levels of analysis become, the more necessary collaborative and interdisciplinary research methods are. Another option is to knowingly exclude certain elements, moments, people, factors, words and concepts from the analysis (Candea 2007).

The study at hand illustrates that thick ethnographic analysis remains best equipped to capture the complexities of and mechanisms involved in constructing contemporary sociocultural lifeworlds. Manoeuvring within predefined constraints and limited resources of research, the fieldwork conducted for this book was multisited and multitemporal but remained focused on one specific issue: the role of local tour guides in the circulation and (re)production of global imaginaries in tourism and beyond. I operationalize imaginaries as real (networks of) practices: through the ethnographic method, we can assess how imaginary activities, subjects, social relations, et cetera are materialized, enacted and inculcated. While all chapters include ethnographic examples of vertical and lateral linkages and their sociocultural effects, chapters 2, 3 and 5 concentrate on scaling up, while chapters 4 and 6 are exemplary illustrations of scaling out.

## Tour Itinerary

> The world is a book and those who do not travel read only one page.
> —Augustine of Hippo (theologian; 354–430)

As a reminder, let me give you a brief overview of what is to come. In chapter 2, I invite you to explore the fuzzy world of tourism imaginaries. What are these fantasies and their discourses about? Who or what is behind them? How are they spreading across the globe? Because tourism imaginaries are not free floating, but linked to specific places, I take you to two top destinations, one in Asia, the other in Africa. You will receive a full briefing of the socioculturally constructed tourismscapes of Yogyakarta, Indonesia, and Arusha, Tanzania, and a brief genealogy of the images and ideas surrounding both glocalized sites. Having set the scene, we will turn our attention to the mechanics of circulation. I focus on local tour guides, and the instrumental role these cultural intermediaries play in replicating as well as contesting and ingeniously altering tourism fantasies. Chapter 3 addresses the question how guides learn to translate tourism imaginaries into seductive guiding narratives. I analyze how both formal schooling and informal learning serve to familiarize them with globally circulating tourism fantasies and I show that transnationally networked guides are clearly at an advantage.

The next chapter presents an ethnographic and discourse-centred analysis of the guide-guest encounter. I rely on linguistic anthropology to examine the (meta)-discursive toolbox of local tour guides. This reveals there are other than tourism imaginaries at play in guiding and leads to a surprising finding about cosmopolitanism. In chapter 5, I situate the role of tour guiding in its larger historical context and briefly review some previous research on the topic. I then move on to discuss how guiding in Indonesia and Tanzania is increasingly regulated and controlled, and this at different levels. In chapter 6, I use a similar analysis as in chapter 4 to unravel the multiple frictions and issues of power and agency involved in the circulation of tourism fantasies and the occasional clash with imaginations held by destination residents or the guides themselves. Chapter 7 acts as the journey's debriefing, in which I propose to take a step back from the micro-level and reflect on what these findings tell us, more generally, about the current interconnected condition in which many (but not all) of us nowadays live.

It is important to reiterate that this book does not pretend to resolve the many unanswered questions surrounding globalization or cultural mobilities. Instead, I want to explore critically one specific issue: the analytical purchase of some of the dominant metaphors in contemporary anthropological theorizing.

The concern with mobility, for instance, has made some scholars lose sight of the continued importance of place-based practices and modes of consciousness for the (re)production of culture and society. Taking international tourism as an analytical entry, I argue that a focus on immobility is at least as important as a research focus that is limited to movement alone. What started as a multisited ethnography of local tour guiding leads to unanticipated corollaries about the seducing force of imaginaries, qualified cosmopolitanism, the growing mediating power of regional trade blocs and organizations over national and global processes and some striking similarities between local guides and foreign socio-cultural anthropologists.

# 2
# TWO DESTINATIONS, ONE DESTINY

Sulawesi is exotic but approachable.
Kenya is intense but refreshing.
Java is exotic and wild.

You might be misled by thinking the tag lines above are taken from a stylish tourism brochure or upscale travel website. In reality, they are Starbucks Coffee descriptors used in the company's global marketing literature (Elliott 2001: 377). Reading these catchphrases reinforced my impression that signs of exoticized difference are present all around us. Undeniably, international tourism is 'the quintessential business of "difference projection" and the interpretive vehicle of "othering" par excellence' (Hollinshead 1998: 121). No matter what budget you possess or how much time you have, the range of possibilities offered by the tourism and travel sector to spend your money and leisure time is staggering. What about flying to your destination entirely naked, touring around one of the world's biggest slums in an air-conditioned vehicle or sleeping in a hotel that is completely made of salt or ice? These days, the Internet allows us to verify that even the craziest holiday ideas are more than a fancy; they exist for real and you can try them out if you wish (and have enough cash or credit).

In a global market characterized by rapidly changing trends, the products and packages on sale vary widely, but the image-making machinery behind them shares well-established strategies and scripts. Whatever communication medium is used, the discourse of tourism is one of persuasion, merging the macroeconomic goals of highly decentralized commercial service industries with attributed need satisfactions of potential clients (Dann 1996b). Seductive stories and imaginaries about peoples and places are so predominant that without them there probably would be little tourism at all (Bishop and Robinson 1999; Lengkeek 2001). Marketers eagerly rely on them to represent and sell dreams of the world's limitless destinations, activities, types of accommodation and peoples to discover and experience. Prospective tourists are invited to imagine themselves in a paradisiacal environment, a vanished Eden, where the local landscape and population are to be consumed through observation, embodied sensation and imagination (Amirou 1995). If anything, tourism is part of the 'image production industry' (Harvey 1989: 290–93), in which identities of travel destinations and their inhabitants are endlessly (re)invented, (re)produced, (re)captured and (re)created in a bid to obtain a piece of the lucrative tourism pie.

In this chapter, I sketch how places such as Yogyakarta and Arusha have developed as popular tourism gateways near famous World Heritage Sites.[1] This gives us a tangible introduction into the fuzzy world of tourism imaginaries—widespread representational assemblages that are used as meaning-making devices (mediating how people act, cognize, and value the world). Before setting foot on Indonesian or Tanzanian soil, tourists already have a mental picture and preconception of what things will be like. Their pretrip impressions and preferred meta-narratives are the result of years of exposure to the most diverse representations about the destination and geographically or culturally related areas. All these images—from tourism marketing, the media, popular culture and so on—help people to connect places with certain values, connotations and feelings, and these themselves create expectations. After all, Yogyakarta and Arusha are destinations through which not only foreign tourists and currencies but also images and ideas pass. What are these imaginaries and their discourses about? Who or what is behind them? How are they spreading ideologies of difference (and similarity) across the globe?

## Java's Cultural Heart

Yogyakarta is the name of one of Indonesia's thirty-three provinces and its capital, situated in central Java (Map 1). The earliest signs of habitation in this fertile area between Mount Merapi and the South Sea (Indian Ocean) are prehistoric.[2] From the seventh century, the region was dominated by Hindu and Buddhist kingdoms, giving rise to the eighth-century Buddhist shrine of Borobudur, the tenth-century Hindu temple complex of Prambanan, and many other sanctuaries and palaces, including Ratu Boko, Kalasan and Sambisari. Around the same period, the Javanese started developing their own language and script.[3] Islam, coming mainly via India, gained ground in the inner areas of the island during the sixteenth century. The Dutch began to colonize the archipelago in the early seventeenth century. Yogyakarta came into being in 1755, when a succession dispute divided the power of the mighty Kingdom of Mataram between the sultanates of Yogyakarta and Surakarta or Solo. Sultan Hamengku Buwono I built a *Kraton* (a vast, walled palace) that later became the focus of a revolt against the Dutch (1825–30). The British established a brief presence on Java under Sir Thomas Stamford Raffles (1811–16), but the Dutch retained control until Indonesia's independence 130 years later.[4]

Before the Japanese occupation of Java (1942–45), Yogyakarta was a Dutch protectorate. When the Dutch reoccupied Jakarta after the Second World War (1946–49), the city functioned as the stronghold of the independence movement by becoming the provisional capital of the newly declared Republic of Indonesia. In return for this unfailing support, the first Indonesian central government passed a law in 1950 granting Yogyakarta the status of Special Province, recognizing the power of Sultan Hamengku Buwono IX in his domestic affairs by making him governor for life. His son, Hamengku Buwono X, was elected as governor in 1998. The Sultan's Palace is still the hub of Java's traditional life. Together with neighbouring Solo, Yogyakarta is considered to be the supreme centre of Javanese culture, known for its sophisticated artistic traditions, particularly its drama and classical dance festivals, and handicraft industries (Smithies 1986). Because it cherishes its cultural roots, the city attracts large numbers of musicians, dancers, writers and all kinds of craftspeople. They assure the continuity of *gamelan* orchestras, traditional court dances, *wayang* plays, woodcarving and the production of batik clothes and decorations.[5] The silverware from Kotagede and the pottery from Kasongan are well known too. At the core of big annual festivals (e.g., Sekaten and Labuhan) are long-established syncretic rituals containing elements of both Islam and Javanese mysticism, in which the Kraton and its king play major roles.[6]

The city of Yogyakarta, with its rapidly growing population of about half a million people (over 3 million in the entire province), is often characterized as a big village because the great majority of its buildings are single-storey structures and many people live in village-like, off-street urban neighbourhoods. Economically, Yogyakarta is marked by small-scale enterprises, cottage industries and self-employed people in a large informal sector. Situated only a couple of degrees south of the equator, the area has a hot and humid tropical climate all year long (more moderate in the highlands of Mount Merapi). Agricultural produce in the province includes rice, corn, peanuts and soybeans, and there are many plantations of cacao, coconuts, coffee, cotton, kapok, pepper, rubber, tobacco and vanilla. Farmers also raise buffaloes, cows, goats, hogs, horses and poultry. The city, with its multiple markets and shopping areas, functions as a local trade hub. Larger commercial enterprises are mostly in the hands of entrepreneurial ethnic Chinese.[7] Much of the existing manufacturing is related to tourism, one of the region's major sources of income. Because of the absence of any substantial industrial infrastructure, the province's prosperity greatly depends on its ability to capitalize on its tangible as well as intangible cultural heritage.

Not surprisingly, Yogyakarta's main product is heritage tourism. The three Indonesian cultural sites on UNESCO's World Heritage List—the Prambanan Temple Compounds (1991), the Borobudur Temple Compounds (1991) and Sangiran Early Man Site (1996)—are all located in central Java. While promoted by the Yogyakarta Provincial Tourism Office (BAPARDA), Prambanan is partly and Borobudur completely located outside the province, in neighbouring Central Java.[8] These heritage sites are must-sees, and most tourists pay visits to the Sultan's Palace and the adjacent Water Castle as well. All these tourist attractions can be toured easily in one day and are commonly offered as daytrips from Bali. The province of Yogyakarta offers much more than cultural heritage monuments: village tourism, agro-tourism (coffee, snake fruit and other plantations), trekking and hiking (especially in the cooler Mt. Merapi areas of Kaliurang and Kaliadem), sports (biking, caving, golf and kayaking or rafting), museums (including the ethnographic Sonobudoyo Museum, the Affandi Museum of painting and the Batik Research Centre), and beaches (Parangtritis, Baron and Krakal). For shopaholics, Malioboro Street is the main area to buy bags, leather goods, clothes and souvenirs. There are also multiple cottage-industry facilities where one can observe the manufacturing process, participate and purchase products directly from the craftspeople.

Although processes of sociocultural change and glocalization are clearly visible in many domains of daily life (Salazar 2005), the existing tourism imaginaries mainly focus on a few selected heritage sites and the traditional arts and crafts, performed or produced in the city itself or in its vicinity (Dahles 2001). The region is usually depicted as the centre of timeless Javanese tradition.[9] As I show below, the creation of Yogyakarta's image abroad is, of course, not the sole responsibility of destination marketing companies, travel agents or tour operators.

## An Oriental Archipelago

During my childhood (most of which I spent in Belgium), I learned many things at school and through the media about East Asia (China and Japan) and South Asia (India). I was much older when I realized that there existed an equally (if not more) exotic region in between, Southeast Asia. During my introductory course in anthropology at university, I was taught that many of the discipline's scholarly analyses and debates were associated with particular Southeast Asian societies, mainly in Thailand, Malaysia, the Philippines and Indonesia. It captured my imagination that the illustrious Clifford Geertz, whose writings I much admire, had started his ethnographic career in Yogyakarta. I had seen the occasional documentary about Indonesia on television, and in secondary school we had read Multatuli's *Max Havelaar* (1860). In addition, I had come across Indonesian migrants and products on city trips to the Netherlands. These vague impressions of a remote Southeast Asian country became much livelier when I started working as a volunteer in an intercultural youth project in France where I happened to share my daily tasks with Yusuf, a young Javanese man. We became close friends and exchanged heartily about our cultural backgrounds. When we finished our volunteering, Yusuf and I returned to our respective countries. I got married a couple of years later and almost instinctively suggested to my spouse spending our honeymoon in Indonesia. As a newlywed couple, we first visited the island of Bali (a preferred nuptial destination). Yusuf's family hosted us in Yogyakarta, and Yusuf himself gave us an unforgettable tour of Java. In 2001, our Indonesian friend had a chance to visit us in Europe so that we could show him around. These fragments of my own past nicely illustrate how the image one has of particular peoples and places is the result of a long historical process involving many contributions from a variety of sources.

For most Europeans, perceptions and stereotypes of Asia began with the earliest contact of Europeans and crystallized in European minds from the late eighteenth century, as an outcome of the growth of European hegemonic power following the Industrial Revolution and the rapid expansion of trade and colonialism. Oriental studies, the forerunner of Asian studies, was motivated by the need to understand the countries of the Orient, defined as those countries situated to the east of the Mediterranean Sea—the Near, Middle, and Far East.[10] These regions provided a backdrop or a coherent and culturally distinct Other against which a diverse and fragmented Europe could define itself. Many Western representations depict Asia in general as exotic (Lombard 1993) and erotic (Prasso 2005), an image that attracts travellers, adventurers and tourists (Michel 2001). In the Western imaginary, noble savages inhabited the Asian (and Pacific) islands. From Portuguese and Dutch colonizers, traders and missionaries, Europeans learned in detail about Indonesia, and many of its islands occupied a special place in their imagination (e.g., the Spice Islands and Bali). Like so many other remote islands across the globe, Java was portrayed as reflecting the Western archetype of paradise: 'warm, bountiful and promising a life free from anxiety and need, and full of leisure and sexuality' (Costa 1998: 323); 'With its abundance of clear, running water, and the brilliant fresh foliage of its rice-fields, its plantations of coffee and sugar-cane, it gives the impression of a Garden of Eden' (Cabaton 1911: 71).[11]

Few have represented Java as primitive or tribal, recognizing the early cultural influences from India—a 'high' civilization because complex and literate—and the adoption of Islam several centuries ago. The civilized image is also due to a concerted effort by Indonesian authorities in the 1980s and early 1990s to send gamelan orchestras and traditional dance troupes around the world, advertising the country's high culture. During that time, above all Javanese cultural expressions received wide coverage in documentaries and in performances and museum exhibitions abroad. Yogyakarta in particular became known through the influences of travel writing, coffee table books, art exhibitions, impressions of diplomats and anthropologists.[12] As mentioned before, Yogyakarta is the place where Geertz became familiar with Indonesian language and culture. This influential anthropological theorist illustrated many of his conceptual ideas with case material from Java (e.g., Geertz 1973, 1983). The widely read Geertz, together with the work of Anderson (1972, 1991), put Java firmly on the map of anthropology and other related disciplines.

In the case of Indonesia as a whole, the ideal representation of a friendly, hospitable and vibrantly diverse archipelago has suffered tremendously from receiving a great deal of negative reporting in the global news media. The country is now commonly portrayed and perceived as a distant world at once attractive because of its exotic landscapes and repellent because of its current environmental and political problems. Given widespread anti-Islamic feelings in the West, it is no wonder that in Java's tourism imagery, pre-Islamic heritage is played up whereas the Islamic one is silenced. The dominant imaginary is also highly age dependent. For people in their seventies, this results from the events of the Second World War, including the Japanese invasion (and, in the particular case of the Dutch colonial nostalgia). Today, new imaginaries are related to the frequency with which the country, island or province appear in glossy magazines, travel programmes and feature films. Given its amazing natural sceneries and incredible cultural heritage, it is surprising that Yogyakarta barely features in movies and that even *National Geographic* has only recently featured the province in a major article (Marshall 2008).

## 'Jogja, Never Ending Asia'

> It stretches from the slopes of mighty Mount Merapi in the north to the wave-swept beaches of the powerful Indian Ocean to the south. It was the mighty Javanese Empire of Mataram, Ngayogyakarto Hadiningrat … The Kraton is still the hub of Yogyakarta's traditional life despite the advances of the 20th century; it still radiates the spirit of refinement which has been the hallmark of its art and people for centuries. Yogyakarta is one of the supreme cultural centres of Java. Gamelan orchestras keep alive the rhythms the past, classical Javanese dances entrance with visions of beauty and poise, shadows come to life in the stories of the wayang kulit and a myriad of traditional visual art forms keep locals and visitors alike spellbound.
> –BAPARDA Leaflet

Tourism to Yogyakarta was first developed under Dutch colonial rule, mainly through the Vereeniging Toeristenverkeer (Association of Tourist Traffic of the Dutch East Indies), which opened an Official Tourist Bureau in Weltevreden (now Jakarta) in 1908, and published informative guides such as *Java, the Wonderland* (1910). After independence, the new Indonesian government continued to promote international tourism, although President Sukarno's political rhetoric was markedly anti-Western and the unstable political and economic climate did not really encourage this development. The opening of the luxurious Ambarrukmo Palace Hotel in 1966—built with funds provided by war reparations from Japan on land owned by the sultan's family—marks the beginning of mass tourism in Yogyakarta. Under Major General Suharto's New Order government (1966–98), long-term planning and a relatively stable environment for business transformed the country. A National Tourism Awareness Campaign taught Indonesians how to play the role of good hosts. Through brochures, newspapers and television advertisements, the Ministry of Tourism, Post and Telecommunications diffused *Sapta Pesona,* the Seven Charms, to please tourists: security, orderliness, cleanliness, comfort, beauty, hospitality and thoughtfulness. Such campaigns still exist, but not on the same pervasive scale as before. By the mid-1990s, *pariwisata* (tourism) had become Indonesia's third most important source of foreign revenue (Dahles 2001). At the same time, tourism contributes only 2.5 per cent to the gross domestic product, and employs not even 2 million people, a mere 2 per cent of total employment (WTTC 2007: 26).

After actively participating in mass tourism for over thirty years, Yogyakarta has become a major gateway to central and east Java, both for international and domestic visitors. The most loyal tourist markets are from the Netherlands, France, Germany and Japan. Repeated travel warnings keep numbers from Australia, the United States and the United Kingdom low. Targeted new markets include China, India, Russia, the Middle East and Eastern Europe. The province has an entire infrastructure in place to receive large quantities of visitors. The Adisucipto Airport became international in 2004.[13] Apart from locally owned hotels and guesthouses, there are star-rated transnational chain hotels (Accor, Choice, Hyatt, Melía, Radisson and Sheraton) and major Indonesian brand names such as Santika, Sahid and Inna. The transport system is extensive, with trains, taxis, buses, bicycles and motorbikes, but also the more traditional cycle rickshaws and horse carts. There are expensive restaurants and fast-food chains (including Dunkin' Donuts, McDonalds, Pizza Hut, Wendy's, and California, Kentucky and Texas Fried Chicken), as well as cheaper local eateries and popular sidewalk food stalls. At the start of the new millennium, 'Jogja' was introduced as a brand name because the letter *Y* was believed to be a more difficult alphabetical start for most international audiences. The brand name also appears in 'Jogja, Never Ending Asia', the catchphrase used by the provincial authorities to attract investors, traders and tourists to the region (Figure 3).[14] With this promotional line, Jogja joins other destinations in Southeast Asia. Singapore and Malaysia, for instance, have been using 'New Asia' and 'Truly Asia' as their respective promotional slogans. This linking of travel destinations to Asia as a whole is a strategy clearly aimed at markets outside the continent.

As a fashionable venue for conventions, Jogja has had its share of key tourism conferences. In 1992, for instance, the International Conference on Cultural Tourism led to the Yogyakarta Declaration on National Cultures and Universal Tourism. This was followed up in 1995 by an Indonesian-Swiss Forum on Cultural and International Tourism and, in 2006, by an UNWTO-sponsored International Conference on Cultural Tourism and Local Communities, lead-

FIGURE 3 • *'Indonesia, the Ultimate in Diversity' and 'Jogja, Never Ending Asia'*

ing to the Yogyakarta Declaration on Cultural Tourism, Local Communities and Poverty Alleviation. In 1994, the city hosted the APEC Tourism Working Group meeting and, in 2001, it welcomed the East Asia Inter-Regional Tourism Forum. In 2002, Jogja housed the ASEAN Tourism Forum. For that occasion, the city built a brand new facility, the Jogja Expo Centre. In the same venue, Jogja hosted the 2004 and 2005 Tourism Indonesia Mart and Expo, an event organized by the Indonesian Tourism Promotion Board. Jogja's participation in international travel marts has become a major strategy to increase international visits to the region. BAPARDA annually sells its products at the rotating Pacific Asia Travel Association travel mart and in Berlin, London, Dubai and Shanghai.

As Dahles points out in her study on the politics of cultural tourism in Indonesia, 'the cultural heritage of the Yogyakarta area has shaped the (international) images of Indonesia, as government propaganda has used architectural structures like the temples and the sultan's palace and expressions of art like the Ramayana dance to promote Indonesian tourism world-wide' (2001: 20). This particularly happened during the New Order era, when the central government (led by Javanese) strongly favoured Jogja in their (re)invention of Java, promoting it as the 'cultural heart' of Java and even Indonesia as a whole. The current planning of Jogja's tourism is in the hands of many stakeholders at various levels: city (Yogyakarta City Department of Tourism, Arts, and Culture), provincial (BAPARDA), Java (Jawa Promo), national (Ministry of Culture and Tourism), regional (ASEAN Committee on Trade and Tourism, APEC Tourism Working Group) and global (UNWTO, UNESCO) levels. Because policy-makers at these different echelons have diverse interests, decisions taken at one level are often contested at another.

The impact of global governance should not be underestimated. UNESCO, for instance, has a long-standing history of involvement in Java's heritage. In 1972, it launched a US$25 million safeguarding campaign to restore Borobudur, often listed as one of the seven (forgotten) wonders of the world. Concurrent with the elevation of Borobudur and Prambanan to World Heritage sites in 1991, it collaborated with UNDP and the former Indonesian Directorate General of Tourism in the ambitious Cultural Tourism Development Central Java-Yogyakarta project (1991–94). This led to increased cooperation between the provinces of Central Java and Yogyakarta in the planning and promotion of cultural tourism. Since the May 2006 earthquake in Jogja, UNESCO has been actively involved in the rehabilitation of the structurally damaged Prambanan temple complex (see chapter 6). Other related global players in Jogja's tourism include the nongovernmental International Council on Monuments and Sites (with an Indonesian secretariat in Bandung) and the nonprofit World Monuments Fund. The latter listed Kotagede Heritage District, which suffered severe damage after the 2006 quake, on its 2008 World Monuments Watch list of 100 most endangered sites. It is probably no coincidence that Borobudur and Prambanan appear on UNESCO's list, but the Sultan's Palace is not (yet) included. After all, the central government in Jakarta advises UNESCO (an intergovernmental organization), and it is in their interest to nominate politically safe heritage sites such as Hindu or Buddhist monuments, rather than a palace where current politics are being played out.[15] This serves as a reminder that, ultimately, a World Heritage Site is the product of agency on the national level. In any case, the Indonesian government has its own heritage politics and national list of *cagar budaya* (heritage conservation).

## Trading Tradition

It was a happy coincidence that the tour guide event I stumbled upon in the spring of 2002 in Belgium (see Preface) involved Indonesian guides from Jogja. In all, I visited the Indonesian province three times over a period of six years (in 2000, 2003 and 2006). This gave me an opportunity to experience how quickly Jogja is changing, while at the same time retaining its old charm. Some personal stories illustrate the ongoing tensions between rapid modernization and tradition. In 2006, a journalist from *Kedaulatan Rakyat*, the city's oldest and most widely read newspaper, interviewed me about my research. Shortly after publication of the article, I received a call from Lestari, a young woman active in a cultural association trying to revive the traditional Javanese arts. She wanted to hear my opinion on the future of Javanese culture and proposed to meet in a Kentucky Fried Chicken (not the Javanese copycat version). I was intrigued that somebody concerned about the disappearance of traditional culture would want to meet at a place I thought of as a typical icon of Americanization. As soon as we started our conversation, I asked her to explain this. Lestari told me that she occasionally meets at KFC with friends (foreign fast food is rather pricy for Indonesian standards) and simply assumed that I, a Westerner, would have felt less comfortable in a more Javanese (non–air-conditioned) setting. A couple of weeks later, I bumped into Jean-Pierre, a French anthropologist and expert in everything Javanese. This time, I chose the meeting place and proposed a new stylish eatery that is extremely popular among the city's young working population. Jean-Pierre ordered a jasmine tea and was deeply offended when the waiter told him the diner did not have the traditional *tutup gelas* (glass lid) to cover his drink. These are just two anecdotes exemplifying how Jogja, like so many places, is a glocal crossroads of the old and the new and how people react to this in different ways.

Apart from being the cultural cradle of Java, Jogja is the Indonesian pacesetter for the progressive and the populist. It is home to the Indonesian Institute of Fine Arts and one of the most active contemporary art scenes in the country, giving space to young artists to experiment both with visual expressions and interpretations of current events (e.g., through public murals and exhibitions in art galleries). The city is also a major centre of higher education, with over thirty universities and more than seventy institutes of higher learning, and an estimated student population of around 250,000. This young—both temporary (mobile) and contemporary—population heavily influences Yogyakarta's cityscape and facilitates the influx of global popular culture and technologies (e.g., Internet cafés can be found in virtually every main street). Contrary to the rather homogeneous rural population, only 30 to 40 per cent of the city's current inhabitants are Javanese. The rest of the population comes from all over Indonesia or from abroad. The steady increase of students and the massive arrival of migrants from conflict zones on other Indonesian islands over the last decade have profoundly changed Jogja's demographics and cultural impact. For one, you hear less Javanese and more Indonesian on the street.[16]

Yogyakarta has alliances with sister provinces in various parts of the world: Kyoto Prefecture, Japan (1985); the Ismailia Governate, Egypt (1990); the State of California, United States (1997); Tirol Province, Austria (1999); and Chiang Mai, Thailand (2007). The city is twinned with Savannah, Georgia (2002); Honolulu, Hawai'i (2003); and Baalbeck, Lebanon (2008). Common areas of collaboration include economy and trade, industry, culture and tourism. In addition, the presence of transnational multidepartment stores such as Carrefour (France), Makro (the Netherlands), Superindo (Belgium) or Hero (Malaysia), and multistorey shopping malls has made the city lose some of its village-like character and, in the process, has also widened the gap between the small capitalist economic sector and the vast informal economy. The city's diverse expatriate community is principally comprised of artists, exchange students, teachers, aid workers, volunteers and exporters of furniture and handicrafts. There is currently one international school (but there are plans to build a second one). As with many other cultural crossroads, Jogja is the playground of ongoing tensions between global, regional, national and local imaginaries and interests—processes of globalization, regionalization, Indonesianization, and localization—coupled with the advance of modernization, consumerism, mass media and tourism. None of these forces, which are primarily the result of changes in the world in the last fifty years, act independently of one another. On the contrary, they often interact and support each other. Changes to the social fabric are not necessarily new, but have been a long time in the making (Mulder 1994).

What happens to tourism in the province is a nice example of translocal connectedness and dependence. Growth rates declined in the 1990s, at first only slightly after the Gulf War, but then there was a more pronounced decline after an outbreak of cholera amongst returning Japanese tourists in 1994 and 1996. The Southeast Asian economic crisis of 1997 and the national political turmoil of 1998 further slowed growth considerably. Challenges facing tourism today include the low volume of tourists, the harsh competition with neighbouring countries offering similar products and an international image of Indonesia that is political instead of a promotional asset. Although it was once one of the destinations favoured by the six five-year economic development plans of the New Order government, Yogyakarta cannot count any longer on much central government support. This has much to do with the ongoing process of decentralization, a direct result of the country's democratization process after the fall of Suharto in 1998.

More recently, the Bali bomb blasts of 2002 and 2005, the outbreak of SARS (Severe Acute Respiratory Syndrome) and the Iraq War in 2003, the tsunami of 2004, the earthquake of 2006 and the outbreak of avian influenza have had major negative impacts on the province's tourism. The Bali bombs indirectly affected Yogyakarta because Bali is one of the main entry gates for in-bound tourism. The other entry gate, the nearby international airport of Solo, was affected by SARS, as many flights coming from SARS-affected Singapore—a major regional connection hub—were cancelled. In addition, the government introduced visas on arrival in 2003, stopping two decades of an open-door policy. Before 1997, Jogja received 10 per cent (300,000) of Indonesia's foreign visitors (3 million). Since then, tourism development halted and there have only been small increases. In 2005 (before the disasters of 2006), the number of foreign tourists in the province was down to 115,000, a mere 2.5 per cent of Indonesia's total of 5 million tourists, and receiving a similar small fraction of the US$4.5 million in national receipts (UNWTO 2006). Some of the shortfall in foreign tourists has been met by a rise in domestic tourism.

## Tanzania's Safari Capital

Arusha is the name both of one of Tanzania's twenty-six administrative regions, situated in the north of the country (on the eastern edge of the Great Rift Valley), and of its capital city (Map 2). Archaeological finds in this area, particularly those of Oldupai Gorge (a variety of *Homo* specimens) and Laetoli (hominid footprints), suggest that people have been living in this fertile volcanic area since the beginning of humankind. Between three and five thousand years ago, Cushitic herdsmen and cultivators from the north absorbed the indigenous Khoisan hunter-gatherer communities. About two thousand years ago, Bantu-speaking people began to arrive from West Africa. At roughly the same time, Nilotic pastoralists appeared and continued to immigrate into the area well into the eighteenth century. The Arusha Region still contains members of each of Africa's four major ethnolinguistic families: Bantu (e.g., Rwa), Nilotic (e.g., Maa), Cushitic (e.g., Iraqw) and Khoisan (e.g., Hadza). Initially established in the early nineteenth century as a market for trading local agricultural produce, Arusha became the site of a garrison around 1900, when Tanganyika was under German colonial rule as part of its East Africa Protectorate (1884–1918). Following Germany's defeat in the First World War, the country was handed over to the United Kingdom as a mandate territory by the League of Nations and, after 1946, a UN trust territory. Arusha's clock tower is supposedly situated at the midpoint between Cairo and Cape Town (3,940 kilometres from each), representing the halfway point between the two termini of the old British Empire in Africa. It was in Arusha, then the British administrative headquarters for northern Tanganyika, that the United Kingdom signed the official documents ceding independence in 1961. Three years later, Tanganyika and Zanzibar merged to form the United Republic of Tanzania. In 1967, the country's first president, Julius Nyerere, proclaimed his renowned Arusha Declaration for self-reliance, outlining the principles of *Ujamaa*.[17]

Arusha has become a major trading hub for Tanzanite gemstones as well as the commercial centre of a large farming area producing half of the country's wheat and substantial amounts of coffee, flowers, beans and pyrethrum for export, along with bananas, maize, millet and vegetables for domestic use. Larger commercial enterprises in the city are mainly in the hands of a prosperous South Asian diaspora. Tourism is one of the major income generators, with the region playing host to numerous safari companies, hotels and lodges. Despite its closeness to the equator, the city's elevation of 1,400 metres on the southern slopes of Mt. Meru keeps temperatures down and alleviates humidity. The estimated population is about 300,000 (in a region calculated at over 1,300,000). The Maasai are the largest ethnic group—approximately 400,000 in the region—followed by the *Waarusha* (Arusha people) and *Wameru* (Meru people).[18] Arusha's prosperity draws migrants from throughout the country, and while they all speak their own languages or dialects, Swahili is the main language of communication.[19] Newcomers from coastal areas are increasing the presence of Islam in an area that has known extensive Christian missionary activity since the arrival of the German colonizers.

## Safari Dreams

In contrast with my rather blurred childhood images of (Southeast) Asia, from early on I was inundated with European images and ideas of Africa. This can be explained in part because I grew up in a country with a colonial past it had not fully digested.[20] However, only when taking graduate courses in African Studies in the United States was I really confronted with the many atrocities committed by Belgian colonizers. As a child, I had heard very different stories, for instance about how dedicated missionaries had civilized the African people (Dr. Albert Schweitzer being presented as an iconic figure). My primary school teachers seemed proud of the fact that no other region in the world had sent out a larger proportion of Catholic missionaries than Flanders. Belgian popular culture was, and still is, full of references to central Africa. As everybody else, I avidly read Hervé's classic but controversial comic-strip album *The Adventures of Tintin in the*

*Congo* (1931) and I watched innumerable documentaries and movies about Africa. Gazing at the colonial trophies on display in the renowned Royal Museum of Central Africa in Tervuren only added to the imagined mysteries of the 'dark continent'. I vividly remember how awkward it felt as a kid to go sightseeing in Matongé, the colourful district of Brussels (named after one of Kinshasha's most vibrant commercial areas) where the Congolese community congregates with other African immigrants. As an undergraduate, I lived together with students from Zaire (now the Democratic Republic of Congo), Cameroon and Nigeria, and during my volunteer work in France I met not only Yusuf but many young people from various African countries as well. My first trip to sub-Saharan Africa took place in 1999. At the time, I was working for an international NGO dealing with refugee issues, and I was sent to Nairobi, Kenya, to co-organize a workshop for international volunteers working in African refugee camps. After the training, I visited a refugee settlement near Adjumani, on the border between Uganda and Sudan. It was on the flight from Nairobi to Entebbe that I caught an initial glimpse of Tanzania (Lake Victoria). On the adventurous journey from Kampala to northern Uganda, I was confronted for the first time with safari tourism.

Tanzania seems to be well aware of the imaginaries of Africa that circulate the globe as it cleverly capitalizes on the world-known iconology of its natural and cultural heritage. The country's promotional campaigns for the global market, 'Tanzania—Authentic Africa' and 'Tanzania: Land of Kilimanjaro and Zanzibar', powerfully encapsulate its most famous landmarks (Figure 4).[21] Many of the northern region's wildlife landscapes, especially that of the wide plains of the Serengeti, have become popular icons for Africa as a whole, in the form of nature documentaries, Hollywood entertainment and autobiographic movies, with their perfect romantic and nostalgic vision of an unexplored and time-frozen wild Eden (Staples 2006).[22] Ngorongoro, for instance, is often referred to as 'Africa's garden of Eden'. It is a common anecdote that when Noah left his (Biblical) Ark, he let all the animals he had taken with him disperse from the Ngorongoro crater. Humans are remarkably absent in these imaginaries (Århem 1985; Shetler 2007), although many of the oldest human remains—sometimes imaginatively called mitochondrial or African Eve (Tierney 1992)—were discovered in and around the Rift Valley, and some scholars have concluded that the true Garden of Eden or cradle of humankind must have been located in East Africa.

The Western imagery of sub-Saharan Africa has often been presented in the most literal sense of the word, in visual forms. Such cultural representations, which flourished especially during the colonial era, are at the basis of stereotypical us-them categorizations. During colonial rule, for example, the British highlighted Maasai life because as colonizers they wanted to promote an image of Africans as different and as nobly primitive. And even though the image of the dark continent has changed and evolved over time (Palmberg 2001; Mengara 2001), some authors have interpreted contemporary tourism as a silent continuation and perpetuation of these old processes of stereotyping and measuring African culture in hierarchical relation to Western civilization (Wels 2002). Westerners long for pristine African landscapes dotted with picturesque huts topped by grass-thatched roofs. They expect to hear the sound of drums the minute they arrive in Africa, and to see natives rhythmically dancing to the ongoing cadence, representing 'real' and quintessential Africa (Norton 1996). Anthropology has historically been implicated in such (re)invention of Africa. As Ferguson reminds us, the discipline was 'one of a number of sites for the elaboration of ideas of Africa as a continent defined by "tradition," "simple societies," and "societies without history," even as "Africa" itself was a central site for the development of key ideas in anthropology' (2006: 2). Mbembe observes that, when it comes to the category of Africa, the 'oscillation between the real and the imaginary, the imaginary realized and the real imagined, does not take place solely in writing. This interweaving also takes place in life' (2001: 241–42). In East Africa, for instance, colonial anthropologists, together with explorers and Christian missionaries, helped create a normative Maasai ethnicity (Spear and Waller 1993; Hughes 2006).

Tanzania has often figured in *National Geographic*. Many of the stories covered deal with archaeological finds or wildlife. The country was also the focus of a scandal that shook the magazine's readers. In July 2004, it published a photo essay about elephant hunting by the spear-wielding Barabaig people (Aposporos 2004). Images portrayed the Barabaig, dressed in traditional clothes carrying elephant tusks, as if fresh from a hunt. Vigilant readers, however, pointed out that the tusks were stamped with various numbers, and the editor's subsequent apology (Allen 2004) admitted that the tusks had actually been borrowed from the Department of Wildlife. A French photographer had staged the photographs, to make the Barabaig look more like the stereotypical image that Westerners have of fierce African hunters. Although photographic safaris have largely replaced hunting, most tourists still travel to Tanzania hoping to see the 'Big Five', a hunting term historically used to denote the five most dangerous African animals: lion, leopard, rhinoceros, elephant, and buffalo. Little (1991) points out how tourism discourse has been influenced by hunting vocabulary: as the camera substitutes for the gun, tourists shoot their pictures and capture images in order to fill photo albums with trophies.

Not without irony, some have expanded the Big Five to the Big Six by including the Maasai people.[23] Alongside the amazing wildlife, the Maasai are the flagbearer of Tanzanian tourism (Figure 4). The relationship between tourism and Maasai has been largely determined by safari imaginaries. Due to countless coffee-table books, movies and snapshots, everybody seems to know the Maasai—a fact some business-minded Maasai themselves exploit (Salazar 2009a).[24] To tourists, the sight of a virile Maasai warrior, dressed in colourful red blankets and beaded jewellery, evokes the romantic image of a modern noble savage (Bruner

FIGURE 4 • *'Tanzania, Authentic Africa' and the Cultural Tourism Programme*

2005: 33–100; Hughes 2006; Bachmann 1988). The Maasai are also the main attraction of Tanzania's award-winning Cultural Tourism Programme (CTP), a project launched in 1995 by SNV, the Netherlands Development Organization (Figure 4). They set up CTP as a network of local communities—mainly Maasai in northern Tanzania—that operate independently from each other, offering individually developed meet-the-people tour packages. Widely praised in travel guides such as *Lonely Planet* and *The Rough Guide,* the programme received an international Award for Socially Responsible Tourism in 1999. In 2002, the International Year of Ecotourism, the World Tourism Organization (2002: 237–40) heralded CTP as Tanzania's good practice example of sustainable development, even though some modules had to close down because they received too little visitors.

## 'Arusha, the Centre of Africa'

> Few places in the world conjure up such rich images as the magnificent peaks, valleys and plains of Northern Tanzania. The highest mountains ... the wildest lakes ... the most abundant and varied wildlife—everything is here. Whether it's the contented roar of a big cat across the water at dusk, the timid face of an antelope calf seen through the rushes, or the sheer beauty of a thousand flamingos taking flight—the magic of this untamed earthly paradise will leave memories you will never forget ... Arusha, where all good things start (and finish).
> —Tanzania Tourist Board brochure

The emergence and growth of *utalii* (tourism) in Safariland, as the area of northern Tanzania and southern Kenya is commonly known, is closely interwoven with the history of environmental conservation (Salazar 2009b). The local face of tourism is largely determined by the distribution of wildlife and the safari business that has grown around it, and the safari concept itself is inseparably linked with the coming of Europeans (Figure 11).[25] Under German and British colonial rule, tourism was first established as a service industry catering to Westerners coming to observe and hunt exotic animals, and the age of Africa's national parks, specifically designed for tourism, began with a 1933 international agreement.[26] Under the British, tourism in East Africa developed on a regional basis encompassing all colonies (Tanganyika, Kenya and Uganda). Tanganyika was only included in this planning after becoming a British protectorate in 1919, marking the initial point of Kenya's superior position in regional development. Colonial administrators decided what was valuable natural heritage and what was not. Early in the twentieth century, the Germans declared Mount Kilimanjaro, the world's highest freestanding peak, and the surrounding forests a Game Reserve. The British designated the snow-capped mountain to be a Forest Reserve (1921), Tarangire as a

Game Reserve (1957), Ngorongoro as a Conservation Area (1959) and Serengeti (1951), Lake Manyara (1960) and Ngurdoto Crater (Arusha) (1960) as National Parks.[27] The establishment of protected areas, in other words, was as much a process of 'Nature' production as nature preservation (Neumann 1998).

The government of independent Tanzania continued conservation policies along the same lines. Already in 1961, President Nyerere released his Arusha Manifesto in which he pledged the protection of wildlife. His government changed Arusha (1967), Tarangire (1970) and Kilimanjaro (1973) into national parks, and added new forest reserves, game controlled areas and game reserves. Despite growing population pressures, Tanzanian authorities dedicated more than 42,000 square kilometres of the country's territory to the formal protection of wildlife. For a while, tourism was a major element of Tanzania's development strategy. The colonial legacy, however, gave Europeans and South Asians, who had the most experience in the hospitality industry, the advantage over inexperienced Tanzanians. While independence did not diminish regional cooperation, Uganda and Tanzania felt that the East African collaboration was benefiting Kenya at their expense.[28] As the three countries pursued autonomous courses, their policies were to magnify rather than reduce the differences in the performances of their respective tourism sectors. Under the 1967 Arusha Declaration, Tanzania declared international tourism to be incompatible with its socialist ideology. Tourism was also discouraged on conservation grounds, because visitors would gradually destroy the wildlife. Already by 1900, the historical record had proved that foreign tourists were most swiftly and systematically killing off Africa's wildlife (Honey 1999: 223).

Despite the change of policy, Tanzania managed to increase its tourism capacity at the end of the 1960s. In 1971, a Tourism Master Plan was presented and, in the same year, the Kilimanjaro International Airport was constructed. Paradoxically, the country's isolationist state-run hospitality industry was heavily dependent on foreign experts, capital and imports. The decline of the economy in the 1970s saw the introduction of bureaucratic procedures at airports and other points of entry that subjected visitors to declarations, searches and demands for form filling. On top of all this, in 1973 the government issued an overnight ban on all hunting and photographic safaris within its territory. Tanzania also had to endure strong competition with Kenya. While the former had the best attractions, the latter had the tourists (Honey 1999: 231). International visitors often crossed the border but their dollars did not. After the collapse of the East African Community (EAC) in 1977, Tanzania closed its border with Kenya, virtually ending foreign tourist traffic at once. Although not originally foreseen by President Nyerere, this border closure set in motion a process that would gradually lead to privatizing Tanzanian's tourism service industries (Honey 1999: 234). This began with new investments from local capital, followed by more substantial investments of foreign capital when Nyerere stepped down in 1985.

With an increasing economic crisis and subsequent political reforms, the new government decided to change its policy, reopen the border with Kenya, and begin again seriously investing in tourism. A major step in this direction was the enactment of the National Policy on Tourism in 1991, the first real tourism planning by independent Tanzania. In 1992, the government launched an ambitious programme to reverse its earlier image. It established the Tanzania Tourist Board (TTB), started a publicity campaign, and liberalized and privatized the tourism sector. In 1996, the administration drew up an Integrated Tourism Master Plan with the focus on improving, developing and refurbishing existing attractions and facilities. In 1999, a revised policy was issued, a result of the involvement of a variety of stakeholders through a number of workshops conducted in Arusha and Dar es Salaam between 1994 and 1998.

In 2002, the Ministry of Natural Resources and Tourism (MNRT) launched a new Tourism Master Plan. To strengthen the private sector, the government assisted in the formation of the Tourism Confederation of Tanzania (TCT), an apex body of all subsector associations in the travel and tourism service industries. There is little evidence, however, that during the privatization of the state enterprises, Tanzanian entrepreneurship was actually promoted. Tourism is now the country's fastest growing economic sector and, together with mining, the leading source of foreign exchange. In Tanzania's Poverty Reduction Strategy Papers, tourism is indicated as a major vehicle for pro-poor growth and poverty reduction. However, while contributing around 4 per cent to the gross domestic product, the sector employs only 290,000 people, a mere 3 per cent of total employment (WTTC 2007: 26). The government is exploring ways to make tourism more pro-poor, though the strategy to be followed is unclear.

For tourists, Arusha is the gateway to nearby national parks (Serengeti, Lake Manyara, Tarangire, Arusha and Mt. Kilimanjaro) as well as the Ngorongoro Conservation Area. As such, the city is often called the country's safari capital. Arusha also strategically markets the imaginary that, being situated halfway between Cairo and Cape Town, it is 'the centre of Africa' (cf. Merrington 2001). Like Jogja, Arusha is well equipped to receive visitors. It is served by the Kilimanjaro International Airport for international connections and the small but expanding Arusha Airport for domestic flights. There are also daily shuttle busses to and from Jomo Kenyatta International Airport in Nairobi, located just across the border. Within the city, there are taxis, 4x4 safari vehicles and the commonly used public transport minivans (imported second-hand vehicles from Japan and the Middle East). In and around Arusha, one can taste an eclectic menu of local and ethnic food (Indian, Chinese, Japanese, Mexican and Continental). The only Western-style fast-food restaurant in town is Steers, a South African flame-grilled burger chain—and there is one McDonald's copycat restaurant, called McMoody's (Figure 2). There are plenty of hotels, lodges, guesthouses and permanent or semipermanent tented camps, the more expensive accommodations mostly owned and managed by foreigners. The city also offers plenty of Internet cafés, increasingly including wireless technology.

Over two hundred safari companies offer activities as varied as game drives; walking, camel, and balloon safaris; cultural tours; mountain biking and climbing; bird watching; canoeing and caving. Commonly bought souvenirs include baskets, weaving, pottery, musical instruments, Maasai curiosa (blankets, spears, and beaded jewellery), Makonde woodcarvings (figurines and masks), Barabaig goatskin garments and *tingatinga* paintings.[29] In 2007, Tanzania welcomed around 692,000 tourists and cashed over US$1 billion in receipts (UNWTO 2008). Around 70 per cent of all tourists arriving in Tanzania visit the Arusha Region.[30] Most visitors come from Europe (Germany, Austria, France, Italy, the Netherlands, the United Kingdom and Spain) and North America. Promotion and marketing happens mainly through websites and the presence at annual international trade fairs, primarily in the United Kingdom, Germany, South Africa and Dubai. In 2008, Tanzania launched its first major televised campaign in the United States. A New York-based advertising, marketing and public relations company handled the promotional strategy.[31] New targeted markets include China, Japan, Russia and India.

## International Mediation

My first visit to Arusha took place in 2004 (and I returned to northern Tanzania in 2007 and 2009). During my initial stay, I was introduced to Lenana, a Maasai chief from a remote settlement in the highlands of Monduli. When he heard that I had expertise in tourism, he immediately invited me to his *boma* (homestead). A couple of days later, Lenana picked me up in his rusty 4x4 Toyota pickup. Before leaving Arusha, he visited town to run a couple of errands. He carefully chose the nonpaved roads, telling me that he was not used to driving on hard surfaces and did not like it. On our way, we stopped at the Meserani cattle market because Lenana wanted to ensure that his younger brother was following his SMS instructions for selling some of the family's cows. After having left the main road in Monduli, we continued along a dirt track for another half an hour, until the last twenty minutes when we had to walk uphill. Lenana's boma, newly built in 2001, was strategically located on top of an escarpment, with stunning views over the Rift Valley. We greeted the elders and had tea in his mother's hut. The location was beautiful, but how to develop tourism there? Access was difficult and there was neither electricity nor water. While sipping the delicious drink, enjoying the outlook and pondering the problem of tourism development, my cell phone started buzzing. It was a message from my spouse in the United States, asking me how things were going in Africa. The whole situation gave me a weird feeling of connectedness and illustrated how, in the Arusha Region too, there is a seemingly paradoxical mix of 'tradition' and rapid modernization.

Due to its central geographical location, Arusha housed the headquarters of the erstwhile East African Community (1967–77), which joined Tanzania, Kenya and Uganda in an economic, communications and customs union. This intergovernmental organization was revived in 2000 (with its secretariat again located in Arusha), and, since 2007, has included Rwanda and Burundi. The city hosts other nongovernmental and international organizations as well, most notably the UN International Criminal Tribunal for Rwanda. Because of all the international activity, and the fact that Arusha is a popular international conference venue, it has been nicknamed the 'Geneva of Africa'. The city has town-twinning linkages with Mürzzuschlag, Austria (1978); Durham, North Carolina (1991); and Kansas City, Missouri (1995). Cooperation includes, but is not restricted to, the fields of government and administration, business and economic development, art(s) and culture, science and technology, education and health. The presence of a large expatriate community—businesspeople, UN staff, missionaries, aid workers and volunteers—has greatly benefited the local economy and has helped to turn burgeoning Arusha into a small cosmopolis. To cater to the needs of the mobile foreign community, there are three international schools and an increasing number of shopping centres and stores with imported goods. The city also counts numerous colleges and some smaller universities, many of which were founded by Christian missionaries from a variety of denominations.

Arusha's cityscape is typical of many other East African towns, with dusty streets, rows of shops run by East African Asians, noisy and colourful markets, mosques and churches and a vibrant street life. The relatively young population has given rise to a lively music scene, notably *bongo flava* (Tanzanian hip-hop originating in Dar es Salaam), mostly performed in Swahili, with various genres influenced by African American music. Perhaps because Arusha has always been a patchwork of cultures and because the general population lacks a common cultural heritage, there seem to be fewer visible tensions between global, regional, national and local interests than in Jogja. However, being located in one of the poorest countries in the world also creates a series of more pressing problems, as, for example, excess mortality from AIDS (leading to lower life expectancy, higher infant mortality and death rates and lower population growth rates). In addition, dependence on foreign donor assistance has made it difficult for people to make the transition from socialism to a free market system, a trend that began when President Nyerere stepped down in 1985.

Tanzania's tourism development is being assisted by strategically placed foreign aid from United States (United States Agency for International Development), British (Department for International Development), Dutch (Netherlands Development Organization), German (Gesellschaft für Technische Zusammenarbeit) and Swedish (Swedish International Development Cooperation Agency) aid programmes. With the help of the World Bank, the country has upgraded its infrastructure, including accommodation in the protected areas, access roads and passenger facilities at harbours and airports. To a lesser degree, also international

NGOs have also been involved. Despite all the assistance, donors' financial contributions to tourism have been marginal, as compared to other sectors. With the liberalizations, the country's tourism has grown faster than Kenya's, to the extent that Tanzania has now become a standalone destination rather than an add-on. Nevertheless, there is a long way to go before the country catches up to the levels of its neighbour.

Although planning bodies are both local (TTB Arusha Branch, Ngorongoro Conservation Area Authority) and national (Ministry of Natural Resources and Tourism, Tourism Confederation of Tanzania, Tanzania National Parks), tourism development is increasingly stimulated by regional, continental and global alliances (Salazar 2009b). The new EAC Treaty, signed in 1999, has an entire chapter devoted to co-operation in tourism and wildlife management. The EAC Sectoral Council on Tourism and Wildlife Management is undertaking steps to harmonize the tourism operations of its member states and promote East Africa as a single destination.[32] Since 1995, Tanzania has been a member of the Southern African Development Community (SADC), which has two tourism-related bodies: a Tourism Coordination Unit and the Regional Tourism Organization of Southern Africa. On a continental scale, tourism is encouraged at different levels. Tanzania is member of the Africa Travel Association and the African Economic Community, which has a special committee on transport, communication and tourism. Even the New Partnership for Africa's Development (NEPAD), the African Union's strategic plan to foster the continent's economic growth, pays specific attention to tourism.

On the global level, Tanzania is a member of the UNWTO and bodies like the Multilateral Investment Guarantee Agency (MIGA), which have tourism-related programmes. These and other organizations have had important meetings in Arusha: the Africa Travel Association annual congress (1998, 2008), the MIGA-Swiss Investment Forum on Tourism (2002), the Association for Tourism and Leisure Education (Africa) Community Tourism conference (2003), the UNTWO Seminar-workshop on Sustainable Tourism Development and Poverty Alleviation (2004), the UNEP International Seminar on Sustainable Consumption and Production (2006) with a working group on ecotourism in developing countries and the Leon H. Sullivan Foundation summit on Tourism and Infrastructure Development (2008). Arusha also hosts the annual Karibu Travel and Tourism Fair, which started locally but has become a regional event with travel representatives from neighbouring countries. As in Indonesia, UNESCO is an influential intergovernmental body in Tanzania. Around Arusha, it designated the Ngorongoro Conservation Area (1979, 2010), Serengeti National Park (1981) and Kilimanjaro National Park (1987) to be World Heritage sites, and the UNESCO Man and Biosphere Programme recognized Serengeti-Ngorongoro (1981) and Lake Manyara National Park (1981) as Biosphere Reserves. Under the International Convention on Wetlands, the Lake Natron Basin was recognized to be a Wetland of International Importance (2001). The World Conservation Monitoring Centre, the biodiversity information and assessment arm of the UN Environment Programme, is monitoring the conservation of all these protected areas.

## Picturing Paradise

As the cases of Jogja and Arusha illustrate, the imagery surrounding tourism to developing countries is about fantasies, and often about an ambivalent nostalgia for the past—ambivalent because returning to the past is not what people actually desire.[33] Modern myths—nature, the noble savage, art, individual freedom and self-realization, equality, and paradise—all have special significance for and are manifested in the practices of international tourism (Hennig 2002). The three recurring myths in the marketing of tourism to developing countries, as identified by Echtner and Prasad (2003), are clearly present in the case of Indonesia and Tanzania: the myth of the unchanged, the myth of the unrestrained and the myth of the uncivilized. Moreover, discourses of the past—orientalism, colonialism and imperialism—seem to be extremely fertile ground for nostalgic and romantic dreams (Edensor 1998; Desmond 1999; Henderson and Weisgrau 2007). Dann (1976) distinguishes two basic characteristics underlying all tourist fantasies. On the one hand, there is the overcoming of monotony, anomie and meaninglessness of everyday life with more satisfying experiences—escapism and the desire for exotism or difference. On the other hand, there is the boosting of personality—ego-enhancement, leading to the accumulation of symbolic capital.[34] Such desires, however, are not simply internalized wishes but, rather, part of widely shared imaginaries that are articulated through constellations of social practice and the media (Crouch, Jackson and Thompson 2005).

My own experiences with European images of Asia and Africa illustrate that destination marketers have no monopoly over 'manufacturing the exotic' (Rossel 1988). Tourism fantasies are always situated within wider sociocultural frameworks (Hutnyk 1996). They emerge not from the realm of concrete, everyday experience but in the circulation of more collectively held imaginaries. Critical scholarship reveals how broader cultural and ideological structures create and mediate tourism representations.[35] Images of difference have been (re)constructed over centuries of cross-cultural contact. In the case of Western tourism to developing countries, the circulating representations cater to certain images within Western consciousness about how the Other is imagined to be. Such imaginaries form a 'representational loop' (Sturma 2002: 137) that heavily relies upon the fictional worlds of literature, film and the fine arts to give 'authenticity' to peoples and places (Urbain 1994; Robinson and Andersen 2002; Hennig 2002). Not surprisingly, the currently dominant tourism discourses draw upon and extend mythologized (colonial) visions of Otherness from popular culture, (travel) literature and academic writings in disciplines such as anthropology, archaeology and history (Clifford 1997; Desmond 1999; Said 1994; Pratt 1992; Torgovnick 1990). The discourses surrounding ecotourism, for example, are closely related to the much wider 'global ecological imaginary' (Conklin and Graham 1995) of late twentieth-century environmentalism, while nostalgia tourism often taps into commoditized '(neo)colonial imaginaries' (Nederveen Pieterse and Parekh 1995). The latter often evokes and mimics the trope of 'first contact' that was common in colonial travel narratives (Pratt 1992).

Popular culture and global entertainment media have the biggest influence on tourist fantasies: the visual and textual content of documentaries and fiction movies; art, museum exhibitions and fairs; trade cards, video games and animation; photographs, slides, video and postcards; travelogues, blogs and other websites; guidebooks and tourism brochures; literature, coffee-table books and magazines; news coverage and advertising; official documents; and quasi-scientific media such as *National Geographic*. The role of the latter in constructing popular attitudes towards the past and towards exotic cultures is well known and has been extensively studied (e.g., Lutz and Collins 1993). All these cultural representations are mixed together, consumed and interpreted. In his study on contemporary media productions of Tibet, Mercille (2005), for instance, shows the remarkable homogeneity of Shangri-La imaginaries in a movie (*Seven Years in Tibet*), a guidebook (*Lonely Planet*), and a magazine (*National Geographic*).[36] One master image of Tibet seems to circulate by the various representations of it. In a similar vein, Bruner talks about tourism imaginaries in terms of 'metanarratives', and calls them 'the largest conceptual frame within which tourism operates. They are not attached to any locality or to any particular tour, and they are usually taken for granted, not brought to consciousness' (Bruner 2005: 21).

If the metaphor of flow is badly chosen to describe global phenomena in general (chapter 1), it is certainly not adequate for capturing the movement of tourism imaginaries. These images and ideas travel, together with tourists, from tourism-generating regions (which are also destination regions) to tourism-destination regions (which also generate fantasies) and back. In other words, imaginaries do not flow like water in a river, but circulate like blood in a living organism—moving through well-established conduits, leaving certain elements behind and picking up new ones along the way, and continuously returning to their points of origin. Such circulation 'takes time—historical time—and is not instantaneously achieved' (Urban 2001: 105). Empowered by imagined vistas of mass-mediated master narratives, tourism imaginaries have become global.[37] They are now sent, circulated, transferred, received, accumulated, converted and stored around the world.

Tourism narratives travel throughout a self-perpetuating 'touristic cycle', by people and organizations with very different stakes in tourism: marketers, service providers, government agencies, the media and tourists (Bruner 2005). All narratives, appearing at different times (pre-tour, on-tour and post-tour) and places (at home and away), and in various modalities (oral, written, pictorial, symbolic or graphic), can be traced back to the same 'master narrative'. While there is ample scholarship on the production and consumption of tourism discourses and images, much less attention has been given to their actual distribution. This book tries to fill part of the gap by focusing on the role of local tour guides in the circulation of tourism imaginaries. Using a combination of glocal ethnography and discourse-centred analysis, I trace in what directions tourism images and ideas travel, how they spread and are transformed (translated) during circulation, and I disentangle the mechanisms that keep them on the move.

## Back to Reality

How to write about Africa . . . Always use the word 'Africa' or 'Darkness' or 'Safari' in your title. Subtitles may include the words 'Zanzibar', 'Masai', 'Zulu', 'Zambezi', 'Congo', 'Nile', 'Big', 'Sky', 'Shadow', 'Drum', 'Sun' or 'Bygone'. Also useful are words such as 'Guerrillas', 'Timeless', 'Primordial' and 'Tribal'.
–Binyavanga Wainaina (writer; 1971– )

The quote above contains the first lines of a satirical text in which Kenyan author Binyavanga Wainaina instructs fellow writers how to create bestsellers about the African continent. Many of the keywords he proposes are widespread in tourism discourse too, whereas others, like guerrillas, are shunned at all costs. This serves as a reminder that tourism imaginaries do not exist in a vacuum, but have to contend with other circulating images and ideas. Global media streams overwhelm us with thousands of impressions of the world, in real time. In the case of developing countries, the competing imagery is often negative and the media can be very selective in what they show or do not show their audiences (cf. Barnes 2005). Tanzania, like other African countries, stands for disease (primarily malaria and AIDS) and abject poverty; Indonesia connotes natural disasters, environmental degradation, mass traffic accidents, avian flu, copyright infringements and human rights abuses. Both share an image of Islamic terrorism and corruption. In the eyes of Western tourists, Africa is seen as dangerous and to be avoided, while Asia is constructed as simultaneously risky but also exotic and worth experiencing (Carter 1998). This does not mean that such imaginaries enter into public circulation with their meanings already defined according to some preexisting cultural matrix; nor are they innocent of history. As new forms of circulation come to shape our world to an unprecedented degree, understanding the historical specificities of these global processes is a central problem for anthropology. I concur with Gaonkar and Povinelli that, in any given culture of circulation, 'it is more important to track the proliferating co-presence of varied textual/cultural forms in all their mobility and mutability than to attempt a delineation of their fragile autonomy and specificity' (2003: 391).

As the above sketches of Jogja and Arusha illustrate, tourism imaginaries of peoples and places cannot be considered simply as commoditized or commercial representations with an interpretative or symbolic content. They often propagate historically inherited stereotypes that are based on widely circulating (colonial) myths and fantasies. In addition, they are powerful propellers of sociocultural and environmental change, and essential elements in the process of (g)local identity formation, the making of place and the perpetual (re)invention of culture (Erb 2000; Adams 2004). Imaginaries become incarnated in institutions, from archaeological sites, museums and monuments to hotels, media and cultural productions (Wynn 2007: 21). In other words, peoples and places are constructed in both the imaginative and the material sense; destination making is as much about meaning or culture as it is about hard cash and politics.

During the colonial era, the Dutch commoditized Java's cultural past and the Germans and British exoticized the great open spaces and natural resources of the 'Dark Continent' in Tanganyika. Postcolonial tourism policies have continued along the same lines. While government propaganda has used the cultural heritage around Jogja to shape the image of Indonesia, Tanzanian authorities have used the natural heritage around Arusha for the same purposes. The difference in accent is reflected in the names of the respective ministries in charge of tourism: the Ministry of Culture and Tourism in Indonesia versus the Ministry of Natural Resources and Tourism in Tanzania. Even the national emblems—Indonesia's Garuda (mythical bird) versus Tanzania's giraffe (wildlife)—suggest preferences for cultural and natural heritage, respectively. These imaginaries are not just shared within a nation, but spread around the region and the globe, creating complex dynamics of power and conflicting interests. The politics of representation in international tourism are clearly linked to regional and global changes, while drawing inspiration from local and national imaginations of tradition. The tensions this creates are particularly visible in young postcolonial states such as Indonesia and Tanzania where national authorities have little control over imaginaries (less in the latter than in the former).

In detailing Jogja and Arusha and the dominant imaginaries that exist about these destinations, I have set the broader context in which local tour guides have to operate. In both destinations, global tourism imaginaries interact with and become embedded in glocalities in which the local is continuously reinvented through processes of globalization and localization while struggling to project its reclaimed self back into the global (Robertson 1995). While the specific contents might be different, the mechanisms that turn the two places into destinations are very similar and the tourism imaginaries surrounding them share common histories and ways of circulation and (re)production. The stage being set, we can now devote our full attention to local tour guiding, in which the narratives and practices of guides interrelate in fascinating ways with global tourism imaginaries.

# 3
# 'SEDUCATION'

⤎⧜⤏

It is no wonder that such a vast territory stretching between the Indian Ocean
and the great lakes of Victoria and Tanganyika should offer an extremely rich
and varied assortment of tourist attractions, ranging from the snow-capped Mt.
Kilimanjaro and spacious volcano craters to the vast open plains, and from the
arid bush to the rain forests and the warm emerald ocean with its white sand
beaches fringed by palm groves. Some of the finest wildlife areas in the world
are concentrated in the North and others are scattered all over the country in
national parks and game reserves well stocked with animals, in most fascinating
scenery. Big game hunting, deep-sea fishing, underwater fishing and goggling in
the Indian Ocean, trout fishing, shopping for sculptured ebony and carved ivory,
handbags of crocodile, leopard, lion, ostrich, elephant and zebra skins, gold and
silver jewellery with locally-mined precious and semi-precious stones, Maasai
spears and shields and inexpensive textile printed in striking patterns, will delight
overseas visitors and so will the friendliness and innate courtesy of the people.

Are you sold yet? Ready to book a luxurious safari and spend your next vacation
exploring the wonders of East Africa? While the quotation above could have come
straight from a glossy travel brochure promoting Tanzania's natural and cultural
heritage, it is actually taken from an old report of the UN Economic Commission for Africa, entitled *Tourism in Eastern Africa,* in which the author colourfully
describes Tanzania's enormous tourism potential (Popovic 1972: 151).

Ponder this for a moment. Tourism offers prospective tourist-consumers
a rather unusual type of commodity, because travel for leisure exists only as a
projected future activity at the time the sale is initially made. This wonderfully
packaged dream, usually a combination of linguistic and supporting visual elements, creates, codifies and communicates certain mythical experiences (Selwyn
1996). Tourism marketing therefore relies heavily on imagined scenarios to turn
places and peoples into easily consumable attractions, providing simplified and
historically fixed versions of local heritage and culture. Whatever communication
medium is used, the language of tourism is one of persuasion, merging macroeconomic goals of growth with attributed individual need satisfactions, imaginaries with imaginations. Seducing images and discourses are so predominant that

without them there probably would be little tourism at all (Morgan, Pritchard and Pride 2002; Jaworski and Pritchard 2005).

I described in the previous chapter how the representations that picture and situate Jogja and Arusha as exotic destinations have a historical foundation and are, as such, linked to wider cultural imaginaries and profoundly affect the expectations of tourists. An in-depth exploration of how local guides become acquainted with these images and ideas will be the basic task in front of us for this chapter. In the world of guiding, tourism imaginaries are expressed and become most tangible through tour commentaries and storytelling; in the next chapter, I will discuss other practices through which tourism imaginaries are enacted and circulated, while here I will look at how apprentice guides familiarize themselves with tourism discourse(s). Once again, discussing data from Indonesia and Tanzania side by side will allow for a more complex and holistic analysis.

## Global Tourism Discourses

> The tourist thought about how wonderful a picture he had taken—a dirty, scrawny, Balinese woman who was once a famous dancer ... but now with her basket on her head, her skirt hitched up to her knees, her swollen feet, wearing an old t-shirt with the printed message: 'Paradise'.
> —Sukanta (2000: 30).

Language can act as a force that does not merely reflect but shapes social relations. As I will illustrate with tour guiding, such language use involves complex indexical signalling, projecting oneself into events and roles, enactments of evaluative models of social life, and so forth. Tourism representations in general draw upon wider cultural imaginaries, and are themselves what MacCannell calls 'an ideological framing of history, nature and tradition' (1992: 1). If the tourism sector has developed its own homogenizing ideologies, how are its workers and service providers familiarized with its traditions, practices and expressions? How do they learn to understand and copy tourism talk, how are they taught to produce the scripts of tourism space and to construct the narratives and signs to locate sites and objects? How are tourism workers trained to perceive and represent the world with a 'tourist gaze'? In short, how are the foundational discourses of tourism circulated and perpetuated?

While there is ample scholarship on the production and consumption of tourism discourse, much less attention has been paid to its distribution and circulation.[1] Exceptions include Bruner (2005), who devoted many years to tracking the spread of tourism narratives. According to him, all tales circulating in the self-perpetuating 'touristic cycle' can be traced back to the same 'master narrative'. However, that archetypical story is continuously transformed and transposed through an intricate system of artefacts and communication devices (chapter 2).

Local tour guides step in this circle by refashioning general discourses as tourism tales, which are 'less encompassing in scope and more attached to particular regions' (Bruner 2005: 22).

The replication and dissemination of discourse is generally a multifaceted process, and globalization has added extra layers of complexity to the way words and ideas travel (Silverstein and Urban 1996). The more global tourism grows, the more its selective representations of life become the codified and authorized versions of local culture and knowledge (Salazar 2009a).[2] There is therefore something highly paradoxical about this process. Destinations worldwide might be adapting themselves to the standardizing trends of global tourism, but, at the same time, they have to commoditize their local distinctiveness in order to compete with other destinations. As a result, tourism becomes an 'arena for discourse construction and manipulation' (Norton 1996: 370).

It cannot be simply assumed there is one universal tourism discourse that sends undifferentiated messages to a homogenized global audience. Because the logic of the global market prescribes diversification and the creation of multiple consumer identities (cf. Bourdieu 1984), the language of tourism contains a wide number of registers, each one addressing a particular type of client with particular interests (Dann 1996b; Morgan and Pritchard 1998). As discourses are being '(re)entextualized' (reproduced with an altered form) or '(re)contextualized' (reproduced identically in another context), innumerable factors intervene, and the copy is often distinct from the original (Bauman and Briggs 1990). Because there is frequently an asymmetrical power relationship between the originator(s) and the copier(s), the original discourse is not only copied but is reacted or responded to (Goffman 1981). As I will show in the following chapters, these general rules apply remarkably well to tourism discourse.

Local tour guides are not without a stake in the (re)creation and promotion of profitable myth-making tourism tales (Fine and Speer 1985). They tailor and glocalize their services—interpretations of local natural and cultural heritage—to constantly changing foreign audiences. Ironically, many guides in developing countries rely on widely fashionable discourses such as nostalgia-talk or eco-babble as a way of capitalizing on their own background and signalling their authenticity as truly 'local'—pretending to be living an imagined immobile life far away from the Western world of capitalism and modernity. In so doing, guides unconsciously become key vehicles in the perpetuation of tourism imaginaries, becoming true mechanics of glocalization (chapter 5). In order to understand how exactly they (re)produce these representations while guiding (as I will discuss in the next chapter), we first need to disentangle how they are acquainted with them through formal schooling and informal learning. Where and how do they learn to tell seductive tourism tales? How do they become skilled at the poetics of closely matching their imaged version of a local Eden to the paradises imagined by the wide array of tourists they are serving? I search for answers to these questions by analyzing how guides in Jogja and Arusha are schooled and trained, what kind of information sources they rely on to prepare their tours and where they obtain their information (Figure 5).

**FIGURE 5 •**
*Inspiration
Sources for
Tourism
Imaginaries*

## The Rhetoric of Interpretation

> Storytelling reveals meaning without committing the error of defining it.
> —Hannah Arendt (political theorist; 1906–1975)

I grew up with international tourism, living the first two decades of my life in Bruges, Belgium. The historical centre of this beautifully conserved medieval town is a heavily visited World Heritage site. Many of my secondary school teachers earned extra money working as tour guides during the weekends and school holidays, and I vividly remember the day when the news spread among pupils that our German teacher had failed the tour guide examination. The rumour had it that he had passed all subjects but the German language test. When I was a graduate student at the University of Leuven many years later, my spouse and I had the privilege of living inside Leuven's historical Great Beguinage, another cultural site inscribed on UNESCO's list. Our apartment happened to be situated just next to a small bridge where tour groups usually paused to take pictures of the scenic environment. We sometimes listened in on the tour guide commentaries and were amazed at the elaborate historical untruths some were fabricating about the site. These personal anecdotes reinforce the common idea that the path to becoming a professional guide is long and arduous and that language and discourse play a major role in this accomplishment. To achieve the international standards set by the tourism sector and the authorities (chapter 5), appropriate instruction is required.[3]

Most tour guide training is an adult education activity, and much of it is competency based with an emphasis on knowledge transmission and skill acquisition. Yet does acquiring skills guarantee success as a guide? A quarter of a century ago, Blanton was already criticizing tourism training for being focused too narrowly on vocational and technical skills. Some of his observations are pertinent for the discussion here (1981: 124; emphasis added):

> For someone who has his roots in the countryside, it is hard to *imagine* the romantic allure of nature. Likewise, it is difficult for someone who has never experienced winter to *imagine* the appeal of a warm climate or to understand the curious practice of sunbathing. In the cities of the temperate zone, warm weather is associated with pleasure, social activity, and renewal; in East Africa the association is with drought; and in Asia it is associated with hard work.

How do guides learn to perceive the everyday world around them through the eyes of tourists? How do they know which objects of attention to select, what details to elaborate on, and which jokes to tell?

To a certain extent, one can think of tour guides as knowledge workers. Their knowledge of the local natural and cultural heritage, however, is not limited to facts, figures, and *couleur locale;* it includes the art of network building, of monopolizing contacts, a familiarity with the operations of the tipping and commission system and a notion of trends in tourism and of the characteristics of tourists and the countries they come from. Aside from building up technical expertise, guides need to understand the currency of their services in a global market that is highly unstable and influenced by continuous changes in consumer preferences. This requires them to endlessly vary, reinvent and customize their services. In this context, mastering the currently fashionable tourism discourses (e.g., the vocabulary of nostalgia and ecotourism) is an asset. In other words, guides need to learn how to tell seducing tourism tales. This includes the use of common keywords and clichés (Dann 1996b, 2001).[4]

In her book on the dynamics of guiding, Pond (1993) stresses the importance of the skills of delivery over actual knowledge when claiming all guides are interpreters first: having the 'ability to interpret by painting mental pictures' (93), they are subject specialists second. Others have similarly argued that face-to-face interpretation lies 'at the heart and soul' of what guides can and should be doing (Weiler and Ham 2001: 549). This suggests that the poetics and performance of guiding are more important than the actual content they transmit. The scope of what is meant by *interpretation,* though, is broad and complex. Over fifty years ago, Tilden outlined its core elements, describing interpretation as 'an art', a 'revelation based upon information', and 'an educational activity which aims to reveal meanings and relationships … rather than simply communicating factual information' (1957: 3–9). Tilden made painstaking efforts to distinguish interpretation from the 'teacher-tell' model of information transfer, asserting that interpretation should inspire or even provoke, because 'any interpretation that does not somehow relate what is being displayed or described to something within the personality or experience of the visitor will be sterile' (1957: 11). Pivotal to the interpreter's approach is the art of storytelling.[5] As Benjamin (1969) reminds us in his essay *The Storyteller,* telling a tale is more than merely communicating information. A story is not a product but, rather, an activity, a 'craft' form of communication.[6] For guides, the best interpretative storytelling is persuasive in that it engages tourists both intellectually and emotionally, as well as being personal, relevant and meaningful for them.

Guides engage in the act of interpretation by means of planned spoken commentary, which is delivered during a visit or tour. Amato nicely describes how such commentaries make strategic use of widespread tourism imaginaries (2002: 68; emphasis added):

> With this type of commentary the tourist guide may attempt to tap into the *nostalgic feelings* of the visitor. This continuously positive commentary may make a seemingly ordinary and practical task, such as farming, appear *special* and almost *romantic.* The tourist guide's commentary can then ignite an *exotic flavour* to the subjects that may help to convey information or just bring down an image into the visitors memory of a certain, perhaps exceptionally beautiful, area of the country.

In sum, guides should be 'at least semi-skilled as story tellers' (Reilly 1991: 142), narrating their tales in a way that is informative and entertaining, what otherwise might be known as infotainment or edutainment. While the delivery of tour commentaries is part of every guide's job, the extent to which guides are expected to practice principles of effective and persuasive interpretation varies widely. Can the rhetoric of interpretation be formally instructed? How and where do guides learn the nameless techniques, gimmicks, gadgets, tricks and approaches? In what follows, I sketch various processes by which tour guides in Jogja and Arusha are 'seducated', learning the art of telling seducing tales. I describe how apprentice guides first encounter tourism imaginaries and associated discourses and how they learn to use them, often through trial and error. I also show that the more transnationally networked guides are, the easier and more successful their learning process becomes.

## À la Javanaise

> I studied Japanese during an intensive two-year course because, at that time [over fifteen years ago], there were still many tourists from Japan and not enough guides. At that time, the sultan went to Japan to promote Jogja ... Before becoming a guide I worked as a clerk at a local travel agency. I have been a guide for eight years now. I learned about the sites by reading books about them. In order to obtain my license, I took part in a short three-month course.
> –Pak Nano (senior tour guide)

Although Jogja is Indonesia's second most important destination after Bali, none of the province's institutions of higher learning currently offers a degree pro-gramme in guiding or interpretation. There are guide-related courses at some vo-cational senior high schools and at various levels of higher education: universities, schools of higher learning, polytechnics and academies. However, as Pak Yono, a senior cultural guide and teacher in several of these institutions, tells me with some disappointment: 'These courses are not about how to become a guide but only to give future tourism workers a general idea of what guiding is about'. In his opinion, tourism education in general is superficial, focusing on giving prac-titioners a broad knowledge base rather than specialized skills. According to the heads of tourism schools and academies that I interviewed, the absence of tour guide training in their institutions is the result of a simple market rule: 'There is no demand for it'. While the nonexistence of these programs might be justified because of the crisis in the local tourism scene since 1997 (chapter 2), the lack of training has existed ever since tourism began to boom in the region.

During the golden years (1980s to mid-1990s), tourism in and around Jogja expanded under the patronage of international actors and organizations. Con-current with the elevation of the Borobudur and Prambanan temple complexes to World Heritage sites in 1991, UNESCO and UNDP launched the ambitious Cultural Tourism Development Central Java-Yogyakarta project (1991–94). As part of this venture, an Italian consultant named Professor Amato reviewed the state of affairs of tour guiding, and found, among other things, that the apparent shortage of guides was a problem of quality rather than quantity, and ultimately a result of insufficient training. He therefore organized a three-month upgrading course for licensed guides at one of Jogja's universities in the fall of 1993. Amato also wrote general job descriptions for guides and tour managers and helped create the first national occupational skill standards, including the design of national tourism training standards and programs. Finally, Amato proposed to constitute an Institute of National Tourist Guides and Tour Managers, providing a two-year course in guiding (1992: 15).[7] Sadly, tourism went downhill shortly after the finishing of the megaproject and Amato died in a tragic motorcycle accident in 1998. The Indonesian authorities never approved consequent attempts to formalize a degree programme in guiding, neither in Jogja nor elsewhere. And it is fair to say that this absence of institutionalized tour guide training is, above all, a lack of political goodwill. While young Indonesians motivated to become guides search desperately for materials and practice opportunities, the UNESCO-UNDP manuals and curricula proposals are gathering dust in rarely consulted specialized libraries.

BAPARDA (Provincial Tourism Office) used to provide short courses for guides too. Since 2002, however, they have outsourced these to the semiprivate Jogja Tourism Training Centre. This is a government-sponsored initiative of Gadjah Mada University's Centre for Tourism Studies and the Jogja chapters of the Association of Indonesian Tour and Travel Agencies (ASITA) and the Indonesian Hotel and Restaurant Association. The centre organizes trainings, assessments and the professional certification of various tourism-related occupations. It is supposed to provide courses and certification for new guides and refreshment sessions for already licensed ones, but during the year I stayed in Jogja, no courses at all were offered. Besides, senior guides consider the compulsory course insufficient to obtain the required knowledge and skills. The materials still include the New Order's Seven Charms to please tourists (see chapter 2). The former practice of Jogja-based travel agents to send their guides to the ASITA training centre in Jakarta seems to have stopped. In response to the need for training, Himpunan Pramuwisata Indonesia (HPI), the Indonesian Tourist Guide Association, is planning a national training centre in the capital. HPI also holds practical workshops during its annual national convention.

## According to the Book

It is early Wednesday morning at the Jogja Tourism Academy (a pseudonym) and the first-year students of the Bachelor programme in Hospitality and Tourism are all excited because today starts the first of a series of lessons on tour guiding.

Since the school has asked me to give a guest lecture at the end of the course, I am allowed to sit in. While we are waiting for the lecturer to show up, I have time to familiarize with the students. I am surprised to hear that the group is so diverse, with people coming from Sumatra to Papua. I make a mental note about how studying together at the same institution undoubtedly facilitates the nationwide circulation of uniform tourism imaginaries and discourses. But what images and ideas are being taught? I notice that some of the course materials have already been distributed: copies from Prabowohadi's 1983 classic training manual *Teknik Memandu Wisata* (Guiding Techniques) and parts of a booklet produced in 1993 by HPI Yogyakarta. Some diligent students have brought along their personal copies of the newest manuals available.[8] Because the teacher is late, I have plenty of time to flip through the books and I become fascinated by their contents. Most of the Indonesian manuals draw heavily on, or are even literal translations of, often-outdated English-language materials. Bibliographies include well-known guiding manuals and rather obscure writings or publications with a destination-specific focus (frequently from neighbouring Australia).[9] While the books are in Indonesian, most of the technical terminology is in English. The authors even include entire English text fragments, usually examples from tourism narratives in other cultural contexts. The conversation section of one practical manual, for instance, starts with *Mini-tours through India,* in which a tour guide, Mr. Singh, and his group of tourists are in the lobby of a certain Emir Hotel arguing with the desk clerk. Not only do these publications lack cultural translation, they actually reinforce the idea that guiding is a globally standardized practice (Salazar 2005).

Before I can ponder the question whether the available materials teach the students anything at all about tourism imaginaries, Pak Marwoto walks into the classroom. He has a long career in tour guiding and teaches the subject at various institutions around Jogja. Pak Marwoto quickly explains which subjects will be covered in the short course and starts his first lecture by telling anecdotes of some embarrassing moments he experienced while guiding. Since many of the examples involve cultural or linguistic misunderstandings, the teacher proposes to start by practising language skills. For this purpose, he distributes copied passages from a tour guide conversation manual and lets students read aloud in turns. When I hear the students speak in their broken English, I realize this is not just a foreign language exercise but an indirect introduction to tourism discourse too. A textbook example will make this clear:

On the bus:

Guide: Ladies and gentlemen, I welcome you aboard. I am delighted that you could join our tour.

G: For the next few hours, I will be your guide and I hope you will have a pleasant trip.

G: Today we will explore the seventh wonder of the world: that is the Borobudur temple.

At the Borobudur temple:

G: Ladies and gentlemen, the Borobudur temple was built in the 9th century during the Syailendra dynasty.

G: We can find reliefs on every wall: for example on this side, we find a description of the life of the holy Buddha.

At the stupa:

G: Now we are on the highest level of the temple. On this level are the stupas. Inside each stupa, there is a statue of the holy Buddha.

G: There is a story about these stupas. It is said that if you can touch the right hand of the holy Buddha, you will have good luck.

G: For about four centuries, the Temple was buried; it was discovered again by Sir Stamford Raffles in 1814.

G: I think that will be enough for today. But before we descend, I will give you an extra ten minutes to look around the stupas.

Tourist 1: These stupas are really magnificent.

T2: Yes, they sure are.

The passage is taken from *English for Special Purposes: Tour Guides* (Nurcahya 2006: 9–11). Texts like the one above may give apprentice guides an inaccurate sense of how guiding actually works. In reality, stretches of interpretative narration are much longer and alternate with interactive small talk (chapter 4). Besides, tours of Borobudur do not end at the upper level of the monument but continue all the way to the exit gate. The example also completely ignores the current politics of guiding at Borobudur, which favours on-site guides from Magelang Regency over others arriving by coach from elsewhere (chapter 5).

Apart from conveying important historical details, however, the fragment does a remarkably good job at teaching tourism imaginaries. Borobudur, for instance, is presented as 'the seventh wonder of the world'. Interestingly, the notes to this unit include a list of 'some of the wonders of the Western World': (1) Pyramid at Giza, Egypt; (2) Athena Statue in Acropolis, Greece; (3) Temple of Diana at Ephesus; (4) Hanging Garden of Babylon, Iraq; (5) Lighthouse of Pharos at Alexandria, Egypt; and (6) Colossus of Rhodes, Greece.[10] Various such precursors to UNESCO's World Heritage list have been compiled over the ages to catalogue the most spectacular natural and cultural heritage in the world. Observe that the Indonesian author labels the list as 'Western' (which is accurate from an Asian perspective). A second list, 'to compare with the ancient wonders' includes exclusively Asian wonders: (1) Borobudur temple, Indonesia; (2) Taj Mahal, India; (3) Angkor Wat, Cambodia; (4) the Great Wall of China; and (5) the golden Buddha in Yangon (Rangoon), Myanmar. Such lists serve the purpose of giving guides translocal references for their narratives, something they avidly use (chapter 4). The story about touching the Buddha statue with your hand to be blessed with good luck is classic and told by all tour guides in Borobudur. It shows the importance of being 'deep into the lore of the area' (Reilly 1991: 143).

Other manuals produced in Indonesia do a much poorer job at teaching the art of seductive interpretation. Suntoro's *Conversations on Tourism Objects* (2002), for example, does not go far beyond sharing a few unconnected details about well-known sights. This is how the booklet handles Borobudur:

One of the world's wonders

A: Is the Borobudur temple influenced by Hinduism?

B: No, it is influenced by Buddhism.

A: Where is it located?

B: Near the town of Magelang.

A: Why is it said to be one of the world's wonders?

B: Because of its unique style and because there is nothing like it anywhere else in the world.

A: When was it completed?

B: In the middle of the ninth century.

A: When was the temple discovered?

B: In 1814.

A guided tour of Borobudur would never take the artificial form of the balanced conversation above. Such texts merely mimic the way education in Indonesia is traditionally conceived: blindly memorizing facts without necessarily understanding what is learned. Clearly, therefore, people motivated to become storytelling guides need to find their information and inspiration elsewhere.

The same is true for the students of the Jogja Tourism Academy. Their short course only provides them with the bare basics of tour guiding: language skills and some verbal and nonverbal guiding techniques. As Pak Marwoto acknowledges at the end of his lecture series, to become a professional guide in Jogja involves a huge amount of self-study. Tourism imaginaries are appropriated mostly through means of informal learning. The questionnaire on tour guide resources that my assistant and I distributed among guides reveals the most popular information channels they rely upon: foreign televised documentaries (National Geographic Channel, Discovery Channel and History Channel), guidebooks (*Periplus, Insight Guides, Lonely Planet, Le Routard* and *The Rough Guide*), newspapers and magazines (especially *National Geographic*), in-flight and travel magazines (often donated by tourists) and history and geography books (mostly Indonesian translations of standard works in English, French or Dutch) (Figure 5). Younger professionals and apprentice guides, including those studying at the tourism academy, have discovered that the Internet allows them to look up travel information, chat and exchange e-mails with former clients.

## 'It is like climbing a tree'

Because I have become good friends with Pak Marwoto (and have helped him out with the course), he invites me to accompany him on student field trips. The first practice session I witness is a one-day field trip in and around Jogja for second-semester students (Figure 6). Many teachers of the school join, but their role during the tour seems limited to playing tourists who are more interested in chatting among themselves than appreciating the sites visited or supporting the students. In fact, more advanced students have prepared and are managing the whole excursion. Apart from providing a tour leader for each of the two coaches, they also assign 'guides' who have to animate the group throughout the day. This mainly consists of communicating practical information, some of which is much too detailed (e.g., one student mentions one site is 7.8 kilometres from the other). When the appointed guides run out of inspiration, they invite other students to give brief presentations about their places of origin. The psychological threshold of this exercise in public speaking is lowered by allowing everybody to talk in Indonesian, and none of the teachers gives feedback on the students' performance. At the various heritage monuments visited, on-site guides give the group extra detailed information and share with them some tricks of the trade, such as country-specific jokes and anecdotes. At sites without guides, Pak Marwoto delivers long interpretative commentaries. As a whole, this day trip offers a rather passive way of becoming acquainted with tour guide narratives and practices.

A couple of weeks later, I go on a four-day field trip to Bali for graduating third-year students. The journey is organized in ways very similar to the earlier city tour. On the bus, students rehearse their public speaking skills by creating on-the-spot commentaries of the places we are passing. This becomes challenging when the scenery does not offer many cues for interpretation. Once in Bali, Mas Made, a local guide, joins the group and overloads the students with a continuous stream of entertaining stories on various topics. The uneasy mix between a practice trip and a holiday—most students have never been to Bali before and consider the excursion as an early graduation gift—leads many to behave as typical domestic tourists: singing on the bus, spending much time shopping and taking pictures of foreigners (especially of the scantily dressed ones at Kuta Beach). Except for the input by Mas Made, the students learn little about international tourism or, for that matter, the art of seductive interpretation. Financial con-

FIGURE 6 • *Learning the Unfamiliar and Reinterpreting the Familiar*

siderations also seriously narrow the options of the student organizers. They are forced to let the group travel to Bali and back by bus, a long and tiring trip only domestic tourists make. They also have to choose the cheapest overnight option available: a practice hotel from a Balinese hotel school on the outskirts of the island's capital, Denpasar. These and other limitations prevent the students from exploring important facets of international tourism in Bali. What they do learn during these outings is the experience of being (domestic) tourists.

Students from the academy probably learn more about tourism tales at school than during excursions. One of the facilities they have at their disposal for practice sessions is the school's 'interpretation garden', an inner courtyard containing miniature copies of Prambanan statues and Borobudur reliefs. On various occasions, I witness how Pak Marwoto invites students to walk around the garden in small groups and interpret these cultural artefacts while developing a coherent narrative out of the whole experience. Yet because the school has no programme specifically focused on guiding, the students miss a theoretical and methodological basis to do this adequately.

Given that there are almost no courses on guiding and that the focus of the available reference works is on tour management and technical skills, how do guides learn the rhetoric of commentary and interpretation? Hands-on experience seems to be the best mode of learning. Unfortunately, tourism in Jogja is currently facing a hard time and practice tours and on-the-job training opportunities are few. Besides, the presence of a *mengikuti guide* (trainee) who follows and observes the narratives and practices of senior guides is not tolerated everywhere. During the high season (June–August), it is customary for senior technical high school students to frequent the region's main heritage sites in order to practice their English and, if possible, their guiding skills. Because there were so few tourists in the months after the May 2006 earthquake (chapter 6), on-site guides were not too eager to take these students on their tours. At Prambanan, for example, the students were only allowed to offer their free interpretation services to those tourists that had entered the complex without a local guide or to those not wanting a standby guide.

One of the rare formal trainings I came across during my stay in Jogja is a one-day Workshop on Guiding Techniques organized by the student association of the French language department in one of the city's largest universities. In the morning, Pak Padmo and Pak Rintoyo, two seasoned guides who happen to be alumni of the department, share their experiences with the enthusiastic crowd. I am surprised to meet many students of tourism academies at this workshop. Their presence indicates they are hoping the workshop will teach them knowledge and skills that their specialized schools do not offer, but also that many see guiding as their preferred gateway to the world out there (chapter 4). Topics include, among other things, the ethics of guiding, life and opportunities after guiding, the importance of foreign-language proficiency, communication and interaction skills and a profound knowledge of local culture and the psychocultural background of tourists. Pak Rintoyo reassures the audience that 'no guide gets it right from the first time' and that guiding involves 'learning through trial and error'. Pak Padmo stresses 'there are too many books on guiding. What is needed is practice'. Interestingly, the question-and-answer time focuses on the importance of persuasion in guiding narratives, and the afternoon is dedicated to role-play. The crowd is divided into small groups, each group having to prepare a guiding commentary about an attraction of their choice. Pak Padmo and Pak Rintoyo comment upon each performance, their main comments being that people's language skills are good but that they need to work on structuring their narratives. Pak Padmo concludes with a beautiful metaphor that serves as a wise warning: 'Learning to become a guide is like climbing a tree. It takes a long time to climb up, but only a moment to fall'.

At Prambanan, Pak Supriyadi, one of the most experienced guides at the temple complex, recently started offering a private course on guiding. The classes last about six months and the apprentices, all university students learning French or English, meet twice a week. Usually one meeting is devoted to theory, while the second gives the students a chance to put into practice what they have learned. Pak Supriyadi stresses that his students not only need to know history but also must master many other topics: current affairs, fauna and flora, culture, religion, et cetera. The practice sessions take place within the Prambanan Park, and, in later stages, at Borobudur and the Kraton. Apart from correcting their language, Pak Supriyadi places emphasis on the delivery of the message, pointing to linguistic and nonlinguistic markers. His students (only four at the time) are excited about the course but also aware of its challenges. Once they feel confident enough, they will have to try out their narratives on real tourists. It is incredible that, except for learning through actual guiding, this small-scale private initiative is one of the only ones in the whole province really teaching apprentice guides the rhetoric of interpretation.

Yet, the lack of formal training seems to have limited impact on the quality of guiding in Jogja. Because the actual teaching of interpretation is mostly absent from tourism schools, the majority of Jogja's active guides have never formally studied tourism. Although there are many different career paths, virtually all came to work in tourism through their study of a foreign language, whether at university, a private language school, or through intensive self-study. And once they mastered the language, they looked for opportunities to shape it within a tourism mould. Many guides are autodidacts with a genuine interest in the local heritage and culture, which their studies of history, archaeology, or anthropology, and their ability to perform traditional arts (e.g., dance or music) illustrate. They also know what it feels like to be a (domestic) tourist through their own travels across the archipelago. These personal interests and experiences largely compensate for the lack of formal training. Because of this entry path, some of the guides

I interviewed claimed that licensed guides in Jogja have a higher educational level than those in Bali (most of who have been trained in tourism).[11]

## Training in Arusha

We tour guides were trained by Ole Kapolondo, a graduate of the African Wildlife College in Mweka [Tanzania], the only one of its kind at that time in the whole of Africa. We learned about the fauna and flora, not in depth but simply those things that a tourist might want to know as he was driven around. Most Maasai already know these facts in our language, so it was a matter of translating them into English and Latin, and we learned quickly. We toured the sightseeing areas along the Seronera River and the Maasai kopjes and studied the area map well.
–Tepilit Ole Saitoti (1988: 96)

From the many interviews I conducted with tour guides in Arusha, it became clear that many of the older guides have had no formal training at all. They developed the required technical and language skills, plus knowledge about animals, geography and culture, largely on their own. This is not self-evident, because the most common type of package offered—wildlife viewing trips lasting more than one day—requires a variety of competences. Senior driver-guide Willy recalls the situation in the 1980s: '*Mzungu* [Europeans] were coming to see the animals ... There were only drivers, without any other skills ... Ngorongoro had some rangers who were paid five dollars per day to guide and show the drivers where to go'.[12] In 1987, the Tanzania Association of Tour Operators (TATO) started offering a one-month course for drivers (not guides). Topics included ecology, public relations, first aid, custom and immigration regulations, park rules and interpretation skills. Since the mid-1990s, the situation has dramatically changed and it has become impossible to find a job without formal training. In contrast to Jogja, the city of Arusha offers a bewildering array of tour guiding certificates and diplomas, widely ranging in content, evaluation methods, duration and tuition fees. Because the organizing schools or institutions are privately run, many of them come and go depending on the market. Most of the programmes operate below standard, lacking teachers and resources, and not offering field attachment programs or internships.[13]

If the schooling of driver-guides is problematic, young Tanzanians attracted to others types of guiding have even fewer educational opportunities. Take cultural tourism, for example. Senior driver-guide Kondo, an active member of the Tanzania Tour Guides Association (TTGA), acknowledges this: 'Cultural guides, we don't have very many ... The professional guides, the driver-guides, they can speak a little bit about culture. We have some who are trying to do cultural things here. Well, they are trying ...' The guides working for the Cultural Tourism Programme (CTP) in villages around Arusha have never received much training, apart from a few workshops when the programme started at the end of the 1990s. Some of them enrolled in one of the tour guide schools in Arusha. However, these programs focus on wildlife tourism or mountaineering, and there is virtually nothing taught on cultural tourism or culture in general. The Dutch organization that started CTP and still has two tourism consultants working on the programme recognizes that guiding skills are a major problem. The consultants lament not finding people to train the CTP guides, even though interpretation is crucial for those working in cultural tourism.

Edward, an Arusha-based expatriate tour operator, is of the opinion that 'Tanzanian guides don't understand their job is like that of a doctor: you constantly have to study'. As he notes, 'It's no longer enough to point to elephants'. Tourists have become more inquisitive and guides need to be interpretative and creative. Johnny, a white South African guide explains why Tanzanian guides might be at a disadvantage:

> Why are guides in Tanzania on a knowledge base less good than those in South Africa, Botswana or Kenya? Because in those countries there are less animals … if you see a couple of gazelles on a three-hour game drive that's already a success! Guides therefore have to create a virtual experience and talk more. Here [in Tanzania], there are so many animals that guides don't need to talk that much.

Of course, much depends on the attitude of the guide and the eagerness to learn. In his autobiography, *The Worlds of a Maasai Warrior,* Saitoti (1988: 97) nostalgically recalls his time as a park guide in Serengeti National Park: 'Often at the end of the game drive, they [US tourists] would ask for a drink and want to know what they could send me from America when they returned. Wanting to improve my education, I told them to send me the best-seller of the year. I read many American books when I was in the Serengeti'.

## A Model School

Bwana Baraka impresses me from the very first time we meet. He comes to pick me up in his new-looking second-hand Toyota Corolla and brings me to a fancy bar usually frequented only by expats and wealthy Tanzanians. Over a couple of Kilimanjaro beers, he tells me his success story. Bwana Baraka worked many years as a professional guide. Capitalizing on his vast experience and providing an answer to a growing demand, he decided in the mid-1990s to set up a school for tour guides. Up to this date, his family-run Arusha Guide School (pseudonym) remains one of the few institutes in Tanzania that focuses exclusively on guide training (Figure 7). The school offers a one-year diploma programme in tour guiding. The official language of instruction is English, although in practice a confusing mix of Swahili and English is used. The Arusha Guide School has over one hundred students year round, predominantly men in their twenties, who come from rural and urban areas all over the country, and usually belong to the burgeoning Tanzanian middle class.[14] Although having a secondary-education degree is an admission requirement, the headmaster often ignores this prerequisite in order to reach higher enrolment numbers. A US nonprofit foundation provides scholarships for many of the students, and because the school is collaborating with the Mweka College of African Wildlife Management, the brightest students try to continue their studies by pursuing a Certificate or Advanced Diploma in Wildlife Management.

The day after our initial meeting, Bwana Baraka invites me to visit the school—one among many others in Arusha (Salazar 2006c). It is a Saturday, so there are not many students around. The Arusha Guide School is located in an enlarged house in one of the poorer neighbourhoods in the hills surrounding Arusha's city centre. The building is rudimentary and, aside from some student facilities—a bathroom, a kitchen, a dorm for boys and a small dorm for girls—there are only two rooms: a classroom and a room that functions simultaneously as office, library, computer room and second classroom (Figure 7). Even though small, the school's library contains many resources (mainly in English): research reports and books on tourism in Tanzania and elsewhere; animal and plant identification guides; travel guides in various languages; Tanzanian travel magazines and wildlife periodicals, some in-flight magazines; and a vast collection of wildlife documentaries (Figure 5).[15]

Over the years, Bwana Baraka has built up a solid transnational network of contacts and became a board member of a renowned international association for tourism education, connections that allow him to travel abroad regularly. His son Frankie, one of the school's main teachers, also has experience guiding and spent six months in the United States attending specialized courses in a mountaineering school and a leadership institute. For outsiders visiting for the first time, it is hard to believe that this tiny school is so well networked. Its multiple transnational connections greatly facilitate the inflow of tourism imaginaries. When I ask the headmaster whether he uses a handbook, he shows me a practical manual coming from the Canadian Tourism Human Resource Council. Materials like this were donated by foreigners who visited the school or have been collected by Bwana Baraka on his trips abroad. And because virtually all the resources are foreign—primarily from Europe, the United States and South Africa—they actually greatly facilitate the students' exposure to foreign tourism imaginaries. However, even if the school plays a critical role in the transmission of tourism discourse, in the end it is an institution that is itself reconfigured periodically by external discourses.

After having had lengthy conservations with Bwana Baraka and some of the school teachers, I return to the Arusha Guide School on a weekday. It is barely 8 A.M. and I count already over hundred students, all crammed in the small class-

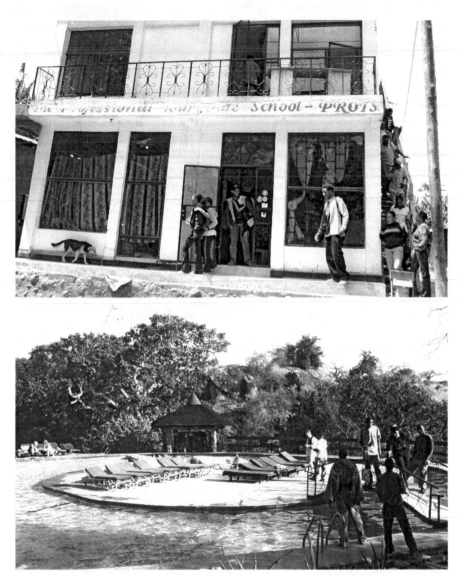

**Figure 7** • *Combining Formal Schooling and Informal Learning*

room upstairs. While waiting for the teacher to show up, the students are practicing their bird identification skills. A small computer screen in a front corner
displays an automated slide show. On each slide, there is a picture of a particular
Tanzanian bird followed by a second slide with the English name of the bird.
Students compete with one another in correctly naming as many birds as pos-

sible. Less by diagnostic key characters, they learn to identify animals by heart, through trial-and-error. Students proudly tell me that Gurisha, the current record holder of the school, is able to distinguish over five hundred different birds. The fact that there are not that many specific words to name different birds in Swahili or other local languages illustrates that the knowledge students are appropriating is not indigenous but foreign—Western and science-based ecological knowledge such as the names of local fauna and flora in both English and Latin.

While chatting with the students, I notice that, in contrast to trainees in Jogja, they tend to lack personal experience in tourism. Most of them have travelled little, have never been inside a national park, and are not familiar with wildlife. The main motivation to become a driver-guide is to earn good money; few express a genuine interest in ecology or cultural heritage (although this might change once they start working as a guide). This reality makes formal tour-guide training an absolute necessity in Tanzania. Thus, regardless of whether they have previous experience with foreigners, the types of knowledge novices have to appropriate to become a tour guide are generally foreign to their own lifeworld.

## *'Aristotle? A Roman Guy or Something'*

Throughout my stay in Tanzania, I repeatedly visit the Arusha Guide School. On multiple occasions, I witness how teachers face challenging situations when they use foreign teaching materials without adapting them to the local context. One day, for example, Frankie is teaching about tourism-related legislation. He immediately acknowledges he is not an expert in this field and is totally at a loss when students start asking him about the 'Workplace Hazardous Materials Information System'—mentioned in the Canadian handbook but completely out of place in a Tanzanian context. I am often struck by the instructors' repeated usage of currently popular tourism discourses, especially the stress on sustainability and ecology (Barron and Prideaux 1998). They know how important it is that guides mirror the imaginations tourists have already acquired about Tanzania before setting foot on its soil, the fantasies that tour operators or travel agencies have already sold to them. The school therefore provides its students with plenty of samples of promotional materials. The teachers use Western wildlife documentaries as powerful tools to indoctrinate student-guides with foreign interpretations of their own natural and cultural heritage (Figure 5). Bwana Baraka emphasizes his students should learn 'to look at things through the eyes of a tourist', to literally emulate the 'tourist gaze' (Urry 2002). One of the methods he uses to do this is to show photographs and ask where they were taken. At one time, for instance, he displays a picture taken inside Steers, Arusha's only Western-style fast-food restaurant. Most students think the picture is shot in New York, somewhere in Europe, or in Dar es Salaam. Not one guesses it right. The principal then uses this example to stress the importance of developing a feel for places and things that are of interest to foreign tourists.[16]

Learning the 'tourist way' also implies familiarizing oneself with the home cultures of tourists. Given the dominance of North American visitors to the region, the headmaster zooms in on US culture and society, often in provoking ways. Commenting upon current politics, he asks, 'Who knows who Obama is? No, not Osama', and adds 'This is important when dealing with American tourists'. On the experience of time, he recalls that 'I saw these [US] series on TV the other day … Life in New York is going so fast that on Saturday you already get Sunday's newspaper!' It is telling that the school uses episodes from the popular sitcom *Friends* to teach spoken English. After all, this soap opera made a notable contribution to slang in the United States (and beyond), and it surely impresses Western tourists when they hear Tanzanian guides mimic that vernacular. According to the principal, openness towards appropriating foreign cultural elements opens all doors: 'You stay Maasai or Chagga and you won't go anywhere'. Finally, a brash statement on tourism imaginaries: 'As I told you two weeks ago, there are people buying a ticket to Tanzania only because they want to see two things: A lion and a Maasai penis … Especially American girls do this'. Sharing this information with the students, the principal teaches them the widely circulating imaginary that Maasai men are well endowed, as well as speaking to their erotic dreams about Westerners.[17]

On a regular basis, Bwana Baraka selects advanced students to guide tourists around Arusha or on other one-day excursions in the region (Figure 7). Those who do not have a chance to engage in these practice opportunities benefit from the in-class reports and evaluations after each trip. The story of Iddi illustrates how students learn the hard way what tourism entails. After his first practice safari with a group of Europeans, Iddi evaluates the trip in front of the whole class. In a rather agitated and slightly angry manner, he explains to his peers how the driver-guides of the tour company had skilfully manipulated the whole wildlife viewing experience. In order to make the five-day safari worthwhile, they made sure the tourists would not see too many animals on one given day. Through radio-contact driver-guides communicated with one another (in Swahili), exchanging the location of Big Five species. This enabled them to carefully monitor and control the amount of wildlife shown to their clients during the trip. While many of the students looked incredulous when hearing the story, teacher Frankie confirms it, but immediately sooths the disillusioned souls by jokingly pointing out that the situation in neighbouring Kenya is much worse, to the extent that certain game parks allegedly put up stuffed wild animals when the real animals are temporarily migrating outside the park boundaries. In such ways, tourism imaginaries are materialized and alter guiding practices in significant ways. Learning to reproduce the language of tourism involves mastering the register of expertise. The guides in Arusha have to build up an extensive knowledge. Bwana Baraka often compares a guide to a 'knowledge bank', a 'library' or an 'information bank', and stresses that 'collecting info is a life-long job'. The teachers themselves still have some way to go in accumulating knowledge. The title of this section, 'Aristotle? A Roman guy or something', is a direct quote from a teacher answering a student's question whether he knew who Aristotle (the Greek philosopher) was.

One day, a student shows up late in class. Instead of scolding, the headmaster praises the boy because he is carrying a copy of *The Safari Companion: A Guide to Watching African Mammals.* This must-have classic on African wildlife, first published in 1993, is written by Richard Estes, a well-known international authority on the behavioural ecology of African mammals. Showing the book to the entire class, the principal shouts enthusiastically: 'This is an example of a good book! It's worth the investment ... but you'll need a couple of months' savings'. Because wildlife tourism is the predominant form, pedagogy necessarily stresses an emphasis on ecology and on mastering the widely popular environmental (or eco-) vocabulary (Dann 1996a; Norton 1996).[18] Students learn that foreign tourists are most interested in big mammals and that this preference is the result of having seen (too) many spectacular wildlife documentaries and movies. In the words of Frankie: 'Small children have watched *The Lion King,* so what do they want to see? Lions!' Consequently, students are taught to represent the Serengeti as the world's greatest 'animal kingdom', and the Ngorongoro Crater as 'the place where Noah's Ark came to rest'.

Apart from naming flora and fauna, the teachers strive to make the novice guides aware of tourism key words, important markers that embody tourism tales. Many hours are devoted to explaining students about world heritage sites, biosphere reserves and conservation areas. Concepts such as authenticity or sustainability are elucidated too. '*Watu wana*—think sustainable' (people think sustainably), is one of Frankie's mantras. As part of the graduation requirements, everybody has to compose a master information file, a long list of words including names of fauna, flora, attractions, people and tourism concepts. This is a very demanding task, forcing students to engage in many hours of reading and organizing the materials (although lists composed by alumni are circulating too). The master list contains plenty of personalities from the colonial era: explorers, mountaineers, missionaries, scientists, writers, German and English administrators, et cetera. The only Tanzanian personalities included are the country's presidents, a couple of traditional chiefs and historical figures from Zanzibar. During the final exam, Bwana Baraka randomly picks out words from the list and asks the student to tell him everything he or she can relate to them. While most collect about 300 key words, the brightest alumni are able to produce lists of more than 1,500.

Another ingenious drilling mechanism is the weekly wildlife video quiz during which everybody receives a sheet with a summary of the video narrator's speech. The students' task is to fill in missing key words in the blanks while watching the video. This makes students focus not only on the content of the story but also on the way the tales are narrated, on the art of delivery. Storytelling is highly encouraged and commented upon in the classroom: 'A good opening sentence makes your clients more curious'; 'Legends are welcome in tour guiding'; 'It's a good story, *mzungu atalala*!' (the foreigner will fall asleep; meant ironically). In this way, students are made aware of the benefits of interpretation. As Bwana Baraka puts it: 'Everywhere [in the world] there are zoos. You make the difference by explaining things'. As an added bonus, apprentice guides realize that telling stories can be used to mask ignorance: Because tour guides are not researchers, the headmaster proposes an easy way out of difficult questions clients might ask: 'This is a mystery, that's how nature is, let's move on'.

## Transnational Advantage

While there are a variety of ways to learn the rhetoric of tour guiding in developing countries, private training programs organized by expatriate-managed travel agencies or tour operators offer huge advantages (Figure 8). These in-house trainings are usually much better attuned to foreign tourism imaginaries, because they are often organized by people who know both sides of the equation, the local reality and the wishes and preferences of the overseas tourist markets. In Jogja, for example, French and German owners of tour operations cater mainly to, respectively, French and German tourists, while in Arusha US and British safari companies have their strongest market shares in their home countries. Realizing the urgent need for a quality schooling that will be sensitive to the home culture of tourists, one exclusive company in Arusha decided to make tour-guide training one of the most important elements of its portfolio.

As I have explained before, I first became involved in studying tourism by coming across a loosely structured, transnational tourism-related network in Belgium. One of the reasons I chose to focus on Indonesia and Tanzania in particular—and not Senegal, Mali, Honduras, Nicaragua, Argentina, Peru, Ecuador or Chile where the network is also active—is the fact that the guides of Jogja and Arusha who are affiliated with the network are the only ones to have met face-to-face. In 2002, the European headquarters invited them for a one-month visit to Western Europe. During this period, they underwent an intense, two-week experience as international tourists—a kind of role-reversal exercise—and participated in an interactive course on guiding and intercultural communication, together with European guides. This experience proved instrumental in giving the guides a more global sense of what tourism entails. They exchanged stories and anecdotes, as well as tips and tricks on the handling of different types of tourists. The mere fact that they were brought together—although coming from very diverse sociocultural backgrounds and dealing with different types of tourism and tourists—illustrates how the people heading the network believe in the universality of tourism and the homogeneous culture of its service providers. Apart from the exchange project, the network is also actively involved in training tour guides in both destinations separately.

## Impersonating the 'Bule'

In Jogja, Jenny is the expatriate representative of the network. She runs a successful travel business that includes a bar-restaurant, a travel agency and an elaborate tour programme. Virtually all the Indonesian guides who travelled to Europe in 2002 are still working for the company and regularly participate in upgrade seminars.[19] Every year during the tourism low season, one of them has the opportunity to travel back to Europe (for periods as long as three months) to deepen guiding skills and the rhetoric of interpretation. Even in times of crisis in tourism (as during the year I was in Jogja), there is an ongoing effort to train new guides. The training itself is led by Jenny, but the senior Indonesian guides play a mayor role too. They take care of the selection process, screening candidates according to language proficiency, availability, communication skills, problem-solving capacities and motivation. Because many participants are working or studying, the training takes place in the evenings and lasts for only two weeks. The sessions focus on topics as diverse as guiding skills, intercultural (mis)communication and conflicts, stereotypes and generalizations, positioning in a group and a (short) discussion of sustainable and eco-tourism.[20] All participants receive a manual and handouts. During the sessions, trainers use PowerPoint presentations and videos. Throughout, the participants engage in role-play to practice guiding techniques (Figure 8), discuss sensitive issues such as dress codes and learn tricks to keep the attention of the tourists.

The training concludes with a practice tour in which the apprentice guides play the role of *bule* (white person) and observe the practices and discourses of experienced guides.[21] This playing-the-*turis* (tourist) helps Javanese youngsters because they are confronted with a whole new range of activities and ways of looking at things: Cycling a whole morning through villages and rice paddies (Javanese generally do not like sustained physical exercise), planting rice (something even the young adults living in villages have never done) and, above all, realizing that what is normal or even boring for them might actually be very exotic and interesting for foreigners (Figure 6). After this practice trip, the aspirant guides are divided in three subgroups, each one having to create a new walking tour in the city centre. This is highly challenging and many participants drop out. Budi, for example, comments that the hardest thing is to look at his surroundings 'with the eyes of a foreign tourist'. Jenny asks me to help prepare these tours. During the first explorations of the different neighbourhoods, I lend the trainees digital cameras and ask them to take pictures of whatever they think would be of interest to tourists. This proves to be quite difficult; they initially do not realize that foreigners are fascinated by the daily life of Javanese people, things they themselves think of as too mundane. Each group presents their results at a meeting and everybody tests the different tours. Under constant guidance by Jenny and some of the senior guides, the tours are fine-tuned until they are all set to be tried on real tourists. Ironically, these new walking tours were ready at the time a heavy earthquake struck the region (chapter 6). Because the regular village tours had to be cancelled, the new city trips became popular among tourists, giving the novice guides opportunities to practice their guiding skills.

FIGURE 8 • *The Transnational Advantage in Tour Guide Training*

## Me and My 'Mzungu'

In Arusha, the European headquarters of the transnational tourism network is heavily involved in the structuring and financing of the Arusha Guide School. Since 1998, European instructors and volunteers have visited the school on a regular basis, not only as guest teachers or syllabus developers, but also as experts who train the teachers. Thanks to an agreement with a European tour operator and collaboration with TATO, the school can offer its students to practice their guiding skills by participating in safaris as junior guides. These connections facilitate the amount of practical experience apprentice guides can gain by going on rehearsal trips with tourists (Figure 8). The practice opportunities are highly valued by the poorly schooled Tanzanian students who are often overwhelmed by having to learn so many new things. Moreover, the teaching materials' lack of adaptation to the local sociocultural context often makes it difficult for the students to appropriate foreign knowledge.

An example of this is Silva, who accompanied a Dutch group to Usa River, an agricultural area near Arusha. When he is telling the tourists about a coffee plantation, he speaks about the 'privatatization' (privatization) by foreigners who are 'investigating' (investing) in Tanzania. While understanding the meaning behind the concepts, Silva is unsuccessful reproducing them (his English not being that fluent), despite his hopes that it will make his narrative seem more expert, helping him connect with his highly schooled clients. During the visit to a sisal plantation, he tells the group that a German man named 'Dr. Himbeer' originally imported the sisal plant from Mexico. Although probably none of the Dutch tourists (who understand German) knows that the right name of the man was Dr. Richard Hindorf (an agronomist working for the German East Africa Company), they all start smiling because they sense that *Himbeer,* German for raspberry, is probably not the correct name. By not laughing out loud, however, they indicate their appreciation for Silva's efforts to reproduce encyclopaedic knowledge.

The Tanzanian students quickly learn, however, how to make tourists feel at home. They do this by strategically using the normative set of genres and strategies they were equipped with at school. The use of touristic key words throughout the guiding narrative gives clients a certain feeling of familiarity, because they are already acquainted with this kind of language. Comparisons are employed to mollify the effects of strangeness associated with a trip abroad, making something alien seem familiar (Cohen 1985: 10). At school, Bwana Baraka gives many examples of how to use comparison. During a lecture entitled 'Hierarchy of Strength: Carnivores' Pursuit of Food', he jokingly refers to Arnold Schwarzenegger (whose old action movies are extremely popular in Tanzania) as a role model when explaining the hierarchy of strength in humans. On another occasion, when talking about cultural differences in human interaction, the headmaster compares different ways of greeting in several African and European cultures. The

72

students pick up many of these classroom examples and test them for popularity in the interaction with tourists. They frequently use comparison to let tourists contrast the visited culture with their own, often as a means of individual status enhancement. Commenting on the public transport minibus, the most common means of transport in urban Tanzania, Solomoni light-heartedly tells his group: 'It is not like in Europe here!' Although Solomoni has never travelled outside his country, he implicitly indicates that he knows how much better organized public transport is in Western countries.

Learning that the interests (and imaginations) of tourists are not necessarily the same as one's own, however, proves to be a more difficult lesson. On a visit to a Maasai boma, Ernest takes his group to the medicine man. This is the last part of the tour and it is already late. The medicine man starts explaining his ritual practices, but everybody is tired and bored. Ernest, who is himself fascinated by the topic, fails to notice the many implicit signs the tourists are giving, indicating they want to leave. Instead, he keeps on asking the medicine man one question after the other. Robert, who accompanies a group on a three-day cultural tourism trip, becomes very annoyed when not everybody shows interest in his long exposé regarding anthills. These examples show the importance of correctly interpreting both the linguistic and nonlinguistic cues provided by tourists. When all of a sudden the topic of female genital mutilation comes up during a trip, Robert does not try to change the subject but instead starts voicing his own opinion (thereby neglecting the headmaster's mantra that 'a tour guide is neutral'). The highly emotional discussion that ensues shows the headmaster's wisdom, as it leaves the whole group very upset. During the evaluation of this practice trip at school, Robert acknowledges his mistakes, allowing the other students to learn a lesson from him as well.

Because the Tanzanian students are still in the process of learning the tricks of the trade and make many mistakes, they soon come to realize that good guiding is often not a matter of getting the details right, but of impressing and seducing the tourists.[22] Evaluating a walking safari, Douglas tells the other students that during the trip, the tour group had seen a very special bird in a tree. He told the tourists it was a buzzard, but he was actually not sure which bird it was. While telling this anecdote in front of the class, the others start laughing, but teacher Frankie only half-teasingly remarks, 'You gave it a name, hey', implicitly indicating that this is a common occurrence. Although Frankie always stresses 'the importance of showing your knowledge', he equally warns his students not to 'mess up with your facts' because he knows from experience that clients often use travel guidebooks as a backup reference. After all, tour guiding is about providing clients a (paid-for) service, and the students are made well aware of the fact that tourists expect quality service.

While the Arusha Guide School is one of the best examples of transnational involvement in Tanzanian tour-guide training, it is by no means the only one. The

73

walking guides of the Ngorongoro Conservation Area, for instance, were trained by the Kenyan wing of the National Outdoor Leadership School (NOLS), a US nonprofit educational organization with headquarters near the Rocky Mountains in Wyoming. The trainings started in 1994 but were suspended in 1998, when the bombing of the US embassies in Dar es Salaam and Nairobi led to a heightened feeling of expatriate insecurity in East Africa and sparked the US NOLS management to close down all their operations in the region. The Kenyan trainer at the time recalls how the NOLS programme was intensively field based. By playing repeated role-playing games (playing both the mzungu and the guide), trainees learned how to deal with different types of clients.

Upscale safari companies owned by expatriates have a strong record of accomplishment in guide training. Some hire trainers and senior guides from South Africa and Kenya to enhance the transfer of knowledge and skills. Other tour operators rely each year on different subject experts to teach their guides specific fields of knowledge. Together with a Tanzanian botanist working for the African Wildlife Foundation, I myself was asked by a large US-owned safari company to lead their annual tour-guide training. The management was most interested in how I could teach cross-cultural awareness and the art of interpretation. Because those programmes are usually very intensive, many Tanzanians apprentice guides do not finish them. The young man who acted as my assistant during my preliminary research in Arusha, for example, had applied successfully for a job as junior tour guide with one of the most prestigious South African companies in town. When he was sent on a three-month intensive training in the bush, he found the whole experience so challenging that he began developing mental problems and was forced to quit the programme.

## Travelling Tourism Tales

Tour guiding demands more than 'the superficial "processing" of a script or a memorized behavioural repertoire that might include smiling and friendly discourse' (Ness 2003: 189). Because becoming an accomplished guide in contemporary global tourism is a never-ending process, novices need much instruction. Language proficiency is an absolute prerequisite for mastering the art of interpretation. As long as guides are not fluent and have to search for the right vocabulary, they cannot pay attention to the subtleties of seductive language use. Although there is no typical career path, it is striking that many guides are self-made autodidacts who stress how their seducation—their training in telling seductive tourism tales—developed slowly, through careful study, the gaining of a great deal of experience and continued practice. The examples from Indonesia and Tanzania discussed in this chapter show that, while imaginaries and their associated discourses circulate through tourism schools and training programmes, there are many other channels of distribution. Depending on availability and personal interest, guides can rely on an entire gamut of information sources to structure their practices and narratives.

In Jogja, the shelves of the guides' private collections feature a variety of textual and audiovisual resources; in Arusha, they primarily are available for consultation at the libraries of the better educational institutions. Guides often receive materials such as maps, guidebooks and travel dictionaries from clients who leave them behind or mail them afterwards as a token of appreciation for the given services. Most of the sources used are not indigenous but foreign, either actually produced abroad or by expatriates living in the country. This lack of indigenization of materials is an old problem in tourism education (Blanton 1981), but it also greatly facilitates the inflow of foreign tourism imaginaries and discourses. In other words, precisely because the resources used are not local, guides are better able to learn about the culture(s) of international tourists and, eventually, the culture(s) of tourism. Apart from oral history (legends, fairytales and beliefs), indigenous knowledge is almost completely absent in the training cycle of tour guides.[23]

Through formal and informal learning, apprentice guides become acquainted with representations of their own culture and heritage that are deeply rooted in foreign ideological imaginaries of Otherness. The tourism master discourse is taken in and processed according to how the local scene can be presented and sold as paradise (chapter 4). The guides in Jogja pick up the idea of the beauty and ingenuity of the ancient Javanese civilization, something Edenic, in its distance from the tumultuous present. In Arusha, the guides benefit from the recent eco-hype, which allows them to interpret their surroundings in terms of an untouched, green Eden, where animals live in harmony (chapter 2). Because of the dire economic conditions in both destinations, materials available are not always the most recent, and some books even date to the colonial era. Yet, being acquainted with colonial views actually turns out to be an asset when working in tourism because natural and cultural heritage are often packaged, represented, and sold in ways that are reminiscent of colonial times (Bruner 2005; Hall and Tucker 2004). Resources from a more recent date are usually not critical academic analyses but illustrated coffee table books and popular literature such as *National Geographic*—which even has an Indonesian-language version—and audiovisual companions such as the National Geographic Channel and home videos (Figure 5). The fact that ethnographies and other anthropological productions are part of the 'circuit of tourism' (Ateljevic 2000) is something that only recently has been acknowledged and researched (Adams 2004; Hitchcock 2004).

The discipline of anthropology has been historically implicated in Western constructions of Africa and Asia. Anthropology has had an intimate relationship to what Trouillot terms 'the geography of imagination of the West' (2003: 8). And the imaginaries of knowledge makers who preceded ethnographers are what the dreams of much contemporary fieldworkers are made of. The internal tropes of anthropology matter much less than this larger discursive field within which it operates and upon whose existence it is premised: The classical Malinowskian image of fieldwork—the lone, white, male fieldworker living for a year or more among native villagers—functions as an archetype for normal anthropological practice (Stocking 1992: 59). At the heart of this image is the notion that ethnography boils down to the ethnographer's personal journey into a strange world, an idea that is also extremely powerful in the imaginaries surrounding tourism to developing countries. The links between power and knowledge, the generation of images of the Other, the creation of natives and authenticity and the consumption of these images are all as basic to ethnographic practice as they are to tourism (Crick 1989).

Until now, Tanzanian guides have been more focused on wildlife and have heard little about anthropology, although some have a personal interest in archaeology. In Jogja, on the other hand, Pak Yono, one of the most senior guides, told me how he used to form study groups with other guides to discuss subjects such as anthropology and history. When he showed me his personal library, I saw photocopied versions of Geertz's famous but outdated *The Religion of Java* and Koentjaraningrat's classic *Kebudayaan Jawa* (published in English as *Javanese Culture*).[24] Pak Hardi, the Yogyakarta chairperson of HPI, has a bachelor's degree in anthropology from Gadjah Mada University. When I was in Tanzania, I received a message from him, proudly telling me he is now using Bruner's *Culture on Tour: Ethnographies of Travel* (2005) in his classes. Ibu Dyah, who works as a Kraton guide and is considered a local expert on Javanese culture, learns about the discipline from anthropologists who come to ask her questions. Junior guide Arifah used to work as a translator—from Javanese or Indonesian to English—for a Norwegian anthropologist doing fieldwork in Jogja. A few months after the fieldwork was finished, the scholar invited her for a three-month stay in Norway to help him translate the transcripts of the interviews he had recorded.

Although not the main aim of this chapter (or the book in general), the comparison between Indonesian and Tanzanian guides teaches us that there are different paths to learning the art of telling tourism tales. In Indonesia, there are more and more locally produced materials, but these are published cheaply and have little means to promote themselves. Younger guides in both Jogja and Arusha often try to bypass the lack of printed resources by resorting to the Internet. While this is a much more affordable way to find information, what is obtained is not always reliable. And while the guides in Jogja have more access to resources, they have fewer formal training opportunities. They may be familiar with the seductive narratives of tourism but do not always know how to use them while guiding. On top of this, they are hindered by the traditional Javanese culture of self-restraint (Koentjaraningrat 1985), and often they need more time to feel at ease as a convincing tourism spokesperson or ambassador in the encounter with foreigners. On the other hand, the refined Javanese culture helps them present themselves as charming guides, neatly dressed and always smiling. Tanzanians tend to be much less reserved and even if the guides in Arusha have fewer educational materials at their disposal, they learn quickly while practicing, through trial and much error. Encyclopaedic knowledge, together with physical strength and seduction, prevail over elegance.

Unlike countries where the content of tour-guide schooling may be controlled by the government, thereby ensuring that guides deliver a uniform, politically and ideologically correct commentary (e.g., Bowman 1992), the governments of Indonesia and Tanzania seem at this stage to have little control over such matters (although both states certainly desire it). Moreover, my observations of training programs in both Jogja and Arusha suggest that the planned curriculum is often very different from the one that is actually enacted. In other words, while schools and training institutes play an important role in the circulation of tourism imaginaries, one-way transmission of ideas is not possible (chapter 7). Students are transformed in the process of becoming tour guides but they also contribute to the transformation and glocalization of tourism discourses. Nevertheless, they all learn to think of tourists as 'clients', even as they address and treat them as 'guests'. Not only do they have to learn to look at their surroundings through the eyes of tourists, they also need to become aware that the imaginaries of *wazungu* and *bule* that circulate in local popular culture are stereotypes. Changing these widely spread preconceptions of tourists in particular, and foreigners in general, takes some time. Bwana Baraka in Arusha always stresses the need for cross-cultural respect and understanding, while Jenny in Jogja teaches her guides to interact 'normally' with tourists and with her expatriate friends.

Even if guides are exposed to widely circulating tourism imaginaries and discourses, the question remains why they would be so eager to copy them. I suggest in the next chapter that the dynamics of ownership involved in the encounter between collectively held tourism imaginaries and the individual imaginations of tourists and guides are much more complex than is usually presented in the literature. For now, it is important to remember that tourism fantasies and discourses come to guides through a variety of channels. No matter how many resources they have at their disposal, ultimately it is in the interaction with tourists that the imaginaries become tangible and are circulated—perpetuated as well as contested. It is to this interactive guide-guest encounter that I will turn next.

# 4
# IMAGING AND IMAGINING
# OTHER WORLDS

Fill a mixing glass, cocktail shaker or pitcher two-thirds full with ice cubes. Add two parts citrus-flavoured vodka, one part Cointreau, one part cranberry juice, and half a part lime juice. Stir well and pour into large cocktail glasses ... You have created a 'cosmopolitan'; the cocktail, that is. Preparing or drinking it, though, does not automatically make you a cosmopolite or world citizen, and neither does reading *Cosmopolitan* magazine.[1] If you want to achieve 'real' cosmopolitan status, you should consider travelling abroad. You already contemplated a cheap package deal around continental Europe or an overbooked Caribbean cruise? No, aim for something more stylish. A cultural heritage trip in central Java or an eco-safari through the savannah of northern Tanzania, for example, could do ...

Derived from the ancient Greek words *kosmos* (universe) and *polis* (city), cosmopolitanism literally means 'universal citizenship'.[2] Scholars from across the social sciences and the humanities have long been captivated by the concept (Beck and Sznaider 2006), variously invoking it as: (1) a sociocultural condition; (2) a kind of philosophy or world view; (3) a political project towards building transnational institutions; (4) a political project for recognizing multiple identities; (5) an attitudinal or dispositional orientation; and (6) a mode of practice or competence (Vertovec and Cohen 2002: 8–14). I am particularly interested in the latter two perspectives because they allow a focus on the ways people perform and enact cosmopolitanisms in their everyday lives (cf. Hannerz 2004).

How does one become cosmopolitan? How to accrue and display this 'stance in the management of cultural experience' (Hannerz 2004: 71)? First, 'the perspective of the cosmopolitan must entail relationships to a plurality of cultures', including 'an orientation, a willingness to engage with the Other' (Hannerz 1990: 239). This capacity to interact across cultural lines necessitates a flexible intellectual and aesthetic openness towards divergent cultural experiences, towards contrasts (difference) rather than uniformity (sameness), and towards the allure of elsewhere and Otherness. Cosmopolitanism requires not only tolerance, respect and enjoyment of cultural difference but also a concomitant sense of global belonging, a kind of global consciousness that can be integrated into everyday life practices (Tomlinson 1999: 185). It is widely believed that such a cosmopolitan outlook or disposition—a desirable form of contemporary cultural capital—is largely acquired through experience, especially through travel (Molz 2005; Notar 2008).[3] International travel is thus a prime example of cosmopolitanism-as-practice, enabling the accumulation of knowledge about 'Other' worlds.

If social theory suggests tight links between travel and cosmopolitanism, how (if at all) is this connection achieved in practice? A microanalysis of cultural tours in central Java and safari journeys in southern Maasailand may provide some surprising answers. In this chapter, I explore the narrative strategies and performative techniques that local guides use to turn tours into cosmopolitan-enhancing experiences, in rather unexpected ways. I show how their practices are firmly steered by the tourism imaginaries and discourses discussed in previous chapters. Before setting foot on Indonesian or Tanzanian soil, tourists already have a mental image of what the place will look like and tour operators organize trips with these widely circulating, ideal-type representations in mind. Local guides have to ensure their clients experience exactly what they expect, receiving the images and fantasies that travel agencies or tour operators originally sold to them when they booked their trip. Guides necessarily understand quite well that holidays are essentially 'experiences in fantasy' (Dann 1976: 19).

How exactly do guides realize the travel dreams of tourists, skilfully mediating the gap between expectations and actual experience? How do they link sites with what tourists expect from them, integrating visited peoples into broader tourism imaginaries, and rendering them continuous with their imagined context? In the previous chapter, I described how guides familiarize themselves with seductive imaginaries and discourses via both formal schooling and informal learning. Yet what is learned in the classroom is one thing, and the way in which these scripts play out in practice is another. In this chapter, I show how guides strategically use the normative set of genres and strategies they were equipped with to assure the (re)production of tourism fantasies during their encounter with tourists. In order to grasp the internal mechanics of this process, I pay particular attention to the metacommunicative dimension and pragmatics of guiding narratives and practices. As I will show, the tools on which guides rely are eclectic, and their toolbox can sometimes be cluttered (chapter 6).

## Framing the Encounter

Guiding narratives are preceded and succeeded by numerous other 'texts', pieces of discourse that both implicate them and render them interpretable. At the same time, tour commentaries are quite different from other tourism language genres (Dann 1996b). There is a distinctive rhetoric to guide-speak that is critical to how its success is perceived (to wit, return requests for guiding services and larger tips). Most commonly, guiding consists of rather complex speech chains whereby long stretches of interpretative monologue are interspersed with moments of intense interaction and various kinds of dialogue. Tourists might ask questions, and the guides themselves often engage in small talk. Guides typically use the latter to fill the gap between bits and pieces of explanatory narrative. In contrast to marketing discourse, they profit from dramatic audiovisual aids, that is, the actual sights that surround the tourists.

A guided tour has far more immediacy than any other genre of tourism language could ever have. The credible illusion of authenticity created depends on a tourist's feeling of being in an immediate indexical relationship with the site. The nearness is assured by the site's presence, to which the guide can point. Nor is this a purely visual matter, because all the senses add to the verisimilitude of the experience. A face-to-face interpretation by a skilled tour guide can be particularly powerful in influencing what tourists think and feel about the people and places they encounter. However, what actually happens during the interaction between guides and guests is nuanced and open-ended, allowing both sides to manipulate expectations and preconceived patterns creatively. While this chapter mainly focuses on the ways that guides, as mediating actors, mobilize tourism imaginaries and discourses, in chapter 6 I discuss how various agents modify and contest them.

## Narrative Performance

Few scholars have explicitly studied naturally occurring discourse in the meeting ground between tourists and service providers. This is a missing link if one wants to understand fully how tourism imaginaries circulate and how tourism workers 'commodify and sell potential narratable memories to travellers' (Bendix 2002: 469). The conceptual tools to conduct such studies are at hand. Over the years, linguistic anthropologists have built up a formidable expertise in the analysis of the transportability of discourse from one context to another, as well as the conditions that enable their 'decontextualization' and 'recontextualization' (Bauman and Briggs 1990; Lucy 1993; Silverstein and Urban 1996). At the heart of these processes lies entextualization, 'the process of rendering discourse extractable, of making a stretch of linguistic production into a unit—a text—that can be lifted out of its interactional setting' (Bauman and Briggs 1990: 73). Entextualization may incorporate aspects of context, such that the resultant text (discourse rendered decontextualizable) carries elements of its history of use within it. This type of conceptualization is extremely useful when studying tour-guide narratives. How are decontextualization (decentring) and recontextualization (recentring) of tourism discourses possible? What does the recontextualized text—the guiding narrative—bring with it from its earlier context(s)? What formal, functional and semantic changes do these discourses undergo as they are recentred?

The study of tour-guide narratives and practices in this way is all the more pertinent since performance has become a privileged metaphor in analyzing the dialectics of tourism production and consumption.[4] It therefore makes sense to conceive a guided tour as a 'mutually satisfying performance' (Feldman 2007), a negotiated relationship between producers and consumers. What takes place during the tour is produced and interpreted as, or by analogy to, a stage performance (MacCannell 1973). The guide-guest encounter can be seen as a scripted performance involving both a guide-performer engaged in a make-believe monologue and interaction, and that performer's tourist audience. Every member of the audience collaborates as a spectator in framing the 'unreality onstage' (Goffman 1974: 130) or what in dramaturgical terms is known as the suspension of disbelief. In other words, tourists are essential constituents or co-creators of tourism performance, because it is only through them that guiding narratives and practices can be ratified. The tour as performance becomes a locus through which old meanings are tested and new ones are negotiated; where rules are enforced, broken and rewritten (Bauman and Briggs 1990).

Conceiving guiding narratives as performances, I am more interested in their metapragmatic framing—the comments and evaluations by which the stories are made to make profound sense and to involve their audience—than the core of the stories themselves.[5] The management of the social in and through the narrative performance is achieved via the ability of competent guides to index two realms of experience simultaneously: On the one hand, the then-and-there of the narrated events (tourism imaginaries) and, on the other hand, the (indexical) here-and-now of the performance and narration—what Young (1987) calls the 'taleworld' versus the 'storyrealm'. Although guiding is related to tourism imaginaries and discourses, it is anchored in the social interaction, or in the storyrealm, by which the taleworld assumes its meaning and vividness (Salazar, Bryon and Van Den Branden 2009).

## Touring Languages

Most of the tours in central Java and northern Tanzania are multilingual experiences. International tourists receive explanations and instructions from their guides in a localized version of a foreign language, with occasional insertions of Indonesian or Swahili words, mostly to indicate a certain local craft, food or plant. Among each other, tourists speak their native tongue (if the group shares a common language) or international English (if the group is mixed). Guides communicate in Indonesian or Swahili if they come from different regions, or either in Javanese or a Tanzanian language (e.g., Maa) if they share the same ethnic background. In the interactions between guides and locals, these same language combinations are used. In general, tourists are incapable of distinguishing between these languages. Given the language barrier (and the limited practical use of foreign language phrasebooks), the direct contact between tourists and locals is often minimal, making them dependent on the guide for communication mediation.

Guides in both central Java and northern Tanzania are conversant in at least two languages. However, language proficiencies differ widely. In Jogja, for example, many guides were not able or willing to be interviewed in the language they use while guiding, which could indicate that their foreign language ability does not go much beyond the fixed commentaries and jokes necessary to do their job. When tourists notice that guides are struggling with their language, they often kindly correct them. In some cases, guides understand the tourists' mother tongue (e.g., Dutch in Indonesia) without telling them. Indeed, the possibility of listening silently in on conversations enables guides not only to enhance their language skills but also to collect useful background information about the tourists' home culture. In other instances, guides will downplay their language proficiency, converging downward to the language level of their clients. They also subtly adapt the depth of information provided to the average interest level of the group. Such a high degree of linguistic accommodation to foreign tourists has also been noted elsewhere (Cohen and Cooper 1986: 533).

Guides constantly swap between local languages and their commentary language in order to manipulate the tourist experience and give the tour a more authentically local flavour.[6] The value of the local language during a tour is less in its utility as a medium for communication than in its symbolic or metonymic representation of the foreignness of the destination (Jaworski and Thurlow 2004: 315). By offering tourists playful, transient crossings into local languages, guides enable their clients to take some of the foreignness home, further positioning themselves as well-versed cosmopolitans. By using this type of language crossing, guides reduce the local language to 'the status of a handful of fixed phrases found in guidebook glossaries and exoticized linguascapes' (Jaworski et al. 2003: 5), offering the thrill of difference without the discomfort of incomprehension.

Take the example of Swahili, Tanzania's national language. For many foreigners, Swahili is not the language of a particular country or people, but a symbol of Africa as a whole, of the safari (also a Swahili word) and its related images of romance, adventure and fun under the African sun (Bruner 2005: 71–100). Tanzanian guides therefore represent Swahili as simple and easy (not to say primitive or backward), and always skilfully insert some simplified Swahili into their interactions. The greeting *jambo*, for instance, is used as both salutation and reply to a single individual or group. In grammatically correct Swahili, however, one greets *hujambo* (singular) or *hamjambo* (plural) 'How are you?' and answers *sijambo* (singular) or *hatujambo* (plural) 'I am (or We) are fine'. 'On safari, it is *jambo jambo* everywhere' (Eastman 1995: 178). Guides also teach their clients simple Swahili words such as *karibu* (welcome), *asante* (thank you), *rafiki* (friend) and *hapana, asante* (no, thank you; as one guide explains: 'To use when you [tourists] are harassed by street vendors'). Guides particularly love to reiterate Swahili phrases that have spread globally through popular culture. For example, they will often sing or let tourists listen to the popular tourist song *Jambo Bwana.*[7] The overly simple lyrics make it easy for tourists to participate and sing along (Eastman 1995: 180; Bruner 2005: 85–86).

When guides really master the foreign language in which they conduct tours, their commentaries can be linguistically refined and playful.[8]

Pointing to some light-coloured figures in one of the ancient rock paintings on a hill near the village of Kolo:
A01. They look like the *Warangi* tribe or *Wagogo*. You know the *Warangi* tribe? [silence] … You know the *Wazungu* tribe, you know [laughing]?

Explaining to French tourists the Javanese numerical symbology found in various decorations of the Sultan's Palace in Yogyakarta (Figure 14):
Y01. It's a bit like the old houses in France, with house numbers like this [writing with a stick in the sand]: 1 3 7 6 1 2 … [tourists looking at each other with expressions of incomprehension] … do mi si la do re [tourists still not understanding] … *domicile adoré* (F; treasured house)! That's a good one isn't it?

The first fragment is a typical example of codeswitching, in which the Swahili names of the Rangi and Gogo people are mingled with an utterance in English. While the guide mentions these two small Tanzanian ethnic groups, he assumes his European clients have never heard of them. He therefore teasingly asks the tourists if they know the *wazungu*, the Swahili word referring to whites or, more generally, to everyone behaving like a Westerner, no matter the person's race or ethnicity. Of course, his remark is meant ironically, because no Tanzanian would speak of whites in terms of a 'tribe'. By associating the light-coloured figures of the rock painting with the Rangi people (who have a lighter skin colour than other ethnic groups in the area; *rangi* in Swahili means 'colour'), he indexically connects 'white' people (*wazungu*) with the more recently painted graffiti message—WELCOME in big white capital letters—that defiles the rock painting in question. The second piece of narrative shows that the multimodal discourse of a guide can be so sophisticated—in this case the cryptic use of numerical equivalence for solfege syllables—that tourists have difficulty following.[9]

Humour (including self-mockery) is probably the most common device that guides draw on to relieve tensions and to manage the unfamiliar, as well as to align themselves with their clients.

During a pretour briefing of a cultural tour to a village nearby Jogja:
Y02. Our trip will start from here and last four hours, more or less [laughing and stressing], more or less!

Taking a group picture of European tourists who are heavily sweating in the tropical heat:
Y03. One … two … <u>smell</u> [laughing]!

At the last Ramayana wall relief in the Shiva temple at Prambanan:[10]
Y04. So, that's the end of the Ramayana story. Now if you go to the [Ramayana] theatre this evening, you can follow the story. <u>Even if you sleep well</u> [during the performance], <u>you'll be able to follow</u> [laughing].

While visiting a Maasai boma near the Ngorongoro Crater:
A02. This Maasai family has <u>only</u> fifteen children! [everybody laughing]

Y02 is a witty form of self-critique of the Indonesian concept of *jam karet* (flexible time), a reference to the continuous uncertainty of scheduled time arrangements. It is an affirmation that Indonesians traditionally do not think in the time-is-money mode common to the societies many tourists come from. The guide uses humour here to inform the clients that if the planned tour runs a little late, this is part of the cultural experience. In Y03, the guide empathically indicates she has noticed her clients are suffering from the heat (and already a bit smelly). The tourists laugh because they understand the guide has jokingly replaced smile (the word they expected to hear) with its homonym smell. Y04 contains an implicit recognition that the Ramayana Ballet performance in the open-air theatre next to the Prambanan temple complex is long and can be boring, especially for tourists who lack the cultural cues to grasp the subtleties of the show and who are tired at the end of a long day of touring. The Maasai joke in A02 additionally shows that humour is a culturally sensitive mechanism. In this case, it works because the joke is based on a shared assumption: Maasai families have more children than families in developed countries. In other words, the trick in cross-cultural interaction is to rely on shared frames of reference, because 'as long as guides feel they are sharing an *implicit* understanding with the members of their tour group … they can afford to apply strategies of differentiation in the form of oversimplification, common prejudices, or perhaps cultural self-depreciation' (Glover 2008: 124).

## Supremacy of the Exotic

For the majority of foreign tourists, visiting Indonesia or Tanzania is exotic in the strictest sense of the word: it is alien, strikingly strange or unusual. It is the local tour guide's task to give significance and meaning to the tourist experience by rendering cultural differences as fascinating, but not disorienting; strange and unique, but not too unfamiliar. The language of the exotic has different registers and uses tropes such as orientalism, tropicality, primitiveness and diverse forms of Otherness to metaphorically (re)describe reality. All of these rely heavily on clichés and stereotypes to represent a destination or sight as an Eden on earth (Dann 2001; Costa 1998; Schellhorn and Perkins 2004). The reality of Indonesia and Tanzania as places of poverty and corruption is bracketed and substituted by vivid imaginaries of an exotic paradise. Through narrating sites and facilitating kinaesthetic and sensory experiences, local guides image the local as it is imagined by common tourism imaginaries. This enables tour participants to experience the exotic in recognizable semiotic landscapes, thereby domesticating it.[11]

## *Java's Erotic Eden*

In tours around Jogja, guides make many subtle references to eroticism. I found the best examples of this in the Water Castle, the former pleasure garden of the Sultan's Palace, because comparisons between this heritage site and (popular culture) representations of oriental harems are easy to make. Local guides use the tour around the enchanting pavilions and mesmerizing swimming pools to rouse the erotic and sexual fantasies of their clients, often jokingly.

> Commenting on the sultans and their harem of wives:
> Y05. The sultan chose one woman a day, not two. That was enough.
> Y06. The seventh sultan was the most roguish; he had six wives. Why was he roguish? He had only six wives. That is to say, during every given week he still had one day to rest ... to watch the football game on Sundays!
> Y07. Four wives is polygamy, three wives is trigamy, two wives is bigamy, and only one is monotony ... and when one doesn't have a wife? That's autonomy!

The Water Castle is depicted as a Shangri-La or earthly Garden of Eden with guiltless sexuality and freedom from work and want, and the physical structure perfectly lends itself for tour guides to perform such fantasies. Many guides love enacting the role of the sultan, strolling with an imaginary girl (when possible substituted by a willing female tourist) from the women's swimming pool to the private pool and adjacent quarters:

> Playing the sultan in the castle's watchtower, observing the make-believe harem girls around the pool:
> Y08. [Directed at the tourists] You want to go upstairs? Watch and take pictures.
> Y09. Ah, woman [number] 26, come! ... And on other days he [the sultan] chooses other women: number 12, 3, ...
> Y10. The women were wearing a *sarong*, no bikini [tourists laughing], ya, a long *sarong*.[12]

The pools of the Water Castle are still there but the lovely girls bathing have long disappeared. Yet the visitors are invited to participate in a performance that will bring this imagined past back to life. On one such occasion, for example, a tourist commented upon his playful guide: 'He's full of nostalgia … Before it was better'. One could, indeed, see the eroticized representations of this heritage site as a form of nostalgia, a kind of mourning for the destruction of an imagined traditional culture (or a sexualized and eroticized one) by colonial and other imperialist forces. Yet this is not just a sentiment; it is also a script, performed and enacted on site.

Tourists with more time visit Sukuh Temple, tucked away in the highlands of central Java. This monument, listed on UNESCO's tentative World Heritage inventory, is unique not only in overall design but also in decoration; it is the only known openly erotic temple on Java. Carved into the floor of the entrance gateway is a large linga about to insert itself into a yoni.[13] Around the temple, statues and reliefs of erect male members abound. Guides use the mystery surrounding the building of the temple to tell piquant stories about the presence of a fertility cult that determined the faithfulness of existing wives and the virginity of potential ones. According to a locally circulating legend, if wives were unfaithful or future spouses not virgin, their sarong would either tear or fall on the floor. The visit to Sukuh is often combined with a walk to the nearby Ceto Temple, where the entrance is decorated with a humongous stone linga on the floor.

> Commentary regarding the stone linga of Ceto Temple:
> Y11. This *linga* is also considered a God. Before Islam started coming here [to Indonesia], sexual relations were more open … Like you can see, this *linga*, [hesitantly] it has three balls. During that period, man would insert this [penis with a piercing] to satisfy the woman. But when Islam started to come here, that practice was more suppressed, and with the Dutch people coming things became more civilized. [laughing shyly]

It was not easy for the female Javanese guide in Y11 to talk about this topic to two young, male European tourists. Again, her commentary evokes a certain nostalgia for an imagined pre-Islamic and precolonial past. The erotic fantasies of the tourists at the site are further stimulated by the presence of young Indonesian couples who come to this desolate place in the hills, using it as a perfect hideout to flirt.

Even at the Buddhist shrine of Borobudur, guides have a chance to play with the erotic imagination of their clients. The wall reliefs on the lowest level of the monument contain depictions of human desires and worldly temptations. Naturally, many have a sexual flavour. However, with the exception of one corner, the majority of the 160 reliefs are behind a heavy concrete encasement. Some guides tell their clients this was done for structural reasons, because the stability of the monument was at stake. Others hint that Indonesian authorities thought people should not see these indecent representations, leaving what is concealed behind the wall of stone to the visitor's imagination. There could also be a veiled criticism of the perceived influence that a growing Islamic conservatism is wielding in Indonesia on those in power.[14]

## Northern Tanzania's Ecological Paradise

In Tanzania, there are also occasional erotic allusions, mostly to the imagined potency of Maasai warriors and to their multiple wives, but the dominating imagery has more to do with a lushly green environment in which humans are barely visible or present. Because of the overabundance of wildlife, Tanzanian guides use relatively little narration compared to their colleagues in other African countries, who need convincing tales to make even the empty bush seem alive. Besides, too much talk might interfere with the tourist's 'vision quest' (Almagor 1985) or first-hand communion with Nature.

> Reflecting on nature conservation in Tanzania during a safari in Serengeti National Park:
> A03. A quarter of the country is being reserved for national parks, conservation areas, game controlled areas, and game reserves … It's more than a quarter … [long silence]

A03 exemplifies how compact tour commentaries can be. Guides leave it to nature to do the rest, simply by unveiling itself. This goes against Cohen's (1985) universal model of tour guiding in which he argues the communicative component is becoming the centre of the professional role (see chapter 5). Interpretation has certainly gained ground in wildlife tourism, but the pathfinder role—leading tourists to the best wildlife viewing spots—remains equally important.

To maintain the fantasy of unspoiled nature (cf. Norton 1996; Dann 1996a), it is in the guides' interest not to tell clients how the Maasai and other ethnic groups were originally expelled from their lands in order to create national parks and protected areas. In the Ngorongoro Crater, many driver-guides also choose not to pass by the ruins of the farm of the Siedentopfs, two German brothers who cultivated on the crater floor in the early 1900s. Such practices illustrate how tourism imaginaries offer a perceptual framework that filters out as much as it includes, proposing for the tourist a particular interpretative frame within which local heritage and culture are understood. By highlighting certain elements of the destination over others, guides take control of interpretation, distracting their clients from things they want to keep hidden, things that are, in Goffman's (1959) theatrical metaphor, 'the backstage', where no members of the audience are allowed. Tourists primarily come to Tanzania to spot wild animals, as they have seen on television. I saw the apprentice-guide story about staged wildlife viewing through radio contact (chapter 3) confirmed while accompanying a group of European tourists to the Serengeti. It was our second day in the park, and we had already seen buffaloes and some lions and elephants. After radio contact with another car from the safari company we were travelling with, our driver-guide accelerated. We passed by a large herd of elephants and some tourists wanted to stop to take pictures. However, the driver decided to continue, promising that we would return to the herd later on. The group was baffled at the guide's behaviour but when they spotted a leopard (a hard-to-spot Big Five species) a couple of minutes later, they appreciated the guide's hurry to move on.

The importance that bush guides give to the principles of sustainable development and ecotourism is less detectable in their narratives than in their practices. Take the common situation in which guides, helped by multiple English-language signboards, inform their clients about the rules and regulations to obey within the confines of national parks or other protected areas. Senior bush guide Willie tells me: 'A tour guide is like a nursery school teacher, who teaches small children how to write and read ... *Mzungu* who are fresh to Africa are like these small kids. It's the work of the tour guide to give the tourists exactly appropriate information on everything'. In these instances, the guide-guest interaction indeed resembles a parent-child relationship (Dann 1996b: 132–33), because the guide not only acts as a go-between but also as a role model of what is appropriate behaviour (Yu, Weiler and Ham 2001). As Edensor notes, '"appropriate" behaviour and performative procedures are regulated by guides, who by synthesizing meaning and action reinforce a common-sense praxis and re-encode enactive norms' (2001: 69). The pristine quality of the Edenic landscape is also enhanced by indicating to clients what the best spots are to take unique pictures and by taking them to places where nobody else goes. In the national parks during the high season, this is not an easy task, because there are very few roads and off-road driving is strictly prohibited. A white South African guide working for one of the top-end safari companies confessed to me that he is forced to drive off-road, because it is the only way he can guarantee his select clientele the exclusive experience they paid for: wildlife viewing without any other people around. Off-road driving is normally heavily fined and drivers can be barred park entry for three months, but many guides will go against park regulations if they know that the reward for their transgression—tips from satisfied tourists—will be substantial.

The great advantage in focusing on wildlife and ecology is that it is possible to avoid having to deal with contemporary societal problems like corruption, disease and poverty. Nature does not talk back. In the meantime, the guides' narratives reinforce a stereotypical image of Tanzania as (East) Africa's sanctuary of peace, especially when there is upheaval in neighbouring countries.

Explaining about a village, just outside Lake Manyara National Park:
A04. This area has over seventy tribes within this small village. But they all live <u>harmoniously</u> as far as we have one common language, which is Swahili.

A05. We have more than 120 tribes in this area, and these tribes come from different parts of Tanzania.

Telling about the Makonde people:
A06. When this tribe arrived in Tanzania it was 1975, it was civil war in Mozambique and some of them were escaping. When they arrived, they found Tanzanian people are <u>so friendly</u>.

A04 and A05 show that the details of the narrative do not matter; it is the general idea that counts. If, for instance, visitors would know that the village in question is not only the most multiethnic community but also the place in Tanzania with the highest prevalence of AIDS, they might prefer not to even stop there. Reports about crime and other disturbances are quickly silenced, because they are seen as threats to tourism imaginaries. Instead, problems are exteriorized and attributed to outsiders (chapter 6).

Soothing tourists in Ngorongoro Crater who did not manage to see any rhinoceros:
A07. You should bear in mind that there was more population of rhinos here. Because they were highly poached until the 1970s by <u>Somalis</u>. Asian countries those days believed rhino horn helped the erection [problems] of men. So rhino horn was expensively, expensively sold. <u>Somalis</u> made good money out of this. They [the rhinos] were poached highly. That's one of the reasons why they are endangered right now.

## Worldly Tools

As mechanics of glocalization (chapter 5), with the responsibility of assuring the local continuity and perpetuation of global chains of tourism imaginaries, tour guides have a wide array of strategies and techniques at their disposal. The process of becoming expert users of these tools also brings them a step closer to becoming cosmopolitans: by opening themselves to the world and its many facets, roaming the global web of interpretations and expressions, and recognizing subtle differences vital to the construction of different identities. Not all guides in Indonesia and Tanzania have had the opportunity to travel abroad, but through their contacts with former clients, as well as the knowledge acquired from tourists, they gain an understanding of the societies these people come from. This cosmopolitan comprehension is vital to their work and resembles that of the more stereotypical cosmopolites, experienced travellers. In other words, guides do not physically need to wander around the world to develop a cosmopolitan attitude; the world simply comes to them. This confirms that 'sheer mobility (in and of itself) does not automatically entail cosmopolitanism' (Swain 2009: 513). I describe below how they strategically exploit this accumulated cosmopolitan knowledge in their narratives and practices.

## Foreign Frames of Reference

Guides use transcultural frames of interpretation to translate the perceived strangeness of their own culture into an idiom familiar to the clients, finding connections between what is being experienced and what tourists already know (Reisinger and Steiner 2006). This helps tourists find 'the familiar in an unfamiliar place' (Notar 2008: 616). The examples below are all taken from a French-language tour of the Sultan's Palace with a young Swiss couple. The accompanying guide is Pak Padmo, a seasoned Kraton guide and alumnus of a French-language department at one of Jogja's major universities.

Commenting upon the sultan's servants working inside the palace:
Y12. They wear a dagger, called *keris*. The *keris* is not used as a weapon; it's not only for the guardians of the palace. It's for those who have served over ten years, as a promotional gift and symbol of loyalty ... a Rolex.[15]
Y13. All the servants are barefoot. That's not good when it's really hot. They become TGV's *à la Javanaise.*[16]
Y14. They don't retire. Even if they are old, they work; but, no problem, in general they do the RATP. Do you know RATP? It's *reste assis, t' es photographié* (F; remain seated, you are being photographed).[17]
Y15. They are like the Scots, men wearing skirts."

Explaining the process of electing a new sultan:
Y16. There will be a big meeting with wise men, around forty people in total. They will meditate and wait for God's answer ... It's like a conclave in the Vatican.

About traditional gamelan music ensembles:
Y17. Nowadays they [the court musicians] also play Western instruments because it's not possible to play *La Marseillaise* on *gamelan*.18
Y18. *Gamelan* has nothing to do with the word *gamelle* (F; lunch box). *Gamelles* are like this [taking a small bowl gong and holding it upside down].
Y19. Have you already heard *gamelan* music? It's not like rap!

An explanatory note on the Indonesian tradition of shadow puppets:
Y20. This is Garuda [pointing to one of the puppets]. It's like Superman in the USA. He flies everywhere to do good deeds. Before the Americans had Superman, the Javanese already had Garuda ... Superman is like an adaptation of Garuda.[19]

Commentary on a painting depicting a sultan's coronation:
Y21. He has big pointed ears [indicating the metallic decorations covering the ears of the sultan]. This has nothing to do with Mr. Spock.[20]

Commentary while standing in front of the current sultan's actual residence:
Y22. The doors are closed, indicating he's not in the palace ... like the flag.

It should come as no surprise that pun-loving Pak Padmo is the Kraton's French-language guide in highest demand. In the fragments above, he shows his deep knowledge of both French language and culture in particular and global popular culture in general. Using simile and metaphor, he repeatedly compares traditional Javanese culture with cultural elements that French-speaking tourists can easily recognize, a technique that can be used to mollify the effects of strangeness associated with a trip abroad (Dann 1996b: 171–74). Of course, the strategy only works if the tourists share the same frame of reference. During the tour with the Swiss couple, for instance, the woman had to explain to her husband what the French acronym RATP stands for, and kindly pointed out to the guide that they do not have that transport system in Switzerland. In commentaries like Y22, the guide is actually testing whether his clients are as well versed in global culture as he is. In this case, he had barely finished his phrase when the female tourist started laughing out loudly and said triumphantly: 'Buckingham Palace!' indicating she understood the guide's allusion to the official flag of the reigning British monarch, which only flies over Buckingham when the sovereign is in residence at the palace. The references to Superman and Spock also indicate that the guide assumes these figures belong to global popular culture and, thus, should be known by everybody—certainly by well-travelled European tourists.

The following examples from a tour around the Prambanan temple complex further illustrate the common use of references to global (popular) culture:

Interrupting the narration of the Ramayana story before taking the visitors to the neighbouring temple where the story depicted on the wall reliefs continues:
Y23. Lakshmana [Rama's brother] takes his Swiss knife, ouch no, his Javanese knife, called *keris,* to make a magic circle to protect Sita [Rama's wife] … Rama and Lakshmana leave for the forest, Sita stays alone in the magic circle … to be continued next week! [tourists laughing]

Continuing the Ramayana tale in the adjacent temple:
Y24. Hanuman [king of the ape-like humanoids] tells Rama: *Don't worry, be happy!*

Pointing to a particular geometric pattern on a wall relief panel:
Y25. A mandala, but don't be confused with Mandela.

After the light-hearted comparison between the relatively unknown Javanese keris and the globally renowned Swiss army knife in Y23, the guide started mimicking the genre of a soap opera: briefly summarizing the latest developments in the story and stopping the narration at a dramatic moment. The guide used the time needed to walk to the second temple to promote the nightly performance at the Ramayana Ballet Open Theatre (local advertising time), making the interdiscursive comparison even more striking. This whole tour was a prime example of intertextual narrative performance. Pak Supriyadi, formerly a Ramayana Ballet dancer himself, not only narrated but also enacted (in a very dance-like fashion) parts of the Ramayana story, changing voice pitch when talking about different characters. In addition, he imitated the chants of a Brahman priest while explaining the Hindu rituals taking place in the temple. Y24 immediately struck my attention because it was uttered during a French-language tour and involved codeswitching (French to English). The guide quickly added the French translation (*'ne vous inquietez pas'*), but it is obvious he was referring to the legendary Bobby McFerrin song, widely used in films, advertising and popular culture. Y25 is a nice pun, although somewhat outdated and out of context—by 2006, South Africa's former President Nelson Mandela had greatly retreated from public life due to his age and health issues. The comment should be seen as the guide trying to show off his cosmopolitan knowledge.[21]

At Borobudur, local guides try equally hard to incorporate global frames of reference in their storytelling. However, their lack of experience and insufficient training (chapters 3 and 5) make this a challenging task.

Introducing the history of the world heritage site:
Y26. After the volcanic eruption, the temple was not used and totally abandoned for almost one thousand years. Exactly like what happened to a small city nearby Rome, Pompeii.

Explaining the (hidden) reliefs about desires and worldly temptations on the ground level of the monument:
Y27. Temptations can destroy our memory. Like me, I have a memory like a Pentium I computer. So, it will be destroyed by many viruses. Viruses are temptations.

Narrating the life of Siddhartha Gautama:
Y28. The history of the life of Siddhartha, of Buddha, is represented in Borobudur in 120 relief panels. It equals the description of Siddhartha's life by a German author, Herman Hesse. The essence of the story is the same.
Y29. It's a bit similar to the history of Christ. A few days after his birth, he was visited by kings as well.
Y30. Buddhists call it the golden Buddha because gold is stainless. The soul is pure, uncontaminated, and free from stress and distress. Like the Catholics, you have the Immaculate Conception of the Virgin Mary.

Small talk on the way to the exit gate:
Y31. Guide: What is Belgium's best-known beer?
Tourist [from Belgium]: Stella Artois.
G: Mhm, internationally known hé, like Heineken, Corona, San Miguel, Felsenschloss, like Paulaner, like Bintang!

Pompeii was a Roman city (now a World Heritage Site), but located close to Naples, and 210 kilometres away from Rome (Y26); computer microprocessors like the ones from the Pentium brand include more than just a memory management unit (Y27); and the name of the German beer the guide is trying to recall is not Felsenschloss but Schloss Fels (Y31). In addition, the guide in Y30 wrongly assumes all *bule* (white people) are Catholic, while the particular European clients on that tour were atheists (but with a protestant background). These examples indicate that the local guides at Borobudur seem less versed in cosmopolitan comparisons than their colleagues at other heritage sites in the area. Yet, it is interesting to note that these guides, the majority of whom are Muslim, have not only studied the history of Buddhism (Figure 6), but also seem familiar with elements of Christianity (Y29, Y30), allowing them to create shared frames of religious reference with their Euro-American clientele (cf. Feldman 2007). The last fragment (Y31) gives us some insights as to how small talk during a guided tour gives an opportunity to build (often superficial or banal) cosmopolitan knowledge about other cultures and places. Every time the guide meets clients from another beer-drinking country, he can expand his list. He also jokingly added Bintang, Indonesia's best selling brand of beer (brewed by an Indonesian subsidiary of Heineken).

In general, the Indonesian tour guide narratives seem a confirmation of Brennan's observation that 'the imbalance of historical learning means that citizens of Indonesia … know much more about Europe than Europeans generally know about Indonesia' (2001: 51–52). The acquaintance with the cultural history of the tourists' societies enables guides to focus on aspects of their own culture and traditions that are particularly different, while at the same time lessening the strangeness by using targeted transcultural comparisons and references, sometimes to the surprise of the tourists.

> Trying to handle the stream of questions asked during a village tour:
> Y32. G: Wait, wait, … curiosity kills the cat, ya!
>    T [amused]: An Indonesian proverb!

The tourist in Y32 is startled to hear an English proverb from a junior Indonesian guide, because it runs against the grain of the idea of a guide being 'local', that is, that he or she is knowledgeable about local natural and cultural heritage, but not necessarily of the outside world (including foreign languages). The witty reply is a kind of implicit acknowledgement of the guide's broader knowledge. Guides who have had the opportunity to travel (or even work) abroad, are clearly at an advantage (chapter 3). Given the dire economic situation, an increasing number of professional guides in Jogja are looking for short-term jobs abroad during the low tourist season. Work on cruise ships or in large hotels in Europe or in the United States seems popular. Yet while such cross-cultural experiences help them in their job, local guides will seldom mention their international escapades to their clients (Salazar 2005).

The guides in Tanzania could learn a great deal from their Indonesian counterparts. They use similar 'framing' strategies (Goffman 1974), but less frequently and not always in the appropriate context.

Upon entering the Serengeti National Park:
A08. So, the Serengeti itself, the National Park, is 14,763 square kilometres, almost the size of Ireland.

Commentary on the archaeological findings in Oldupai Gorge:
A09. It belongs to the same species as the skeleton nicknamed Lucy, which was found in Ethiopia in 1974. But the name Lucy, which is a joke name for that skeleton, was given because during that day the scientists were listening and dancing to the Beatles' song 'Lucy in the Sky with Diamonds'.

The guide made commentary A08 to a group of US tourists, to whom the size of Ireland, expressed in kilometres, meant little to nothing (and the actual size of the island of Ireland is 84,430 square kilometres or 32,600 square miles, comparable to the State of Indiana). A09 is a nice anecdote but slightly off-topic because it is not about the archaeological findings at Oldupai Gorge itself. While there are many entertaining stories to be told about the discovery of hominid fossils in Oldupai Gorge, the guide apparently lacks access to the resources that contain them (even though some of the stories are illustrated in the small museum at the site). This type of limitation prevents guides from effectively creating shared frames of reference. During a visit to a Maasai boma, for instance, a group of Maasai warriors was dancing and singing with deep-throated voices. One of the European tourists remarked that the singing men looked like they were taking a course on how to become Tom Waits. The accompanying guide did not know how to react, because he did not know that Tom Waits is a US singer-songwriter famous for his raspy voice.

While the tourism tales told by Tanzanian guides may be enthralling, they are not always historically correct. Take the following example:

Narrating the origins of the Iraqw people:
A10. The history, according to the migration of the tribes, and the movements of societies in Africa and all over the world, this people they actually migrated all the way from the Middle East, following the Great Eastern Rift Valley. They walked all the way for centuries, down to the centre of Tanganyika, around Dodoma and Songea … At that time, they were known as *Wairaki* people, the Iraqw tribe.

Stressing the genuineness of his narrative by using the word *actually,* a 'truth marker' common in tourism discourse (MacCannell 1999: 137–41), this guide reproduces the widespread origin myth of the Iraqw. I not only heard this myth from tour guides but also from an old storyteller in Babati. In this way, an imaginary designed for foreign others becomes accepted by local people as a story about themselves. The legend is based on a well-refuted ethnocentric scientific theory, the Hamitic hypothesis, that argued Caucasoid peoples from the north (Iraq or Mesopotamia) were responsible for a number of precolonial cultural and technological achievements in Africa, serving to legitimize European intervention and colonization on the continent (Rekdal 1998). While the guide does not know the historical context of the story, his retelling it helps to ensure its ever-widening distribution, illustrating his role as a mechanic of circulation.

Examples like the one above help us understand how tourism discourses circulate so widely. As they are being '(re)entextualized' (reproduced with an altered form) or '(re)contextualized' (reproduced identically), innumerable factors intervene, such that the copy is often distinct from the original (Bauman and Briggs 1990). Urban (1996: 40), however, argues that the more that discourse is overtly coded as nonpersonal, and the less it is linked to a present context and circumstances, the more likely the copier will be to replicate it. In the case of tourism, it is extremely difficult to trace the actual producers of its imaginaries and accompanying discourses because they are circulating globally (chapter 2). In addition, the positionality of tourism discourse speakers shifts vis-à-vis layers of social authority. Goffman's (1981) distinction between various speaker roles is useful in this context. He suggested that there are three speaking roles: (1) an animator who makes the sounds; (2) an author who selects the words and the phrasing; and (3) a principal who is responsible for the opinions expressed. Guides can be conceived of as animators, their narratives being scripted by authors like teachers, tour operators or senior guides (chapter 5). Because tourism discourse is part of a much larger 'representational loop' (Sturma 2002: 137), the guide does not know who the principal is, who is the one responsible for the opinions expressed. Because tourism tales like the one above are often situated in a distant past, guides can safely replicate them. This does not mean, however, that no alterations can be made (chapter 6).

### Supralocal Legitimacy

In addition to the use of transcultural frames of reference, local guides give their narratives more weight by stressing the global significance of the places visited. Sites on the UNESCO World Heritage list, for example, all have clearly visible signs indicating their privileged status.[22] Guides will often stop at these signs for a 'photo opportunity', while using the information on the sign to reinforce their own tales. Bruner calls this strategy 'dialogic narration' (2005: 169–88) because the guide's narrative is not just indexically referencing what is actually written on the sign—for instance that Site X is a UNESCO World Heritage site—but takes account of all the stories tourists have heard, read or seen about other World

Heritage sites as well. Explicit comparisons with those other monuments are used
to put the local site on an equal level of global importance.

> Pointing to some stones that were temporarily removed from the Borobudur monu-
> ment for restoration:
> Y33. This is the technique they used to build Borobudur in the eighth century, with-
> out using concrete. It's like a puzzle, exactly <u>like the pyramids in South America
> and in Mexico</u>, the Aztec and Maya culture, and Inca.

> Explaining the structure of the temple complex in Prambanan:
> Y34. For example, also in Cambodia, in <u>Angkor Wat</u>, there are five pillars.
> Y35. Prambanan temple is the largest Hindu temple in the world outside of India. It
> <u>resembles the temples in South India</u>.

In a site without World Heritage status, such as the Water Castle in Jogja,
one guide was quick to stress that the compound was renovated with money
from UNESCO and Portugal (pointing to a big panel at the entrance gate).
The sign actually indicates that not UNESCO but the private World Monument
Fund supported parts of the Water Castle's rehabilitation in 2003. The support
from Portugal came from a private foundation too. At the Kraton, which has
been on UNESCO's tentative list since 1995, guides make sure to mention that
UNESCO is helping with the reconstruction of the pavilions that were destroyed
by the 2006 earthquake.

In northern Tanzania, the driver-guides are blessed by the opportunity to
virtually bring their clients from one World Heritage site or Biosphere Reserve
to the next. At the gate of each park, huge signs publicly announce this international recognition, and guides usually stop at these boards without giving much
commentary. They invite tourists to take pictures and allow the message to sink
in silently. At Serengeti National Park, for example, guides are proud to tell that
the park is not only a World Heritage site and Biosphere Reserve but also one of
the seven New Wonders of the World (as voted by *USA Today* and ABC News's
*Good Morning America* in 2006).[23] At the Kondoa rock-art sites in Kolo, only
inscribed on the World Heritage list in 2006, a local guide is already fantasiz-
ing how the UNESCO recognition will change the place in a couple of years.
Whereas now you need a 4x4 jeep to get close to the painted rocks, the guide
enthusiastically explains how new roads will be built, pointing to good spots to
develop a parking place and tourist facilities such as toilets, a snack bar and a souvenir shop. This is truly an exercise of the imagination because for miles around
there is nothing to see but lush vegetation. While the Kondoa rock paintings are
still relatively unknown, the guide proudly reminds visitors that the paintings
were 'discovered' by nobody less than Dr. Leakey, the famed archaeologist and
naturalist who did groundbreaking research on human evolutionary development in East Africa.[24]

In Serengeti and Ngorongoro, guides pay tribute to Professor Bernard Grzimek and his son Michael, who made the Oscar-winning documentary *Serengeti Shall Not Die* (1959), perhaps the best-known and most influential wildlife movie ever made.

Overlooking the wide Serengeti plains at the Naabi Hill Gate:
A11. The ecological system of the Serengeti … that's how the 'Serengeti shall <u>never</u> die' came about, by Dr. Bernard Grzimek who made Serengeti famous.

In A11, the guide subtly reinforces the romanticized image of the Serengeti as the last wildlife haven on earth by altering the title of the documentary, replacing the original 'not' with the slightly more dramatic 'never'. Guides resort to name dropping famous people who not only worked or lived at certain sites, but also those who simply visited—a technique Dann (1996b: 176–79) calls 'testimony'.

In front of the official reception hall of the Sultan's Palace:
Y36. Before, the sultan used to eat seated at a table while the ordinary visitors were seated on floor mats. But two years ago, <u>Mrs. Clinton</u> came here. Fortunately for <u>Hillary</u>, everybody was seated [at a table]. If she would have had to sit kneeled [on a floor mat], that would have been good for her Bill [tourists laughing], but at that time he was busy with his Monica.

At a souvenir market in a Maasai village:
A12. These things are made by our women here … This one [pointing to a decorated ostrich egg] I gave last time to <u>Bill Clinton</u> when he came to Tanzania. Even <u>Hillary Clinton</u>, she has just been here. Bill Clinton we met in the airport.

In Arusha National Park, driver-guides stop in front of the Hatari Lodge, and explain that the property and its surroundings were the setting for John Wayne's Oscar-winning wildlife adventure movie *Hatari!* (1962). This film is widely believed to have put Tanzania on Hollywood's map of the world, greatly assisting in opening up the country's major tourism attractions.

Foreign publications are another way of giving guiding narratives supralocal legitimacy, another form of intertextuality. At Java's cultural heritage sites, for example, most guides utilize copies of illustrations from scholarly books about archaeology, history or architecture to exemplify their points or to make visual comparisons. The safari guides of northern Tanzania use illustrated fauna and flora field guides to check and prove that they have correctly identified a certain animal or plant. Tourists also use many of these written sources. In other words, both tourists and tourism service providers rely on overlapping sources to (re)produce and authenticate tourism imaginaries. The more access guides have to these sources (more in Indonesia than in Tanzania), the better they are able to create shared frames of reference with their clients.

## The Other and Me

I do not remember the first group of tourists I took out alone, but I guided hundreds, if not thousands, of them during the four years I worked there [Serengeti NP]. I guided ordinary people and lords, kings, senators, and movie stars. For the first time I interacted with white people of all shades and nationalities. I boasted that I knew the typical behaviour of each nationality. For example, Italians were very noisy, but they admitted it. Germans were cruel and arrogant to the point of stupidity. Americans were easygoing, noisy, and arrogant. They measured everything by dollars; they would say things like, 'Ranger, I will give you ten bucks if you will find me a kill and a leopard'. Frenchwomen were like peacocks. They carried little handkerchiefs and you could easily tell that they did not belong there. The British seemed annoyed when ordered not to shout near an animal. You got the feeling that they were annoyed at themselves for not knowing in the first place that it was forbidden.
                                                                    –Tepilit Ole Saitoti (1988: 97)

Local guides in Indonesia and Tanzania have to present their foreign clients with a difficult balance between 'mimesis' (the idea of imitation, adaptation or assimilation) and 'alterity' (the idea of difference and distance from the Other), a complex pair of processes analyzed in detail by Taussig (1993). While Taussig conceives of these concepts broadly, in tourism alterity is constructed as exotic difference and mimesis rarely goes far beyond enacting imagined Others by dressing up (e.g., playing the Maasai or Tarzan) or acting like them (e.g., planting rice in a Javanese rice paddy) (Figure 9).

## *Whose Culture?*

Although certainly not all foreign tourists want to be immersed in alien cultures or meet local people, often it is the human contact, the close encounter with locals, which remains strongly etched in a tourist's mind and keeps surfacing in post-trip anecdotes of a tour. A brief tourist questionnaire revealed the following main motivations for meet-the-people tourism in Jogja: to meet real people, to know more about the daily life of local people, to see Jogja with other eyes, to come closer to culture and to see places one otherwise would not come. These tourist statements can be seen as metadiscursive commentaries, indicating a desire to break out of the common tourism bubble, to look for more genuine intercultural experiences (chapter 7). Of course, what is understood by 'local' needs to be qualified. Both in central Java and northern Tanzania, the local is, and has been for some time, 'glocal' (chapter 2). However, overt glocalization does not sell in a global market that trades on the romance of difference, so the *g* in glocal must remain silent. Guides voluntarily participate in this game of 'staging authenticity' (MacCannell 1973). Ironically, it is their cosmopolitan knowledge

FIGURE 9 •
*Guide-assisted
Mimesis in
Tourism*

that helps them frame the glocal culture around them as distinctively local. This makes them complicit in the perpetuation of global tourism imaginaries as well as the construction of (re)created local identities and traditions (Hobsbawm and Ranger 1992). Even if these processes of globalization and localization seem contradictory, ultimately they are complementary manifestations of the globalist ideology underpinning the mythologies of both globalization and tourism (Jaworski and Thurlow 2004).

The construction of local culture for tourists and the misrepresentation of the complexities of rural societies is clearly visible in village tours around Jogja (Salazar 2005). These are not about how the local is currently being lived and internalized by villagers. Rather, it gives tourists exactly what they want: a mythologized, nostalgic version of premodern rural life. Because tourists want to experience such an imagined local, guides prefer to show them those rice fields where the planting still happens in the traditional way, without the use of modern machinery (Figure 9). Tours are organized by horse cart or bicycles resembling the models imported by the Dutch during colonial times, rather than by car or scooter (the most common means of transport on Java). Guides also facilitate the experiential process—which includes not only seeing, but doing and feeling things—by themselves blending in with the village life that is on display. For instance, during the tours some of the guides wear a traditional conical straw hat that also the villagers working in the fields wear (but is attire that guides would never wear when they are not guiding) (Figure 10). This clear sign of social indexicality helps guides portray themselves as more 'local' than they really are, knowing perfectly well that in many developing countries 'the guide, as much as the sights seen, are one of the attractions' (Ness 2003: xv). While the guides specialize in reproducing widely popular ways of selling heritage and culture, tourists assume the local authenticity of the guides' narratives and knowledge, leaving both parties mostly unaware of the classificatory schemes and scripts behind the generalized representations used.

The make-believe character of tours is enhanced by narrating legends, superstitions and magic—all elements stereotypically linked to premodern cultures.

> Enchanting visitors with the magic of Borobudur:
> Y37. Do you want to see Gunadharma, the architect of Borobudur? Look at the line
> of the mountain there [pointing and giving a detailed description] ... The <u>legend</u>
> says that this mountain is a reincarnation of the architect of Borobudur.
> Y38. This is a special Buddha statue because it brings good luck. But, this is a <u>belief</u>
> outside Buddhism. It's not philosophy, not religion, just <u>superstition</u>. Men touch
> the finger or ring of Buddha while making a wish. Women touch the foot of the
> Buddha. Now, I cannot give you any guarantee. I have short arms and cannot
> reach!

FIGURE 10 • *Staging the (Imagined) Local*

In these examples, again, we see the importance of performance, and the mysterious sphere that is created is not only the result of the guide's narrative, but is also enhanced by the setting in which the service encounter takes place (cf. Arnould and Price 1993).

Jalan Malioboro, Jogja's main shopping street, is another place that speaks to the imagination. Because there is no written record of the naming history of the street, guides can choose which story to tell their clients. The most popular folk etymology is that Malioboro was named after the English soldier and statesman John Churchill (1650–1722), the first Duke of Marlborough, though the man had no relation whatsoever to Indonesia and died long before the short English occupation of Java (1811–16). Another explanation links Malioboro to the Sanskrit phrase *malya bhara*, 'bearing garlands of flowers'. According to this theory, the street used to be decorated with flowers each time the Sultan's Palace (at the end of the street) held ceremonies. This second account has the added narrative benefit that guides can relate it to Javanese cosmology, in which Malioboro Street plays an important connecting spiritual line between the Kraton and Mt. Merapi (the 'fire mountain').[25] However, the Kraton was built only in the eighteenth century, so a Javanese name for the street would be more plausible than a Sanskrit one. A much weaker story links the street name to the Marlboro cigarette brand, an argument indexically supported by the strategically placed advertisements of the company in the Malioboro neighbourhood. Most likely, however, Malioboro is a linguistic deformation of the Dutch *mergelburg* (limestone fortress), referring to Fort Vredeburg, a fortress on Malioboro built in 1765 to protect the Dutch governor. I did not hear any local guide offer this as a plausible interpretation. This could mean either that they have never heard this explanation or they do know it but prefer the other stories because those allow for narrations that are more imaginative and do not necessitate references to the Dutch colonial period.

For guides, it is fun to tell tourists about local popular beliefs and check how much of it they actually 'believe' by performing their instructions.

Commentary about the statue of Kuvera (the Hindu god of wealth) at Prambanan:
Y39. This is a god with plenty of jewels, with a purse. He doesn't hide it but gives to everyone. This is the god of money, or wealth. If you want to become wealthier, you need to pray before Kuvera three times. Like this [demonstrating] … and you put [money] in your pocket, one, two, three. I try already thirteen years, but it doesn't work. It's for tourists maybe … [One tourist doing as instructed] And don't forget 20 per cent commission [for the guide]!

Explaining the folkloristic beliefs surrounding the shrine of Durga (or Loro Jonggrang) at Prambanan:[26]
Y40. If women want to look prettier, you have to touch the face [of the statue] and then [touch] your own face, three times. After the visit, one becomes really pretty.

But it only works for women. For you and you and you [pointing to the men in the party], you can touch, but only here [touching the breasts of the statue], it brings good luck [laughing]. If you touch the face, afterwards you walk like this [imitates a stereotypical gay gait] … The face of Jonggrang is very black because every day girls and women come to touch it. The breasts of Jonggrang are also black because I often come up here. Twice a day! [Everybody laughing]

Sometimes guides create their own folk beliefs, which they are then able to instrumentalize. Having reached the upper terrace of the Borobudur monument, for instance, one guide explained to his clients how a Buddhist procession around the shrine works. He told them that while the complete procession implies walking and meditating for more than five kilometres, some of the spiritual effect could be achieved much more easily: 'You can do a procession like a real pilgrimage. Not ten times, not seven times, but three times is enough. Here on the top terrace you can do the procession, clockwise [around the main stupa], to become pure'. While the tourists were sheepishly following his instructions, the guide could relax, smoke a cigarette and chat with his colleagues.

Apart from framing the wildlife viewing experience, the most important narrative strands of guiding in northern Tanzania are stories about the Maasai and, increasingly, other local ethnic groups (most often groups to which the guides themselves do not belong).

Commenting on the Maasai and other ethnic groups of northern Tanzania:
A13. The Maasai are really scattered … It's very hard. They are scattered in east and central Africa. The Maasai in Kenya have relatives in Uganda, and relatives in Tanzania. So they <u>wander around</u>, they don't have permanent settlements, they are <u>nomadic</u>.
A14. The Datogas are <u>still</u> pastoralists, just like the Maasai. And the [Hadzabe] bushmen, they are <u>still</u> collecting and gathering … But the bushmen and Datoga tribe were not that strong to defend against the <u>strong Maasai</u> invaders. And these Maasai tribe warriors pushed these two weakened tribes down to the southern foothill of the Ngorongoro islands, which is now Lake Eyasi.

While visiting a woodcarving workshop in a village on the road to the national parks:
A15. The <u>Makonde</u> originally come from Mozambique but now from the southern part of Tanzania and here in our village we have a couple of hundred. As you can see, they are making sculptures, different styles, and they use different types of wood. They make sculptures according to the shape of wood and also according to what they are dreaming at night. So whatever they dream, early in the morning they start making it like in the dream. So they make sculptures to represent cultures, traditions, the Maasai, and also they represent the Makonde culture.

In A15, the guide tries to give the woodcarvings on sale more authenticity by claiming that the carvers that the tourists could see at work were actually members of the Makonde people.[27] But while the local carvers might have learned the Makonde style of carving, they belong to a variety of different ethnic groups. Meanwhile, the guiding narratives in A13 and A14 confirm the archetype of the noble Maasai warrior and common depictions of African ethnic groups as un-developed and time-frozen (chapter 2). According to Fabian (2002: 31–32), this 'denial of coevalness', that is, placing the Other in a time frame different from and inferior to that of the commentator (and audience), is a general feature of modern Western thought and has deep historical roots. This kind of representa-tion reappears in the discourses of modernity, modernization and development that divide the contemporary world into portions that are fully of our time, those that unfortunately remain at greater or lesser distances behind it and those who have moved on to a so-called postmodern condition. Local guides rely on such narrative allochronism to connect their tales with widely circulating imaginaries (Dann 2004; Aitchison 2001).

## Liminal Positionality

Any perceivable behaviour can make facts of positionality palpable in social inter-action (Agha 2006). The guide-guest encounter, like all service contacts, is typi-cally asymmetrical. In the encounter between tourists and local service personnel, for example, the former are assigned a high situational status, even if they might otherwise be of a lower status than those who serve them (Cohen and Cooper 1986: 537). By paying the guide for his or her work (and for access to certain areas), tourists expect quality service in return. However, there are many points in the interaction when shifts of role alignment occur and these same asymmetries are blurred or temporarily interrupted. Guides repeatedly rely on dualisms or bi-nary us-them oppositions to position themselves interactionally vis-à-vis tourists and local people, but two different logics are at work simultaneously: A logic of differentiation that creates differences and divisions, and a logic of equivalence that subverts existing differences and divisions. As global marketing prescribes, guides often have no choice but to play the local, even if they are not necessarily natives of the sites where they work (e.g., almost all the guides in and around Arusha are Tanzanians, but many come from other regions and belong to differ-ent ethnic groups). In some instances, guides find creative ways to distance them-selves from locals and align themselves on the side of the tourists. In other words, guided tours are strategic encounters in which guides attempt to 'sell' particular images, not only of the Other but of themselves too (cf. Goffman 1974).

Some examples will help to clarify this point. The dominant global discourse, which tends to treat all Africans alike and, thus, conceptualize the guides as full members of local Tanzanian communities, can be subverted. Many guides in Arusha distance themselves from local people encountered during a trip as a means of aligning themselves with the us-tourist side of the us-them binary. This can be achieved through the subtle use of deictic terms such as demonstrative and personal pronouns, or temporal and spatial expressions.[28] An important function of such metalanguage includes making judgments or expressing attitudes towards others, which serves the purpose of drawing social boundaries between the self and the other, reinforcing similarities and differences respectively.

> Briefing tourists on the way to a village nearby Arusha:
> A16. <u>We</u> will be able to meet <u>the local people</u> at the market place. You can say *habari*, so you can become popular suddenly, and they can respect you because you greet them in their language.

> Commenting on how the Maasai sing and dance:
> A17. I don't know how <u>they</u> do it!

> Explaining the traditional use of local flora:
> A18. This leaf, croton leaf, is edible. <u>Old people</u> use it like toilet paper, very smooth!

The city guide in A16 performatively resists stereotyping by not telling his clients he is very much a local, often frequenting the market they are about to visit to buy his groceries and second-hand clothes. The cultural guide in A17 is actually half Maasai (from his mother's side), but prefers not to be identified as such. Finally, the safari guide in A18 talks about old people to distance himself from the uncivilized practice he is narrating. This last example also includes humour (the most common device guides use to align themselves with tourists).

Interactional positioning is central to narrative self-construction. In a bid to enhance their cosmopolitan status, guides prefer to position themselves as different from the represented locals and more similar to their clients. Similar practices have been noticed elsewhere as well (Jaworski and Thurlow 2004: 316):

> Bumsters on the beach in The Gambia buy into the myth of global citizenship through the discourse of their desire of travel to the UK. In doing so, they stylize themselves in similar ways—through their use of English, which is of course part of their post-colonial legacy, but especially through their displays of cultural references to English football, weather, geography, and so on, yet knowing that, with few exceptions, the asymmetry of economic globalism does not allow them to shrug off their national identity as 'Gambians' and will not transform and transport them into the 'British'.

When tourists expect exactly the opposite, there can be tension, because they grant guides their authority based on (imagined) expressions of nativeness. As a way of avoiding too much friction, guides therefore position themselves in a transitional or liminal space that facilitates shifting between these frames (Feldman 2007).[29] One moment they are playing the native (forced to be looking culturally inwards) (Figure 10), and other moments they are distancing themselves from the locals (dreaming of the wide world out there). Such shifting of alignments or 'footing' (Goffman 1981: 325–26) is common in situations where the speaker roles of animator, author and principal do not coincide. Guides are only animators and sometimes authors, but certainly not principals of tourism discourse.

As guides engage tourists in (re)constructing peoples and places, they also engage in remaking themselves. Their cosmopolitan aspirations are visible outside their guiding jobs as well. Writing about guides in the highlands of Sulawesi, for instance, Adams (2006: 61) notes:

> Although the currency of their livelihood was their knowledge of Toraja traditions, many of these young men found more compelling inspiration in global cosmopolitanism. Dedicated followers of the latest global music and media sensations, and aspiring collectors of foreign tourist 'girlfriends', these young men turned to nonreligious external sources as they constructed their identities.

It looks as if tour guides have to play a Janus-faced role in more than one instance. From a service-oriented point of view, they have to look simultaneously towards their foreign clients and towards their own (or the represented) ancestral culture and tradition. For reasons of self-interest, guides are also liminally positioned in a temporal sense, both representing the past (for tourists) and dreaming of the future (for themselves). This liminal state is characterized by ambiguity, openness and indeterminacy, and sometimes their sense of identity dissolves to some extent, bringing about disorientation. Ironically, it is this characteristic that makes guides look modern and cosmopolitan, especially local guides in developing countries.

The guided tour is the setting where much of the guide's cosmopolitan capital is accrued and tacitly used to better serve foreign clients. The explicit display of their cosmopolitan aspirations and lifestyle—what some have called 'banal cosmopolitanism' (Beck 2002), 'vernacular cosmopolitanism' (Nava 2002) or 'consumer cosmopolitanism' (Hannerz 2004)—happens mainly elsewhere. They can brag to their relatives, friends and colleagues about how up-to-date they are with trends in global popular culture and modern technology. Bringing too much of this into the encounter with Western tourists, however, would disrupt the magic of the tour (Salazar 2005).[30] Yet central Java and northern Tanzania show many signs of advancing glocalization and rapid modernization, with local guides serving as the frontrunners of these developments. Paradoxically, the guides' dreams of moving forward and upward, of becoming more cosmopolitan and also more Western, can only materialize if they represent and sell the lifeworld in which they live as developing little or not at all. And although most guides want to broaden their knowledge of the world in general, they show a particular curiosity for learning more about Western cultures, making their cosmopolitanism somewhat lopsided.

It is clear from the above examples that various schemas of identity and identification are at work while guiding. When talking about the destination as a generalized place, the guides position themselves as locals (respecting the global canon). However, when referring to their own person(a), they prefer to align themselves on the side of the tourists. I argue that this positional shift is mainly caused by the fact that during the guide-tourist interaction, guides have to negotiate between tourism imaginaries and their own imaginations and aspirations of cosmopolitan mobility. Having close contact with (white) tourists is considered to enhance status in both Indonesia and Tanzania, and many guides see foreigners as their gateway into a better (Western) world. The privileged interaction with tourists nourishes their cosmopolitan dreams of escape from the harsh local life. However, as most guides realize, the most realistic chance of improving their quality of life is by becoming successful in their profession. In order to do so, they need to find the right balance in their narratives and practices between their own imaginations and the imaginaries of tourism. I show in chapter 6 that they cannot always do this successfully.

## A Cosmopolitan Edge

This chapter has shown that many successful guides in developing countries are prototypes of imaginative cosmopolitan mobility. Of course, not all of them necessarily have cosmopolitan aspirations, and not all guide settings and professional roles are equally conducive to enacting cosmopolitan values. But the tour is the liminal setting par excellence in which guides can build up their cosmopolitan capital. And, paradoxically perhaps, contemporary international tourism is structured in such a way that tourists seem to lose out in the quest for cosmopolitan status, which brings us back to Hannerz (1990), who also does not consider tourists to be cosmopolitans for their (perceived) lack of interest or competence in participating or translating difference. While this analysis probably fits the majority of tourists, there is a relatively small group intentionally seeking out cosmopolitan-enhancing experiences (Molz 2005; Swain 2009). The many tourists I came across in central Java or northern Tanzania were willing to engage with the Other, factors like their local intermediaries (including guides) and language barriers made the necessary access and dialogue extremely difficult. Guides present tourists (their best teachers in cosmopolitanism) with imagined and staged versions of local culture—mirrors of widely circulating tourism imaginaries.

In his earlier writings, Hannerz (1990) positions (white, middle-class and male) cosmopolitans and (indigenous, native) locals as opposed in the imaginary field demarcated by the global and the local. While the former appears mobile, contemporary and (post)modern, the latter seems rooted, timeless and traditional. This tacit acceptance of the conventional and stereotype-laden distinction between locals and cosmopolitans has been heavily criticized for being normative and elitist (Werbner 2008). Instead, scholars have proposed pluralized and particularized accounts of nonelite 'discrepant cosmopolitanisms' (Clifford 1997) or 'actually existing cosmopolitanisms' (Malcomson 1998) that are geographically grounded, historically and socioeconomically situated, and embedded in material everyday practices (Breckenridge et al. 2002). Appadurai, acknowledging 'the transformation of *natives* into cosmopolites of their own sort' (1996: 57), observes that 'today's cosmopolitanisms combine experience of various media with various forms of experience—cinema, video, restaurants, spectator sports, and tourism, to name just a few—that have different national and transnational genealogies' (1996: 64). Cosmopolitanism is sought after not only by those who travel or those who feel at home in several parts of the world but also by those who stay at home. Indeed, also the study of local tour guides in Indonesia and Tanzania confirms that one becomes cosmopolitan not only through travel and direct contact but through exposure to the rapid circulation of global signs and images (e.g., television). In other words, physical mobility alone is neither a sufficient nor a necessary condition for cosmopolitanism.[31]

It is no coincidence Clifford includes guides in his list of people 'whose cosmopolitan mobility has been overlooked by narrowly defined elitist forms of cosmopolitanism' (1997: 36). Of course, the cosmopolitan mobility of guides in developing countries has to be taken in a figurative sense, as most lack the means to travel abroad. Nevertheless, their profile includes transcultural identifications and aspirations, and an interest in cultural difference. Through personal contacts with tourists, other foreigners and the mass media, they can build up their knowledge of foreign experiences, ways of life, and social conditions. The cultural capital accumulated from their knowledge of foreigners and distant countries is a constitutive part of their identity (cf. Favero 2003). And as an added bonus, this cosmopolitan capital gives them a broader perspective on their own culture. As Urban writes, 'to understand your own culture, immerse yourself, for a time, at least, in another' (2001: 189). This explains the advantage of the transnationally networked guides (chapter 3).

To understand cultural difference is to understand liminal space, the spaces in between the designations of identity, 'the connective tissues that constructs the difference' (Bhabha 1994: 4) between people of different ethnicities and cultures. People able to do this

> are the people who belong to more than one world, speak more than one language (literally and metaphorically), inhabit more than one identity, have more than one home; who have learned to negotiate and translate *between* cultures, and who, because they are irrevocably the product of several interlocking histories and cultures, have learned to live with, and indeed to speak from, *difference*. They speak from the 'in-between' of different cultures, always unsettling the assumptions of one culture from the perspective of another, and thus finding ways of being both *the same as* and at the same time *different* from the others among whom they live. (Hall 1995: 206)

The description above fits most of the successful guides I met remarkably well: this is exactly the role or social persona they enact. Their understanding of the cultural experiences of strangers is more than what they have been told or read about the stereotypical, inauthentic experiences of cultural outsiders (and, after all, working in tourism requires knowing exactly what the inauthentic is all about). The ability to make cosmopolitan connections gives guides a comparative advantage over those who are less familiar with foreign frames of reference. They do not need to travel abroad to experience Otherness (although most would love to if they had the financial means): others are coming to them, giving them plenty of opportunity to actively consume cultural differences in a reflective, intellectualizing manner. In other words, guides do not need physical mobility to become cosmopolitan. Their cosmopolitanism arises out of 'their having to produce a cosmopolitan atmosphere for those who travel to them' (Notar 2008: 639). As I discussed in this chapter, their cosmopolitanism, reflecting exposure to a variety of cultures, becomes evident in the ways they are imaginatively and discursively mobile.

If guiding for foreigners can be seen as a cosmopolitan practice, it comes, once more, close to anthropology (Kuper 1994). Kahn describes how all ethnographic knowledge is 'inevitably cosmopolitan knowledge; that is a construction that emerges out of the encounter between representatives of different cultures' (2003: 411).[32] Such cosmopolitan competence is marked by 'a personal ability to make one's way into other cultures, through listening, looking, intuiting and reflecting' as well as by 'a skill in manoeuvring more or less expertly with a particular system of meanings and meaningful forms' (Hannerz 1990: 239). Ethnographers undoubtedly recognize in this description elements defining the ideal fieldworker (cf. Rabinow 1986: 258), but, as this chapter has shown, such a description also applies well to professional guides (and, perhaps, to the ideal tour guide). Whereas anthropologists need local informants to construct anthropological knowledge, tour guides cannot do without tourists to jointly (re)create tourism imaginaries and build up cosmopolitan knowledge.

The performative space, where tourists and service providers creatively play with culture and invent it, can be thought of as a 'contact zone' (Pratt 1992), 'Third Space' (Bhabha 1994) or 'borderzone' (Bruner 2005: 191–210). Anthropologists have long acknowledged that such transitional, liminal contexts are sites of creative cultural production (e.g., Rosaldo 1993). Although what takes place in tourism encounters is about the local, such performances take account of global and transnational elements: 'Host-tourist interactions and identities embody the essence of globalizing processes in that it is precisely at this level which the global and the local interface, are negotiated and resolved—be it through processes of cultural absorption, appropriation, recognition, acceptance or rejection' (Jaworski and Thurlow 2004: 318). It is through the combination of equivalent microlevel, interactional analyses like the ones described here and in chapter 6 (scaling out) and macrolevel, structural analyses discussed in chapters 2, 3 and 5 (scaling up) that we can come to a more critical understanding of the experiences, changes and identities commonly invoked in the globalization literature.

This chapter has focused on how guided tours are a nice indexical affirmation of the recontextualization of tourism discourse and imaginaries. On the metadiscursive level, guiding narratives help guides position themselves as cosmopolitans. And on the discursive level, they play their role in the global circulation of tourism fantasies, representing destinations as 'different'. In chapter 6, I discuss the multiple flaws in the transmission, the various frictions between the agents involved, and the upsetting moments when tourism imaginaries are not only mirrored but also contested and (re)entextualized. However, before doing so, it is necessary to step back, in order to scrutinize in what ways tour guiding is structured in Indonesia and Tanzania and to disentangle the complex web of mechanisms that try to restrict guides in what they do or say. Building on the documented history and existing theory of tour guiding, I analyze in the next chapter the complicated politics of guiding in Indonesia and Tanzania and I describe how guides are locally, nationally, regionally and globally regulated and controlled.

# 5
# GUIDING ROLES AND RULES

The best tour guide is someone who lives in the place, knows everything about it, is proud of his or her city, but does not work for any agency. Go out into the street, choose the person you want to talk to, and ask them something (Where is the cathedral? Where is the post office?). If nothing comes of it, try someone else—I guarantee that at the end of the day you will have found yourself an excellent companion.
–Paulo Coelho (writer, 1947– )

Paulo Coelho—who, apart from being a prolific writer, is also a seasoned traveller—acknowledges that tour guides can make or break a trip. His experience tells him not to trust guides employed by tour operators; their interpretative practices are perceived as less authentic because they are mediated and controlled by company and government authorities with vested stakes in what guides say and how they say it. How has the role of professional tour guide evolved over time? What guiding roles have been identified in the literature? What is 'local' about local tour guiding? These are some of the questions I seek to address in this chapter. With the history and theory in place, I zoom in on the reality on the ground and analyze the intricate politics of guiding in Indonesia and Tanzania. In the final discussion, I draw some general lines on the work of guiding and its changing scales of organization and control.

## A Pocket Guide

Guiding is not fun only. Of course, people who you guide …. they are here for fun. But you are there for work. You never do one thing for fun for one year … you do something else. So guiding is work, guiding is a job like any other job.
–Zuberi (senior driver-guide, Arusha)

The history of tour guiding illustrates that tourism is older than some scholars acknowledge. In his study of travel in the ancient world, Casson (1974: 264) mentions that the Greeks had two words for guide, *periegetai* (a person who leads around) and *exegetai* (a person who explains).[1] In addition, there was the *prox-*

*emos,* a tour leader accompanying Greek citizens travelling abroad. Guides were needed 'to ensure safe-conduct as much as to show the way' (1974: 319). In their interpretative acts, they were notorious for the embroidering of fact, 'knowing that the average hearer had no way of checking up' (1974: 266). Their frivolous interpretations often came from a 'passion to connect whatever they could with the heroic days of mythological times, a passion no doubt nourished by the eagerness with which the customers lapped up such nonsense' (1974: 266–67). Apparently, tour guides have always gathered mixed reviews. They have been variously described throughout history as 'nuisances, opportunists, charlatans, and zealots' (Pond 1993: 1). The chief complaint seems to be the aggressive manner in which they attempt to gain business. Even if, according to some commentators 'local guides have not improved very much in the course of two thousand years' (Casson 1974: 264), the structural conditions in which they have to operate have changed much over the centuries.

Herodotus of Halicarnassus, the father of history, greatly relied on local guides during his wide-ranging travels around the lands of the Mediterranean and the Black Sea. The stories he recounts are not always accurate, partially because Herodotus depended on guides who had a propensity for reciting, with great authority, dates, dialogues and other specifics about people who had lived hundreds of years earlier. As Plutarch (*The Oracles at Delphi*), Pausanias (*Guide to Greece*) and Lucian (*Amores*) attest, people visiting sanctuaries for festivals or other reasons could always count on the help, or hindrance, of local guides who expounded the significance of buildings, monuments and sacred artefacts. During the Middle Ages, pilgrimages were the most prevalent type of travel for adherents to religions as varied as Hinduism, Buddhism, Christianity and Islam. Pilgrims were accompanied by guides whose roles were not only those of pathfinders but also of 'protectors, safety escorts, and even bribers to assure safe passage' (Pond 1993: 4). In the Holy Land, as in other places of the Orient, 'entrepreneurs known as "dragomen" provided interested travellers with "subsistence services": means of transport, security, and portable field accommodation' (Katz 1985: 53). Because these men had some knowledge of one or more languages (hence the name *dragoman,* which means 'interpreter' in countries where Arabic, Turkish or Persian is spoken), they were able to serve their clients with information and interpretation concerning routes and encountered sights.[2]

From the fourteenth through the eighteenth century, the profession reached new heights in Europe as guides became 'travelling tutors', also called 'bear leaders', 'antiquarii', or 'cicerones' (Pond 1993: 5). Named for the learned Roman orator, Marcus Tullius Cicero, these cicerones were supposed to be erudite, serious and respectable people. They mainly accompanied young gentlemen through Europe on their Grand Tour, a prescribed trip to finish the boys' education, giving them the required social capital for a future as political leaders and ambassadors. The escorting tutors were among 'the most esteemed guides in European society, entrusted with representing their region and its history' (Pond 1993: 2). Thomas Cook, who benefited from new transportation technologies and the socioeconomic changes caused by the industrial revolution to open up the Grand Tour to the British middle classes, achieved his initial success through his services as a package tour guide. In 1856, this father of mass tourism guided the first of many of his tours of mainland Europe.

One of the earliest recorded cases of tour-guide training, evaluation and regulation is found in the United States. After the US Civil War (1861–65), the Battlefield of Gettysburg in Pennsylvania became a national military park in 1885, and visitors employed guides to locate the graves of relatives or acquaintances. In 1915, in order to ensure the capability of the guides and to stop numerous visitor complaints, the War Department put into place regulations stating that only licensed guides would be allowed to conduct visitors through the battleground for a fee. The department established rules covering fees, solicitation, conduct, length of tours and even personal cleanliness (Pond 1993: 8). In addition, guides were required to take an examination proving that they were adequately informed about the battle. Those who passed the test attended classes and were given the opportunity to take a new examination to earn a higher classification. Despite this early example, guiding remains little regulated in the United States.[3]

Whereas guides might have been untrained and unrestrained for centuries, nowadays training, licensing and accreditation are increasingly common worldwide. Even if there remain great local variations in qualifications, there is a global tendency to standardize. In 2003, the World Federation of Tourist Guide Associations (WFTGA) adopted the European Committee for Standardization definition of a tourist guide as 'a person who guides visitors in the language of their choice and interprets the cultural and natural heritage of an area, which person normally possesses an area-specific qualification usually issued and/or recognized by the appropriate authority'.[4] Whereas the WFTGA speaks of *tourist guides,* I prefer the term *tour guide* because it shifts the focus from the service relation—a tourism worker serving clients—to the dynamics of the encounter between guide, tourists and locals while touring.

Guides are often the only local people with whom tourists interact for a considerable amount of time during their trip. During this 'extended service encounter' (Arnould and Price 1993) or 'interactive service work' (Weaver 2005), they can offer their clients more than a superficial introduction to a new environment, country or culture, connecting their clients with those elements (Christie and Mason 2003). Whether visitors feel welcome and satisfied, want to stay longer or decide to come back, depends largely on their guides. The qualifier 'local' does not necessarily imply that guides are natives of the place where they operate (although they are habitually perceived as such by foreign tourists). In the case of Arusha and Jogja, for instance, many were born and raised in the area but some have roots in other parts of the respective countries. Oftentimes, they came to

Arusha or Jogja to study or look for a job and settled. Because they contribute considerably to the perception of a destination, local guides are entrusted with the public relations mission to 'encapsulate the essence of place' (Pond 1993: vii) and to be a window onto the site, city, region or even country or continent. Some take pride in representing and explaining the local natural and cultural heritage, and, as role models for appropriate behaviour, they try to ensure heritage sustainability by making visitors aware of its importance and vulnerability (Jennings and Weiler 2006). Others are more business oriented, merely interested in selling images, knowledge, contacts, souvenirs, access, authenticity, ideology and sometimes even themselves (Bras 2000).

## Spot the Differences

> My guide is a man called Ahmed (everyone here seems to be called either Mohammed or Ahmed). Ahmed does not like to be thought of as a mere guide. He has participated in a number of archaeological expeditions investigating coastal ruins—though in precisely what capacity I am not sure—and so regards himself as something of an expert in antiquarian matters, befriending only those visitors to the island whom he considers to be of 'serious' intent.
> –Shiva Naipaul (1979: 183)

As my fieldwork in Indonesia and Tanzania progressed, I became more and more intrigued by the striking similarities and linkages between tour guiding and anthropology, between the guides' interpretative practices and my interpretive anthropology. Whereas anthropologists are traditionally outsiders trying to access and disclose the 'cultural intimacy' (Herzfeld 2005) of a particular society or group of people, tour guides do the opposite: using their societal position as (relative) insiders and gatekeepers of what is culturally intimate to establish contacts with interested cultural outsiders. Both are often represented as culture brokers, translating and interpreting from one language and culture to the other.[5] What is more, the two occupations seem to need one another to grow professionally (especially in developing countries). It is not rare for those doing ethnographic fieldwork to contract local guides as interpreters or research assistants. One of my assistants in Jogja was a bachelor's student in anthropology who wanted to become a cultural guide, and my main assistant in Arusha was finishing his vocational studies in professional tour guiding. Guides, on the other hand, particularly those working in cultural tourism, rely on anthropological knowledge to give their narratives more depth. In fact, quite a number of guides I encountered in Indonesia and Tanzania have studied anthropology in some way or the other (chapter 3).

Guiding, especially in museums, is often recommended as a great job for anthropology majors. Jafari, a cultural anthropologist with expertise in tourism recounts, 'My tourism vista opened not through an academic door, but through my first job as a tour guide' (2007: 111). He even recalls his good fortune of guiding Margaret Mead in Iran, although at that time he had absolutely no idea who she was. In fact, many anthropologists working in academia or as museum curators have experience in guiding, above all on study or alumni tours to the locales of their expertise. Bruner, for example, guided numerous times. One of these occasions, a trip to Indonesia, turned out to be a defining moment in his theorizing about tourism (2005: 1–7, 191–210). Being a guide also had methodological benefits for him: 'Whatever else may be said of my tour guide role, it had the one overwhelming advantage of allowing me to be the closest I could come to studying tourism from an ethnographic perspective, by actually being there on tour within the tour group' (2005: 1). However, the combination of guiding and doing research was not an easy one. Bruner found 'aspects of the tour guide role uncomfortable and ambiguous' (2005: 204) and, in the end, he was even fired.

Bruner is not the only person to have experienced friction between the roles of ethnographer and guide. Little (2004) worked as a guide in Guatemala during a small field project. He remembers how his subject position was viewed negatively by his Mayan friends: 'They considered my role as guide to be linked to Ladino society. The only exchanges we—the tour group and I—had with Mayas were purely economic' (2004: 20).[6] Anthropologists with little background in tourism are often shocked by the ideas circulating among tourists or tourism workers. Guldin (1989), for instance, accompanied tourists from the United States to China and was struck by the preconceived notions and reactions they had about the country. On an alumni tour to Kenya, Kaspin (1997) even became involved in a dispute with the accompanying local tour guide over issues of cultural representation. Tour guiding has also been used as a fieldwork method. Traweek (1988), for example, studied a community of high-energy physicists. She started her research conducting public tours of a particle accelerator facility. Through this job, she gained access to the world of physics. Traweek wrote the resulting ethnography in the style of a guided tour and devoted an entire chapter—'Touring the Site: Powerful Places in the Laboratory'—to describing the buildings of a high-energy physics lab.

## The Scholar's Stance

Despite the importance of guides in the representation of peoples and places, academics were late in studying tour guiding.[7] Approached from a service-oriented perspective, a dazzling range of tour guide roles has been identified in the literature (Salazar 2008b).[8] A successful guide is a 'facilitator' who knows how and when to fulfil and synthesize different roles, often simultaneously (Pond 1993). Cohen's (1985) sociological model is often cited as the basis for examining tour guide roles. According to him, guides serve four major functions, namely, instrumental, social, interactionary and communicative. Cohen traces the origins of modern guiding roles back to the two types the ancient Greeks distinguished (see above), the pathfinder (leading around) and the mentor (explaining). The two principal concepts that characterize contemporary guiding, leading and mediating combine and expand elements from the earlier roles of pathfinder and mentor. According to Cohen, guiding is evolving and shifting from the logistical aspect to the facilitation of experience, from the pathfinder to the mentor role, away from leadership towards mediating and away from the outer towards the inner-directed sphere, with the communicative component becoming the centre of the professional role. In general, my findings on tour guiding in Jogja and Arusha seem to point in the same direction. However, in the previous chapter, I illustrated how the pathfinder role in wildlife tourism—leading tourists to the best game viewing spots—remains as important as the accompanying interpretative narratives.

The significance of the mediatory role of tour guides is evidenced by the fact that, of all the professional roles, it is probably the most heavily researched one.[9] Yu, Weiler, and Ham (2004: 4–5) categorize the mediating activities of guides in three aspects: (1) mediating access, determining which part of the local environment, heritage, and culture is exposed and which is hidden; (2) mediating encounters between tour group members and between tourists, locals and service providers; and (3) mediating information, by conveying the significance of the visited place, and helping visitors make intellectual and emotional connections with it. By providing a structure within which tourists view, interact with and experience a place and its people, guides organize and limit the tourist gaze and thereby the tourist experience. I illustrate these roles in detail in chapters 4 and 6. Here I want to point out that these various intermediary functions imply that guides have different accountabilities to multiple stakeholders.

In countries where their profession is neither well established nor formalized, guides can go about their activities as they please. In others, the position of interpretative mediator makes them susceptible to outside interference and manipulation. After all, decisions regarding the 'true' story or the 'most appropriate' behaviour are subject to relations of power and dependence. This becomes even more salient if one sees guides as unofficial ambassadors or representatives of a site, city, region or country.[10] It comes as no surprise, then, that an increasing number of regulatory mechanisms are put in place by tour companies and authorities: codes of conduct (a form of soft law), professional associations, awards of excellence, formal training, professional certification (or accreditation) and licensing. Each of these devices has the potential to reinforce certain key guiding roles. While these mechanisms are promoted as tools of 'quality assurance' (Black and Weiler 2005), they also serve the Big Brother purpose of surveillance and control. I will illustrate this below with examples from Indonesia and Tanzania.

It is impossible to encompass all guiding roles within a comprehensive frame-work. Moreover, trying to fit the ephemeral professional activities of guides into a narrow essentializing structure cannot do justice to what actually happens during the dynamic guide-guest encounter, a point that has been repeatedly illustrated by ethnographic research.[11] Such studies reveal that guiding is not just about organizing a tour, socializing with tourists and interpreting what they see and experience in a language they understand. Guides are not necessarily altruistic mediators by vocation, nor can they be expected to submit blindly to government or tour operator rules and regulations exacting them to tell prefabricated stories (Bras 2000). Some scholars have described additional roles that acknowledge the guide's agency and are more self-oriented: salesperson (Gronroos 1978), receiver of tips (Holloway 1981), entrepreneur, friend and even gigolo (Bras and Dahles 1999). Not surprisingly, there are multiple strains and conflicts in trying to com-bine and reconcile the service-oriented with the more self-oriented guiding roles (chapter 6).

I question the role of guides as ambassadors of the 'local', and rather see them as mediators of the glocal (and national), a role that implies some distance, in-tervention and displacement (Mazzarella 2004: 348). Globalization requires the work of particularly positioned 'glocalizers'. In line with the discussion on tour-ism imaginaries in chapter 2, I would like to add yet another role, albeit of a different kind: the tour guide as mechanic of glocalization. I take *mechanic* here in the sense of a skilled technician, working to keep things operating properly. I showed in the previous chapters how local guides are not primary producers of tourism discourse, but in the service encounter with tourists they maintain the tourism system of provisioning as it is, assuring the continuity and perpetuation of the global chain of imaginaries and giving it a local flavour. As such, guides are both producers and consumers of widely travelling tourism fantasies. Their glocalization role can be machine-like because, at times, the circulation of tour-ism imaginaries appears automatic or even involuntary.

In old English slang, the term *mechanic* refers to a person who cheats (at gambling games). As I will show in the next chapter, guides are also mechanics in this sense of the word: independent social actors and cultural producers in their own right, capable of manipulating the narratives they are supposed to deliver to suit their own agendas. Therefore, local guides are more than mere transmit-ters of tourism imaginaries. As Urban (2001: 33) argues in the case of culture in general,

> It is possible for individuals to be regarded as mere transmitters of culture, as the conduits through which culture flows … Yet the view from tradition—as a kind of objective characterization of culture …—focuses only on the inertial side of culture, and, even so, fails to comprehend the decelerative forces acting on that inertial culture. It is a view that comprehends onceness, but fails miserably at futurity. Any cultural

element, to survive, requires that some measure of accelerative force be added to it. Otherwise, it deforms and disintegrates or evolves into something else. Yet culture has a telos: It wants to be carried on.

Tourism imaginaries have a remarkably similar intentionality and tour guides play an important role in realizing this. It is their creative freedom as imaginers, dreaming an unknown but attractive world out there, which motivates local guides to be good imaginarians, ensuring the continuous circulation of tourism imaginaries (chapter 4). Those in charge of tourism development and regulation do not always understand the complex dynamics of these processes. In what follows, I focus on different regimes of control. Some of these tour guide management systems act, in Urban's terms, as decelerative forces in the circulation of tourism fantasies because they try to prevent acceleration. I start with Tanzania, because the guiding profession there has only recently been recognized and regulated, and then move on to discuss the situation in Indonesia.

## Arusha-Style

> A guide is like a soldier and should be ready for everything.
> —Baraka (driver-guide)

In her book *Rehema's Journey: A Visit in Tanzania,* children's writer Barbara Margolies familiarizes her young readers with Tanzania. Nine-year-old Rehema, the heroine of the full-colour photo-essay, leaves her home high up in the Pare Mountains of eastern Tanzania for the first time ever when her father takes her to Arusha and the world-famous Ngorongoro Crater. The little girl is fascinated by Arusha's street life, by the exotic animals inside the crater and by her encounters with other ethnic groups. Such a travel tale would seem unlikely in a country as poor as Tanzania, were it not for one significant detail: Rehema's father is a safari guide. Not only is he the perfect person to introduce his daughter to the wide variety of animal species, but he can also tell her about the problems of poaching, as well as the dangers that have driven some animals into extinction. He is a resourceful person, ready for everything: urban life, dangerous wildlife and sociocultural Others.

### A New Calling in the Wild

When ethnic groups such as the Maasai refused to guide Western hunters and explorers into the Serengeti and other areas, white adventurers became northern Tanzania's first guides. Captain Frederick Selous was one of these bold pioneers.

In 1887, he was contracted as the first game guide for wealthy US and British hunters in South Africa and, in 1909, he served as a guide for Theodore Roosevelt and his entourage in one of the most (in)famous hunting safaris in the history of East Africa. A couple of years earlier, John Hunter, another of these legendary figures, had guided the first paid safari to the Serengeti. He also led the expedition that opened up the Ngorongoro Crater to visitors. After over a century, white bush guides are still there. Usually descendants of Europeans or North Americans who settled in some part of East or Southern Africa, they work for exclusive high-end safari or hunting companies. David, a veteran in the field, told me that 'it's hard to start this job without an African background, except for specialists like birding guys'. As in colonial times, these guides have an aura around them of adventure and bravery. One of them has even become an Animal Planet TV personality.

When hunting became more restricted and expensive in Tanzania, photographic safaris offered an attractive alternative. However, there were very few guides available for this type of tourism, only drivers or local game scouts. The Ngorongoro Crater, for instance, had park rangers whose task it was to show drivers where to go. As Joseph, a senior safari guide, confirms, 'At that time, Tanzanians were not interested in wildlife. They thought the parks were for the British, like *shamba la bibi*, farms belonging to the Queen of England ... People had no awareness of tourism'.[12] Over the years, visitors have grown in number and become more inquisitive, giving rise to the new profession of guide (Figure 11). Zuberi, a beginning driver-guide, reflects on how quickly the situation has changed: 'Five to ten years back, this business was just experience, people [guides] just studying the roads, and not going to school. Nowadays, tour operators have come to realize that there is a big competition out there'. Whereas in the past safari drivers were typically uneducated and had problems communicating with tourists, today all have gone to guiding school first and have studied English or another language (chapter 3).

Guides in northern Tanzania come in many shapes and colours, all referred to locally as *waongoza watalii* (tour guides). The most common are driver-guides—also called safari, game or bush guides—who show clients around in protected areas. Mountain guides mainly operate on Mt. Kilimanjaro and Mt. Meru. Walking safari guides are in charge of hikes in wildlife zones. Given the physically demanding nature of the job, virtually all these positions are filled by men. In addition, there are different kinds of on-site guides: (1) park guides, who join unaccompanied groups entering protected areas; (2) lodge guides, who do basically the same work as driver-guides but are based in a lodge or permanent tented camp; (3) cultural tourism guides, who are affiliated with the Cultural Tourism Programme and show people around in villages and rural areas; and (4) museum guides, who operate in the Arusha Declaration Museum, in the Arusha Natural History Museum and the adjacent Old Boma Museum and in Meserani Snake

FIGURE 11 • *The Natural Environment of Driver-guides*

Park and its Maasai museum. In addition, there are so-called flycatchers, who ignorant tourists sometimes mistake for professional guides (e.g., McCrummen 2007).[13] Some of these young men receive small commissions for each client they deliver to a safari company or another tourism service, and others make money as would-be guides, organizing budget trips for backpackers. For the purposes of this study, I focused on the two types of guides the majority of tourists visiting the area encounter and whose main activity is the interpretation of natural and cultural heritage, that is, driver-guides and the rapidly expanding group of cultural tourism guides.

Because interpretation is an important aspect of the job, many local guides stress their representational role. Issa, a cultural guide, formulates it nicely: 'So guides are standing there as ambassadors, you know, for Tanzania, and to represent people and everything, community and everybody, to outsiders, the visitors who are coming'. Senior safari guide Salim confirms this: 'Guides are actually doing a lot for the government, a lot for the society, because they are the ones speaking about our country. They are ambassadors, Tanzanian ambassadors to whomever they are carrying [in their car]. If it is a Northern American, a British, whoever. They speak to them about our country, culture and people'. Daudi, who has been guiding for many years, points out that 'a guide is actually the centre of the industry ... but people do not know'. Some tour operators do acknowledge the key role of guides in the safari business by including them in their company name: East African Guides, Kibo Guides, Professional Safari Guides and Tanzania Guides.

## Standardizing the Profession

The profession of drivers evolved to that of driver-guides only in the 1990s, and other types of guiding are even newer. That regulation has lagged behind should not come as a surprise. For example, the National Tourism Policy of 1991, reviewed in 1999, does not mention anything regarding guides. The most recent Tourism Master Plan (2002), on the other hand, specifically notes the poor quality of Tanzanian tour guides, their lack of knowledge, inability to communicate and their poor attitudes, in comparison with standards in competitor EAC and SADC destinations such as Kenya, Botswana and Zimbabwe. This latest master plan was prepared with assistance from the EU Institutional Strengthening of the Tanzania Tourism Sector Project (2002–04). According to this planning document, the formalization and upgrading of guides needs to be addressed as a priority because the quality of tour guiding is fundamental to the holiday experience. It proposes to improve existing standards by establishing training programmes (chapter 3) and strengthening institutions by setting up an association of licensed tour guides (see below). The plan further recommends that guides should receive their license only after the successful completion of a formal programme in tour guiding, ideally with external accreditation and validation.

Extending the 1969 Tourist Agents Act (Licensing Regulations) and various Tourist Agents Regulations, the Ministry of Natural Resources and Tourism published guidelines in 2004 on how guides should obtain their Class B tourist agent license, worth US$200. According to these directives, all guides must be Tanzanian nationals, holders of a license recognized by the Tourist Agents Licensing

Authority and have adequate experience (though no details are given to gloss the word 'adequate'). Noncitizen applicants with over ten years' experience may forward their license applications through the tour company for which they work, an exception that looks like an effort to legalize and control those who have been working illegally. At the time of writing, however, the authorities do not forcefully endorse these guidelines.

In 2007, the ministry held consultation meetings in various parts of the country on a bill for a new Tourism Act that would delineate an institutional framework for the administration, regulation, registration and licensing of tourism facilities. The proposed act has an entire section (Part VI) on the registration of tour guides. Those wishing to register for the future Tanzania Tourism Licensing Board will need to be citizens over twenty-one years of age, with Ordinary Level education (middle secondary school until Form 4), holding a valid First Aid Certificate, and with adequate knowledge of the area in the field applied for (again, this is not specified). Registered tour guides will receive an identity badge, and Article 43 states that every guide will be required to: (1) undergo medical examination annually; (2) comply with rules and regulations made by the relevant authority; (3) in the course of work, use approved routes or trails and (4) be polite, hospitable, helpful and friendly to tourists. In case of complaints, guides will be reprimanded, suspended or deregistered. It is noteworthy that Part I of this new Tourism Act urges all stakeholders to promote the UNWTO Global Code of Ethics for Tourism, and emphasizes ecotourism, cultural tourism and any other forms of tourism that provide better sectoral linkages, create employment and foster sustainable development.[14] Using the fashionable keywords of global tourism discourse, the ministry gives a clear signal, particularly to donors, that it is in full agreement with current ways of thinking about tourism planning and development.

Protected area managers are developing their own ways of controlling tour guiding. The parastatal entity Tanzania National Parks (TANAPA), for example, is seriously thinking of introducing its own guide licensing system. Such a scheme is already in place for Kilimanjaro, where only certified guides, registered by the Kilimanjaro National Park Board, can lead climbing expeditions. People can qualify to become registered guides after having worked first as a porter (for around three years) and then as assistant guide (for about two years). TANAPA also provides its own park guides and walking safari guides for visitors entering national parks without professional guides. According to General Notice 12/72 of the Ngorongoro Conservation Area Ordinance, an official guide, who needs to have authorization from the conservator, must accompany all tourists visiting the Ngorongoro Crater. All professional guides and safari attendants are required to be licensed by the conservator. It is not clear, however, how the Ngorongoro Conservation Area Authority (NCAA) is enforcing this ordinance, if at all.

Because the profession of guide is still rather new in Tanzania, there are no fixed payment scales and incomes can vary greatly between and within companies, depending on tipping guidelines, allowances and salaries. As people generally lack the habit of talking openly about their wages, they are short of knowledge about how much their colleagues are earning, which makes it difficult to get a general sense of how much money guides are making. I heard figures as varied as US$20 (low season) to US$2,000 (high season) per month. This stands in sharp contrast with the white bush guides who work for exclusive, high-end safari companies—so-called first-class tourism—and who earn up to US$300 per day. Many Tanzanian guides do not have a monthly salary but rely on shopping commissions and tips for their income. On average, mountain guides earn more than other type of guide (between US$1,000–2,000 per month during the high season), but most Tanzanian guides are comparatively well off in a country where the estimated per capita income per year for 2008 was less than US$450. Nevertheless, the majority cannot survive from guiding alone and require other income-generating activities, especially during the low season. These include, but are not limited to, farming, small-scale business (often part of the informal economy) and teaching.

During his 2005 campaign for the presidency, Jakaya Kikwete promised his electorate that he would create 1 million new jobs. While I was in the country in 2007, President Kikwete had little to show in terms of achievements and his government seemed desperate to create jobs at all costs, even at the expense of antagonizing foreign investors or going against EAC open border politics. Top officials have vowed to weed out foreigners (a vast majority of whom are Kenyans) working in the country without legal permits, and the witch hunt of immigration officers cracking down on safari companies employing foreign workers is also affecting tour guides, some of whom are originally from other East or Southern African countries. The official argument (supported by Tanzanian guides and their associations) is that the country does not need this foreign workforce any longer, because Tanzanians are knowledgeable enough and can do the jobs. Because the authorities are making it more and more difficult for non-Tanzanians to work legally as guides, one way for immigrants to get around this problem is to register themselves with the Tanzania Association of Tour Operators (TATO) as tour leaders or to start up their own safari company.

Among other groups escaping the mazes of bureaucratic control are freelance tour guides who do not bring their clients to protected areas (where they have to show documents) but to adjacent wildlife zones. Flycatchers try to outsmart officials by passing on the few licenses they have to those colleagues who need them to go on safari. At the time of writing, guides working in Cultural Tourism Programmes (CTP) were not subject to any regulations, apart from agreements at the village level (e.g., wearing identification badges or uniforms). However, that is about to change. In 2006, the Tanzania Tourist Board appointed its former Arusha Branch Manager as full-time coordinator of the CTP modules. In collaboration with two consultants, she is developing a whole series of CTP guidelines. Because Tanzanian government regulations on guiding are still in a premature stage, the ones currently exerting most control over guiding are private safari companies (individually or through TATO). Not only do they decide what guides wear (dress code), what behaviour is allowed (code of ethics), which clients they attend, where they sleep on safari and how much they earn, tour operators are increasingly involved in matters of training and accreditation (chapter 3). Recognizing this power, the government is forced to consider and consult the private sector and its organizations in its tourism planning.

## Tanzanian Tour Guides, Unite

At the end of the 1990s when tourism started booming in northern Tanzania, safari guides began to mobilize around employment issues and formed a loose organization. Individual tour operators and TATO, afraid the association would become a powerful labour union, soon sabotaged the initiative.[15] Some guides were fired for their involvement, which had the effect of scaring potential new members away, and these labour issues almost made the group extinct. However, at a 2006 stakeholder meeting organized by the Tourism Confederation of Tanzania, other professional organizations argued that because tour guides play an important role in tourism, they need proper representation.[16] TATO no longer objected when it became clear that the focus would be on training rather than on labour issues, and all parties reached an agreement to create the Tanzania Tour Guides Association (TTGA). This new organization, headed by an executive director and a board of twelve councillors, strives to ensure and promote the highest standards, ethics and professionalism among tour guides (Figure 12). TATO maintains that the TTGA cannot legally form a professional organization and can only have affiliate or associate members, because there is no official certification for guides in Tanzania yet.

From the start, the TTGA has faced many organizational problems. Lack of funds prevents the organization from acquiring office space, paying daily operational costs and setting up membership campaigns. Following the example of TATO, the association contracted a lawyer to represent its interests, but cannot afford to pay him the US$250 per month. Although the TTGA claims to promote higher professional standards and is a strong advocate of standardization, it has no capacity to realize these aims. Because it does not have the financial means to hire specialized consultants, the organization is setting up partnerships with European volunteer organizations that can send experts on short assignments to help them with management and internal organization. Because the TTGA is the

# T.T.G.A.

**OBLIGATIONS:**

The obligations of a tour guide is to **MANAGE, INFORM,** and **ENTERTAIN** Tourists travelling singly or in a group around a given area.

A guide **MANAGES** by providing such services as are needed to ensure the smooth running of events.

A guide **INFORMS** by providing an honest and favourable information confidently and professionally to the satisfaction of his/her clients. also to provide a true picture of our country Tanzania.

A Guide **ENTERTAINS** to increase the clients enjoyment in their stay in Tanzania.

**GUIDELINES:**

Therefore in order to achieve the basic aims and sustain our obligations in Tour Guiding, the following guidelines should be observed:

● A good relationship and respect with:

1 Fellow guides.

2 Employers.

3 Clients.

4 Stake holders e.g. TANAPA, NCAA etc.

5 Service providers e.g. Hotels, Restaurants, Religious sites,Law enforcers etc.

At all times, approved guides are supposed to observe maximum protection of our environments. Should not allow any kind of misbehaviour that will negate our aims and obligations. And must accept full responsibility to our clients for their well being in Tanzania.

For further understanding of your society a copy of Constitution and a Code of conduct will be available with the secretariat. order now and work professionally.

*Neat, smart, practical and professional during work hours, Image is important.....*

**FIGURE 12** • *TTGA Promotional Leaflet (Source: TTGA)*

only guide association recognized by the Tourism Confederation of Tanzania, it would make sense that similar organizations affiliate with them. However, means are limited to reach those working in other areas of the country (especially in Bukoba, Bagamoyo, Dar es Salaam and Zanzibar). Ironically, the TTGA seems to fare better in its international networking efforts, having contacts with the Uganda Safari Guides Association, the Kenya Professional Safari Guides Association and the Zimbabwe Professional Hunters and Guides Association.[17] The TTGA board also wants to join the World Federation of Tourist Guide Associations (WFTGA) as soon as it has the necessary funds to do so (membership fees are EUR 145 per year).

The TTGA is pushing forward the idea of tour guide certification (by a registered institution) and a grading system (by an independent board). Members were alarmed when they heard rumours that TATO planned to organize guide examinations and that some individual safari companies were setting up their own accreditation schemes. In 2007, TTGA had around two hundred members, virtually all of them driver-guides. Many of their colleagues do not want to join the association. They are still afraid of the possible repercussions (because some companies do not allow their employees to join) or they do not see the benefits of a membership. As Akida, an active TTGA member, told me, 'They [those not joining] count the fees as losing their money'. Erasto, a junior driver-guide, has heard (vaguely) about the organization and would like to receive more information before making a decision: 'Some of these associations are just ... I want to work with serious people'. Because little is known about the TTGA, some expect it to handle all their problems and will join only when they are in trouble. Others are enthusiastic but 'forget' to pay their dues.

The TTGA is not the only guide organization around. Professional Safari Guides, for instance, claims to be the association of the best safari guides in Tanzania. Membership is exclusive: applicants are carefully assessed and accepted based on quality, dependability, experience and trust. Of its ten members in 2007, only three were native Tanzanians. In 2002, the UNDP awarded a small three-year grant to the College of African Wildlife Management in Mweka to form and register the Mt. Kilimanjaro Tour Guides Association and to develop a guiding code of conduct for nature interpretation as a tool in promoting sustainable conservation and development. As many as 1,200 local mountain guides participated in the project, but it is unclear where the organization will go from here. Apart from the slowly growing institutionalization of guiding in associations, the profession is internally structured in more informal and tacit ways. I noticed this when I started joining tours and discovered that there is a clear hierarchy among driver-guides and mountaineering guides. Junior driver-guides will do their seniors all kinds of favours, regardless of whether they work for the same safari company or not. This can range from communicating the position of Big Five and other wildlife inside protected areas to sharing food and drinks to leaving the best accommodation in lodges to the ones with most seniority. In the world of mountaineering, assistant guides often end up being the porters for the head guides.

# À la Jogja

Climbing from the lower levels of the monument, whose walls depict the sensuous
pleasures of the flesh and the tortures accruing to bad actions, to the upper strata
displaying the Buddha's progressive enlightenment, our tour-guide waxed more and
more morose. But as we came upon a level crowned with statues of meditating
Buddhas, his face suddenly became animated. Pointing to a statue of the Buddha
with its right arm extended and its fingers drawn into a 'V', he called for our notice.
'In America', he said … 'they call that the peace sign. Or the "V" of victory. But
in Indonesia we have our own sign for victory. When someone makes that sign
in Indonesia, he is showing that he knows two children are enough'.
                                                                    –Leslie Dwyer (2000: 34)

Little did the tour guide in the passage above imagine that one of his clients that
day would remember this particular tour and write about it years later in a chapter on the politics of family planning in Indonesia. Dwyer visited Borobudur in
1993, the year she started ethnographic fieldwork on Islam and gender in Java for
a PhD at Princeton University. She recalls the tour because the local guide implies
that *dua anak cukup* (two children are enough), the Indonesian government's slogan for its family planning programme, can be found victoriously resplendent in
this monument to 'national culture'. Her anecdote illustrates how the New Order
government successfully managed to use tourism for politics (cf. Dahles 2001). I
describe below how things have drastically changed since then.

## From National to Local Politics of Regulation

Local tour guides in Jogja are commonly known as *pramuwisata, pemandu wisata,
guide* or *gaid.* They used to be divided in two broad categories, *guide resmi* (licensed guides) and *guide liar* (self-employed street guides). The former referred to
those with a guiding license from the government, while so-called illegal or wild
guides were those without a license, mainly operating around Malioboro Street
and the Sultan's Palace. I vividly remember how, during my first visit to the city
in 2000, these young men frequently harassed me (some being persevering and
pushy). The distinction between official and unofficial guides has become harder
to make due to increasing control over guiding practices. As I did for Arusha, I
focus here on the types of guides the majority of foreign tourists visiting Jogja are
likely to encounter.

Tour guiding has been subject to government regulations for quite a long time
in Indonesia (Dahles 2001, 2002). Intervention in tourism started in the early
1970s, when the island of Bali was developing rapidly as a popular destination. A
government regulation from 1979 (PP24/1979: Part transfer of government mat-

ters in the field of tourism to provinces) decreed that tour guiding was a provincial matter. However, when tourism in the country boomed at the end of the 1980s, the former Department of Tourism, Post and Telecommunications produced a whole series of letters, ministerial instructions and lower-level decrees regulating guiding in terms of licensing, certification, training, pay and benefits, marketing and conducting tours and the organization and professional ethics of guides (Dahles 2001: 133). The control even extended, at least on paper, to the content of the information and explanation provided. In practice, the national regulations were one thing; the ways in which they were implemented at the provincial and local levels another (Bras 2000; Salazar 2005; Cole 2008; Adams 1997).

Only in 1988 was tour guiding officially recognized as a profession (KM.82/PW102/MPPT-88: Ministerial decree on tour guides and tour leaders). This was followed in 1989 with a policy detailing guide training (Kep-17/U/I/89: Guidelines of tour guide training programs). The New Order government established formal training and the possession of a license to be the decisive criteria in determining who could operate as a guide. Tourism officials also introduced a clearcut guide classification system (Dahles 2001: 139). *Pengatur wisata* (tour leaders) could go anywhere inside or outside the country; *pramuwisata madya* (provincial or senior guides) and *pramuwisata muda* (regency or junior guides) had to operate within provincial boundaries; and *pramuwisata khusus* (on-site guides) could only work at specific sites. Of course, these guide categories overlapped and some people held a number of different licenses. The classificatory system corresponded to government-run courses that prepared guides to pass exams at different levels, while instilling the *Pancasila* state ideology (Dahles 2002).[18]

The fall of Suharto in 1998 had far-reaching consequences for the organization of tourism. After more than three decades under a centralized (and autocratic) national government, the country embarked on a democratization process that quickly gave rise to regional demands for decentralization of power. In response, the central government decided to implement a new policy of decentralization, devolving its authorities in all administrative sectors to local officials at the regency and city level, with the exceptions of security and defence, foreign policy, monetary and fiscal matters, justice and religious affairs. The main objectives of this reform were to promote better delivery of administrative services and to raise the level of local government accountability. The policy of regional autonomy, first outlined in 1999, became effective in 2001, and within a very short period, local administrations had to reform their internal structures to accommodate the huge increase in responsibility that had been passed on from the central government.

Tourism is one of the sectors that now fall under the responsibility of local authorities. In the case of the Yogyakarta province, each of the four regencies (Sleman, Bantul, Gunung Kidul and Kulon Progo) and one city (Yogyakarta) are in charge of tour guide policies, licensing and certification. In 2002, for example, the city issued an ordinance concerning tour guiding, detailing a classification, licensing issues and obligations and prohibitions. The regencies issued similar ordinances around the same period. Local officials took over the existing national classification but, interestingly, added the category of *pengantar wisata* (tour escort). The latter were included in the regulation to provide a place for those who have the potential to become guides but lack the minimum educational requirements. They are the only category not needing a certificate, only a license badge. While the inclusion of street guides is an attempt by the authorities to control the growth of informal activities by legalizing them, this measure has been far from successful. Many street guides told me they are reluctant to obtain a license because they do not see any benefits of doing so. A tour escort license costs money (a nominal IDR 10,000 every three years) and does not guarantee work.[19] Besides, most do not like the idea of being registered and controlled.

The city ordinance of 2002 details the duties of guides: (1) watch over the safety of tourists; (2) use the license badge; (3) behave well, talk properly and dress respectfully; (4) help the government develop tourism; (5) always give information and explain things well; (6) pay the obligatory provincial and national taxes and (7) deliver a periodic (six-month) activity report to the city hall. Certificates are valid for an unlimited period whereas license badges are valid for four years at first and then must be renewed every two years (IDR 20,000 for junior guides and IDR 40,000 for senior guides). License fees vary widely. In Sleman, for instance, guiding licenses cost IDR 100,000 and are valid for three years. To obtain a certificate or upgrade to a higher level, one needs to take a competency-based course and pass a test at a Profession Certification Institute. In Jogja, this is done at the semiprivate Jogja Tourism Training Centre. The certification body consists of qualified assessors from the centre itself, the Indonesian Tourist Guide Association (HPI), the Association of Indonesian Tour and Travel Agencies (ASITA), and the local government. In Indonesia, professional certification seems less voluntary than it is in most other countries (Black and Weiler 2005). One needs both a certificate and a license to work legally as a tour guide, tour escorts being the exception.

The certification courses and tests are based on the competences of guides as outlined in the 2002 Indonesian National Work Competency Standards, a concrete outcome of the Indonesia Australia Partnership for Skills Development Programme (in which the HPI collaborated for the part on tour guiding).[20] To make tourism workers more competitive in the current landscape of international labour circulation, standardization seems to be the way to go. Indonesia has understood this well and is clearly aiming at improving its position in the regional labour market. The Ministry of Culture and Tourism, together with a Jakarta-based consulting company, is playing a principal role in the development of the APEC Tourism Occupational Skill Standards. These are largely overlapping, if not in many cases identical, with the national standards. On top of this,

Indonesia has acted as the lead country in establishing the ASEAN Common Competency Standards for Tourism Professionals Framework (2004–05). Yet, despite the plethora of professional standards, there are as of yet no mechanisms in place to implement them.

## Mas Gaid and the Bird of Paradise

According to regional regulations, licensed guides must be member of a professional organization. The most important one is Himpunan Pramuwisata Indonesia (Indonesian Tourist Guide Association, HPI), established nationally in 1983 as Himpunan Duta Wisata Indonesia (Indonesian Association of Tourism Ambassadors). In the same year, the Yogyakarta Provincial Tourism Office (BAPARDA) established HPI Yogyakarta, mainly as an instrument to apply licensing regulations and to enforce their observance.[21] Consequently, the HPI cannot function as a labour union and has little impact on the employment of guides. Because there is a memorandum of understanding between ASITA and the HPI stating that HPI guides can only work for ASITA member agencies, ASITA fixes the guides' honoraria. In 2006, this was minimum IDR 10,000 per hour. The chairperson of the Yogyakarta ASITA chapter justifies the relation of dependency between tour guides and tour operators by comparing it to general practitioners working for a hospital. The latter also have no say over how the hospital is being managed. Given the fragile economic situation, some freelance guides (who do not have a fixed monthly salary) are willing to work for as little as IDR 3,000 per hour. As in Tanzania, most guides rely on shopping commissions or tips for their income. Solid data on salaries is equally difficult to obtain. In Indonesia, this is partly a legacy of the secrecy of Suharto's regime and partly because of the lack of efficient statistical recording. As in Tanzania, mountain guides earn the most (around IDR 500,000 per day is common), but the number of hikes per year on Mt. Merapi is limited.

The HPI can only offer its paying members (dues are IDR 10,000 per month) a collective insurance and help when they get sick or need financial support. Board members serve a five-year term, although re-elections are possible. Regular members are subdivided in language divisions, each with a chairperson (2006 numbers in parentheses): Japanese (158), English (98), French (52), Mandarin (35), German (28), Italian and Spanish (27), Dutch (16) and Korean (4). The group of Japanese-language guides is the largest, but Japanese tourists most often visit Jogja as day-trippers from Bali (Figure 14), while European tourists tend to stay at least overnight. This increases the amount of time and interaction with local guides. Pak Hardi, the HPI chairperson from 2004 until 2009, told me that, given the precarious economic situation, only an estimated 80 members are still active as guides. Many do not pay their monthly contribution, unless their license has to be renewed. HPI Indonesia is an active member of the World Federation of Tourist Guide Associations (WFTGA) and hosted its 2009 biannual convention in Bali.[22] The association also played an instrumental role in setting up the Southeast Asia Tourist Guide Associations, launched in Indonesia in 2008.

The official HPI logo, the wings of a bird of paradise, indicates an attractive voice and a good-looking appearance (Figure 13).[23] Upon hosting the 2003 annual national workshop, HPI Yogyakarta launched its own logo: 'Mas gaid' is a line drawing of a smiling young Javanese man, dressed in a formal coat, a long batik cloth covering the lower body, slippers, with a typical male batik headdress on his head and wearing an heirloom dagger. Of course, no guide would ever choose to dress like this because it would be highly uncomfortable to walk in such an outfit. Moreover, as in Arusha, tour companies in Jogja determine the dress code and they often ask guides to wear a company uniform. The logo has a more symbolic function, reaffirming the special status of Yogyakarta within

**FIGURE 13** • *The Bird of Paradise and 'Mas Gaid'*

Indonesia (needing a different emblem) and the importance of Javanese culture, which makes it no surprise that the guide represented is male. Femininity on Java is traditionally associated with the domestic sphere, and women still encounter ambiguous and contradictory messages when they seek employment in tourism.

Whereas HPI mainly represents the interests of guides working with international tourists, Paguyuban Pemandu Wisata Nusantara (Archipelagic Association of Tour Guides) is the overarching association of those working with domestic tourists. According to the PAPTA Yogyakarta chairperson, Pak Budi, the organization was started a couple of years ago as 'an attempt to take the tourism business in local hands'. It recently introduced its own licensing system for junior guides. PAPTA Yogyakarta incorporates three neighbourhood sub-branches, two of which were established as loose networks a long time ago. According to some of the members I interviewed, Paguyuban Pemandu Wisata Kraton dan Tamansari (Association of Kraton and Tamansari Tour Guides) has been around since 1974. Paguyuban Pengantar Sosrowijayan (Association of Sosrowijayan Tour Escorts), the association of street guides operating in the popular backpacker neighbourhood of Sosrowijayan, celebrated its tenth anniversary in 2006. Paguyuban Pemandu Wisata Kotagede (Association of Kotagede Tour Guides) is newer and much smaller.

## The Teething Troubles of Regional Autonomy

Of the licensed guides in Jogja, around 80 per cent work as *guide lepas* (freelance guides), scratching together an income by working for a large number of tour operators. The other 20 per cent are *guide tetap* (permanently employed guides) with a fixed contract, usually with a single tour operator. Many older guides recall how during the golden years of tourism (1980s until the mid-1990s), it was the opposite. An expatriate professor in tourism who lives already a couple of decades in Jogja commented on the situation of guides in the 1980s: 'They thought they had the world for themselves. They kept on bringing people to souvenir shops and I told them that people did not like that, but they did not listen. They were proud to say that they had a big car or could build a big house'. Indeed, the senior guides I visited are all living in comfortable, large houses. Had it not been for the earlier tourism boom, they would never have been able to live so cosily; today, junior guides can only dream of the wealth they see accumulated by their seniors. According to Pak Yulisetiono, who works for the Sleman Tourism Office, the selection of guides these days is mainly dependent on market rules. Russian- and German-speaking guides, for instance, are in high demand.

Any Indonesian senior high school graduate above eighteen years of age, with no criminal record and mastery of a foreign language, can enrol in a guide competency course. As in Tanzania, foreign tour guides are not allowed to work in

Indonesia. Of course, some foreign tour leaders partially act as guides when they are touring the country with their groups. Many young Indonesians want to become guides, but are waiting in vain for the regencies to organize the mandatory courses and exams. Access to the courses is restricted and, as some guides acknowledge, often subject to bribes. There is a chronic lack of human resources and expertise in regional bureaucracies and the competition between regencies and provinces is doing tourism more harm than good. According to the new regulations, guides need a certificate from the regency or city where they live and license badges from all the regencies or cities where they operate. To comply with the law, they also need to file activity reports every six months and pay tax levies if they want to maintain their licenses.

These new rules are highly impractical, because virtually all tours cross administrative boundaries. Pak Desky, the chairperson of the Yogyakarta ASITA chapter, stresses how ridiculous it is that guides taking tourists on a tour through different regencies should have licenses from each place. The most common day trip, for example, includes visits to Borobudur (Magelang Regency, Central Java), the Sultan's Palace (Yogyakarta City) and Prambanan (Sleman Regency and Klaten Regency, Central Java). Even if these three places have on-site guides, the accompanying guide is still guiding in between and would need at least four different license badges. Many tourism workers share Pak Desky's opinion that 'tourism is borderless and should not be bound to political regions'. Although political decentralization was seen at first as an opportunity to enjoy the full strength of tourism revenues, it has been a catastrophic development for most people to whom I talked.

In addition, there are other absurdities as a direct result of regional autonomy regulations. In 2002, Magelang Regency passed a directive regarding the management, security and orderliness of its tourism sites. The proposed measures, reinforced by a circular letter in 2005, were intended to improve the conditions of the people living around Borobudur. Among other things, the directive stated that all tourists visiting the complex need to take an on-site guide (licensed by the Magelang Regency), but because most tourists arrive on package tours (with guides from Jogja), this necessitates a change of personnel at the entrance gate, at an extra cost of IDR 40,000. In 2006, when the measure took effect, both ASITA and HPI Yogyakarta protested loudly against the transfer rule, stating that the HPI Magelang guides at Borobudur were 'of a lesser quality' and that this would have a damaging impact on tourist satisfaction in particular and the image of Indonesian tourism in general. They were also upset because they had never been involved as stakeholders in the decision-making process. At the time of writing, the problem has not been entirely resolved. HPI Magelang is much smaller than HPI Yogyakarta. Few on-site guides at Borobudur speak languages other than English, French and German. When other languages are needed, Jogja-based guides are still allowed to operate inside the complex boundaries.

FIGURE 14 • *Guiding à la Javanaise*

One large group of guides (over seventy) is exempted from the aforementioned rules and regulations, namely, those working in the main complex of the Sultan's Palace (Figure 14).[24] The Kraton itself selects them and senior officials give them private training. Working for the sultan is considered a great honour, bestowed mainly on people who belong to different echelons of the Javanese gentry with ties to the royal family. As a result, most guides operating within the Kraton constitute a group of older, honourable people, well educated and intimately familiar with the palace's vicissitudes. Many of them are children of royal court employees, although admission rules nowadays are much less strict than when the Sultan's Palace first opened its doors to the public in the 1970s. While job hours are flexible (every day between 8:30 A.M. and 2:00 P.M.), the pay is insufficient to support a family. Not surprisingly, therefore, there are only ten male guides. The rest are women, satisfied with a job that allows them to manage a household and earn some additional income. Like other on-site guides, the ones at the Kraton wear uniforms that change according to a fixed sequence with the day of the week. Because they are not allowed to have side jobs, palace guides try to arrange deals with fellow senior guides who transfer their guests visiting the Kraton to them and pay them directly from their tour budget.

There are other small groups of guides in Jogja that fall largely outside the control of the authorities, those employed by specialized foreign-owned tour operators that recruit and arrange private trainings (chapter 3). Because these guides have fixed contracts anyway, they do not need to worry about licenses or certificates. The Sultan's Palace, Prambanan and Borobudur are important places for the different types of guides to mix, network and exchange stories and experiences. Jogja's guides, whether licensed or not, are heavily dependent on their personal networks to find clients to make a living from guiding. Street guides rely on an extensive network of contacts to find prospective customers. Those who are fortunate enough to be employed by a tour operator have to be loyal towards and available for their employer in good and bad times. Others have to put a huge amount of effort into maintaining a network of potential employers; often they have to find additional sources of income, because guiding alone does not provide them with sufficient money to survive and feed their families. This situation was aggravated after the disaster year of 2006 (chapter 6).

## Mirroring Mercury?

An old-fashioned term for tour guide is *mercure*, referring to the Roman god Mercury. In Roman mythology, Mercury was the messenger of the gods (Hermes is the analogous Greek deity). His role as a guide consisted of leading departed souls on their journey to the afterlife. Always on the road, wearing winged sandals and a winged hat, Mercury was known for his eloquence, ingenuity and aptitude for commerce. A perfect patron for tour guides, so it seems. We do not know whether the wings of Mercury were those of the bird of paradise (the symbol Indonesian guides chose for their association emblem), or those of a flycatcher (as Tanzanian street guides are called) and the equivalence would, of course, be pure coincidence. But this chapter shows there are similarities between the tour guiding scenes of Arusha and Jogja that are not accidental, produced by wider trends of standardization in global tourism.

Even if the development of the guiding profession and policies regarding tour guides in Tanzania and Indonesia are at different stages, certain parallels are striking. In both cases, increasing control is being exerted over the occupation, an ongoing process that is steered internationally, legalized on the national level and implemented locally (although the local is the weakest element in the chain). It is becoming increasingly difficult to operate lawfully as a guide without formal training and a license issued by government authorities. This is complemented in Indonesia by professional certification, an instrument of control that is still in the making in Tanzania. In addition, guides are urged to adhere to codes of conduct: Tanzania endorses the UNWTO Global Code of Ethics for Tourism while Indonesia's regional autonomy allows local authorities to promote their own rules of conduct (Bras 2000: 28). Finally, the creation of professional associations, the HPI and TTGA, has been a process largely controlled by the government.[25]

The increase of regulatory mechanisms in managing the tour guide profession is a trend that has been noted worldwide over the last decade. To a certain extent, it can be seen as an acknowledgment of the important role that guides play in tourism. Yet, if recognition were the prime motive in Tanzania and Indonesia, awards of excellence would not have been overlooked. Such awards, at the organizational, product or individual level, encourage guides to achieve excellence in a range of roles and are usually intended to 'recognize and reward outstanding individuals, provide role models for the industry, promote excellence in guiding to the industry and the wider community, provide a benchmark for "best practice," and give an incentive for other professionals to improve their skills and performance' (Black and Weiler 2005: 30). A commonly heard argument is that controlling devices are necessary to improve the quality of guiding. However, as I discussed in chapter 3, vocational training—the main tool to transfer the appropriate knowledge, professional skills and the attitude of hospitality—is far from adequate in both Indonesia and Tanzania. In theory, the tour guide associations could contribute to schooling, but in practice, they have limited resources to do so. Instead, they are fully occupied with other activities such as maintaining contact with their members, serving more as a body to control and enforce the licensing process. In Indonesia, membership is even compulsory to acquire and renew licenses.

In her analysis of Suharto's New Order policies of guiding in Indonesia, Dahles (2001, 2002) illustrates how the Indonesian government at that time used tourism as a strategy to address issues of national significance. In earlier research on Israeli and Palestinian guides in Israel and the Occupied Territories, Bowman (1992) has shown that state organizations controlling travel and tourism service industries are ensuring that guides serve the interests of their constituencies and of the state. This helps to explain the resentment of authorities against foreigners working as guides in Jogja or Arusha. Only natives can be true cultural ambassadors or representatives of the country, so the thinking goes. Unlike the Roman god Mercury, guides are seen as the messengers of worldly national ideologies. Moreover, by excluding strangers, the authorities hope more jobs become available for locals.

There is another reason why regulatory mechanisms are becoming increasingly pervasive. For the global system of travel and tourism to work efficiently, international standards need to be imposed across the board. That is why instruments of standardization and control are being developed at the supranational level. One readily understands that this makes sense for sectors such as transport (e.g., the Universal Safety Oversight Audit Programme of the International Civil Aviation Organization) and food (e.g., the International Organization for Standardization Food Safety Management Systems Standard). Global standards of service and customer care, on the other hand, are contested. Although UNWTO and the International Organization for Standardization have been successful in creating international standards in the area of tourism services (ISO 18513:2003), sector-based interest groups see them as redundant and costly. One criticism is that the promotion of standardized services runs contrary to the tourist's desire for diversity in the travel experience, as well as negating cultural and geographical diversity in destinations. As this study makes clear, global tourism cannot do without local mechanics of glocalization to spread and sustain its imaginaries and practices. Yet another mundane messenger function for tour guides to fulfil.

While there is protest against standardization at the global level, homogenizing policies proposed by regional blocs—which are believed to be more culturally uniform—are perceived as less of a problem. Taking Australia as the regional model, Indonesia is actively involved in helping shape the APEC and ASEAN professional standards. For Tanzania, South Africa is the example most people look up to, and EAC the institution increasingly determining the policies of the region (although many Tanzanians do not seem to understand and accept this yet). Behind all these international and regional policy developments, there is a huge moneymaking machinery. It takes a long time and the involvement of numerous well-paid international consultants and national administrators to reach agreements. In other words, it assures bureaucrats of attractive work, involving travelling abroad and meeting new people. Besides, for poor countries like Indonesia and Tanzania, participation in such policy development programs looks good in the eyes of foreign donors. And once the policies are in place, implementing them often becomes a low priority, because other international or regional guidelines are waiting to be developed.

Both Dahles (2002, 2001) and Bowman (1992) acknowledge there are significant limits to the extent that regulatory mechanisms can be enforced and policed. Setting up and making these devices operational is expensive. A small and rich country such as Israel may have the means to do so, but in large developing countries such as Indonesia and Tanzania, this is less the case. These countries might have everything in place on paper, but they are extremely weak when it comes to implementation. A variety of different power relationships therefore influences the character of interactive service work. Samweli, a bright young Maasai, gave the following reason why he decided to give up his job as a driver-guide: 'A guide is like a punch box, hit by rangers and wardens, bosses and managers, police, and clients'. It bothered him that all these interest groups were constantly controlling his actions. His statement confirms that efficient policing of guiding practices can only happen at the local level. While Dahles (2002) forecasted that the more liberal and democratic atmosphere in Indonesia would lead to the easing or even lifting of restrictions, I show in this chapter that, in fact, the reverse is happening. Local authorities compete against each other with a plethora of new rules and regulations. In Tanzania, where the administrative system in general is weak, the private sector (largely in expatriate hands) controls tour guiding. Those working in the informal sector—flycatchers and guide liar—go largely undetected on the controlling radar of authorities and companies.

For tour guides, current developments at the international level do not change very much, relative to their situation on the ground. Guiding in Arusha and Jogja remains a risky profession, depending on highly unstable economic conditions. In both places, there is a clear gender imbalance in that most guides are male and it is very difficult for women to enter the guiding business. In Jogja, the reason is cultural. In Arusha, however, structural and physical constraints prevent women from becoming driver-guides. The trend of creating costly regulatory devices, while giving prestige and international recognition to the administrations developing them, fails to grasp the volatile nature of guiding, particularly in developing countries. Guides have to pay for training, licenses and certificates, although for many their guiding role is as momentary as the one played by tourists. As soon as the clients are gone, income needs to be assured through other activities such as farming, running a small business or teaching. Also the next chapter will illustrate that, rather than resembling the Roman god Mercury, tour guides have to survive in working environments that are decidedly 'mercurial'—unstable and liable to sudden and unpredictable changes.

# 6
# FANTASY MEETS REALITY

⚜

Tanzanian guides are very extravagant and they pretend to know everything ...
They get more money and do very little with it ... Most tour guides are not
qualified ... They don't take their clients seriously ... They don't show the real
life Tanzanians live. Why don't they take them [the tourists] to Internet cafes
or airports? These things show how a country is modern. If I were a guide, I
would show how developed we are! We are not very different from tourists;
the only difference is that we have lions and zebras in open plains.
—Leo (high school student, Arusha)

As the previous chapter and the evocative quote above reveal, guiding foreign
tourists in developing countries cannot be a politically neutral matter. In contrast
to other types of tourism, guided tours do not take place in a sociopolitical vacuum or well-protected tourism bubble. The players involved, the tourists, guides
and locals (and, behind the scene, tour operators, government agencies and law
enforcement), all interact in ways that involve complex dynamics of power, positionality and agency. Destination residents who have contact with tourists (and
become part of the attraction) have often been described in passive terms, for
example *visitee* (Bruner 1991), *travelee* (Pratt 1992) or *touree* (Van den Berghe
1994). Causey (2003) proposes the term *tourate* to indicate that local people
simultaneously have some degree of agency in tourism and are changed by it. In
chapter 4, I discussed how global tourism spreads certain imaginaries about peoples and places, as well as how tour guides try to mirror these images and ideas in
their guiding narratives and practices. In this complementary chapter, I add other
agents to the equation. Tourates, for instance, have fantasies and thoughts about
tourism, tourists and guides too. During guided tours, these multiple imaginations interact in a multivocal dialogue and, occasionally, clash. I zoom in on the
moments of friction in guided tours, showing the unexpected instances when
personal imaginations hamper the nearly flawless (but fragmented) replication
of tourism imaginaries, yet which, in fact, also can facilitate their circulation by
allowing them to be modified.

## Excursion into Power

Acknowledging the performative dimension of representations and the dynamic competition between different representational systems leads one to consider the power relations between the different players involved in tourism encounters (Chatelard 2005). Before delving into the power microdynamics of guided tours, it is necessary to delineate the key concepts of the discussion. Many stakeholders in tourism—individuals, interest groups and several public and private organizations—compete for power and a piece of the lucrative tourism pie. An analysis of the power dynamics and controlling processes that are circulating through a multiplicity of discourses, sites and practices is essential in understanding tourism and its localization.

Few have influenced how social scientists think about power more than Foucault (1980), who considered it as a multiplicity of forces, all of which function as force relations that affect individuals as mechanisms of control. Foucault's insights are popular in critical tourism studies that analyze how productive power generates tourism knowledge and how power is enacted discursively (Ateljevic, Pritchard and Morgan 2007; Cheong and Miller 2000). The performative action of guides, for example, can be conceived as enacted in a setting where power relations both subjectivize and empower the guide, in a performance space where power relationships are enabling and constraining at the same time (Hollinshead 1999). While the work of Foucault has made scholars more aware of everyday forms of power, that of Scott (1985, 1990) has had a similar effect for everyday forms of resistance (Figure 16).[1] With some exceptions (e.g., Adams 2006), Scott's theorizing remains relatively untapped by those studying tourism. Important for the study at hand is that in both Foucault's and Scott's frameworks, power is understood as relational rather than an individual or structural capacity: it is a way of acting on the actions of others. If power is relational, the concept of human agency becomes important.[2]

While Scott reduces agency to actions that resist domination and Foucault leaves little room for agency, Giddens (1984) treats agency and (power) structure as mutually constitutive. This idea of dialectic interplay between individual agency and social structure is also present in Bourdieu's theory of practice, in which he describes the concept of 'habitus' or habitual condition as a generative process that produces practices and representations that are conditioned by the 'structuring structures' from which they emerge (1977: 78). Aspirations are one of the key areas through which habitus is expressed. In other words, embodied practices and entrenched power relationships are deeply intertwined. These various theories offer useful conceptual tools for studying power dynamics in tourism in general and guided tours in particular (Salazar 2006a).

No matter how we name the different parties involved, the relationship between global tourism players and local tourates is severely asymmetrical, for it is the latter who have to bear the burden of economic, social and cultural adjustment. However, it is when focusing on the microinteractions between mediators, locals and tourists that power relations and the mutual interdependence of structure and agency become conspicuous for analysis. Power might be everywhere, but people do seem to have various types of agency to contest and even change existing structures. Microanalyses confirm the dialectical and relational nature of power by illustrating how tourates are neither passive nor unable to influence the character of their interactions with tourists. It would be incorrect to lump all residents of destinations such as Jogja or Arusha (or even the smaller units of urban neighbourhoods or settlements in the area) into a single heading of 'local community', because the interests and stakes in tourism are not the same for everyone within those communities.

## Imaginary Control

The study of power in tourism demands increased analytical attention to the role of brokers or mediators—guides, interpreters, travel agents, accommodation providers, government at all levels and international agencies. Local tour guides, the focus of this book, are both actors and agents of power.[3] They are bound by currently dominant tourism imaginaries but, in some ways, their narratives and practices function as performative 'hidden transcripts', sneakily critiquing established ethnic, (post)colonial, political or other hierarchies and operating as 'weapons of the weak' (Scott 1985, 1990). Their constantly shifting positionality (chapter 4) illustrates the ambivalences and ambiguities of resistance. Guides may be the underdogs in relation to their employers or clients, but with respect to tourates their position is significantly different. There is an almost constant struggle among the various stakeholders over tourism representations, as different groups with (sometimes incompatible) projects, apprehensions, memories and yearnings create, (re)produce and engage with them. When considering the competing stakes of tourists, mediators and tourates, it becomes clear that tourism is a 'complex arena embodying contending discourses concerning identity and hierarchies of authority and power' (Adams 2006: 29). While the practice theories discussed above give us a framework to describe these entangled webs of power, they cannot adequately explain how key figures such as local tour guides manage at times to transform the systems that produce them—how social reproduction can become social transformation. Theorizing from linguistic anthropology can help us to shed light, as Ahearn puts it, on 'the question of how any habitus or structure can produce actions that fundamentally change it' (2001: 119).

As I have shown in previous chapters, guiding narratives and practices do not merely reflect already existing social and cultural realities; they also help to create them. The tourism discourses they rely on both shape and are shaped by sociocultural factors and power dynamics. Their meanings are co-constructed by all participants, emerging from the social interactions taking place before, during and after touring. In other words, agency is located in the dialogic space between people, rather than within individuals themselves. Part of the effectiveness of tourism imaginaries lies in their capacity to become natural or to naturalize what they represent. This process takes place largely through the continuous replication of imaginaries in practice. In this course of action, tourism fantasies become dynamic and regulating form-given dispositions, giving meaning to people's behaviour. How are tourism imaginaries, which often contain elements that are not internal to culture, able to reproduce themselves so easily in various cultural contexts? The examples discussed in chapter 4 seem to indicate that the power in their (re)entextualization resides with the chief copiers (i.e., the local guides), because they have the ability to change the original while replicating it. That is also the common opinion of the local communities in which guides operate, as evidenced by the opening paragraph of this chapter. The fact that guides, and not their employers or the tourism sector in general, are blamed for misrepresenting culture and heritage indicates that tourates identify guides as those with most power over the representations.

The social life of the (linguistic) habitus is mediated by discursive interactions (Agha 2006). Each moment of this process is formed by operations of role alignment that have an irreducibly agentive character, even though the individuals involved differ in their degree of effective freedom. The connection between knowledge and agency is of central importance in this social construction of meaning, and because of a knowledge differential, guides are able to distinguish themselves from other locals, creating a power differential as well. Both groups, however, use (meta)discourse to negotiate their asymmetrical social identities in the encounter with tourists. Ironically, it is precisely that these social relations are asymmetrical that makes them conducive to the transmission and replication of tourism discourse more readily than would be the case within egalitarian or symmetrical ones (Urban 1996: 37).

In this chapter, I show that both tourates and tourists have stakes in the circulation of tourism imaginaries. Because the agents involved have different interests, the discourses through which tourism imaginaries become tangible can be criticized, altered and even stopped. And because local people are not always present during guide-guest encounters, the control they exert is often indirect, through metadiscourse. Urban explains, 'Anyone who contributes metadiscourse about an instance of replication participates in control over the replication process. That metadiscourse is a kind of response to the copy as discourse, and, similarly, the metadiscourse is also itself public, susceptible to criticism as it circulates (by means of replication) in the community' (1996: 41–42). In other words, replication of tourism discourse depends on response, a metadiscursive reaction to the original discourse. Urban rightly remarks that 'control is also lodged in the form of the discourse itself' (1996: 42). Tourism discourse is more replicable because it is overtly coded as nonpersonal and its core imagery is relatively detached from local contexts and circumstances.[4] The examples in this chapter show that guides, indeed, easily mirror tourism imaginaries in their narratives. However, they and other local people also use (meta)discourse to contest and transform those same representations.

## Commentary as Critique

Even if tourism seems to impose monolithic meanings through the relentless circulation of its archetypical images and ideas, each representation of peoples and places is subject to multiple interpretations. The tourism system does exert a great amount of control over its workers, but none of the service provider roles are as rigid as they may seem (Edensor 2001). This is certainly true for tour guiding, an interactive endeavour that can never be fully controlled—neither by the tourism system or authorities, nor by guides themselves. During the guide-guest encounter, the original message can be subtly modified and contested, and the learned scripts can be tempered with unfamiliar elements that are brought out. This makes every meeting with visitors unpredictable and a new challenge, however well trodden the terrain may be by the guide.

Tour guides never serve a neutral role. Their performance invariably has political ramifications, which may sometimes be quite explicit (Bowman 1992: 131), because, even if limited, they often have at least some power to intervene and constrain tourism activities. During their interaction with clients, they may contest in disguise the roles they are expected to play. At the same time, even in circumstances where guides enjoy maximal authority, their interpretations are subject to contestation (Feldman 2007). On some occasions, tourism fantasies are demystified. This may take place in moments of inattentiveness to specific actions or participants and usually results in changing patterns of alignment, or 'footing', among participants (Goffman 1981). Microchanges to the original tourism 'text' in the course of its reproduction can come from tourists, guides or tourates. It is in these (meta)discursive deviations from the expected script that imaginaries are tested and contested. Below, I discuss some examples related to politics, religion and poverty.

### Never Say the P-word

While the general rule for guides is not to talk about politically sensitive issues and remain neutral (chapters 3 and 5), some cannot refrain from voicing their opinion. In Arusha, for example, I heard one driver-guide give his clients a lengthy exposé on how European imperialists consciously exploited Africa, leading to the modern underdevelopment of most of the continent. He was lucky to find among his educated US group a receptive audience that did not perceive this intervention as a disruption to the 'magic' of the tour. As mentioned before, tour guide discourse sometimes works as a hidden transcript, expressing socioeconomic and political dissatisfaction without directly confronting or challenging the authorities (Schwenkel 2006: 20). This type of subtle agency is extremely popular on Java, where people continue adhering to traditional ideas of deference and hierarchy. Although there are new forms of social mobility, hierarchical order remains very important in Javanese culture. Deference must be paid to those who have high status; they are not challenged directly or openly. The operational directive is often *asal bapak senang* (I, as long as the boss is happy).

> Commenting upon the traditional attire the soldiers of the Sultan's Palace wear:
> Y41. It's not at all easy to go to war in such a costume!

> Brief remark regarding the royal batik motive of the sultan of Yogyakarta:
> Y42. It's nothing very special.

> Remark on a commemorative plaque thanking those who financially sponsored the restoration of Borobudur:
> Y43. [President] Suharto didn't pay anything but still has his signature here … Madame, if you want to contribute more than Rockefeller, you will have a bigger signature, on top!" [points to the back of the plaque where there still is plenty of space].

The attire the sultan's soldiers are wearing (only during special ceremonies) is a heritage from the Dutch colonial period (1619–1945): heavy and thick clothes that are not at all appropriate for the tropical weather conditions of central Java. While humorous, the guide's comment implicitly questions why those in power have never opted to change the old-fashioned costumes for something more fitting to the local circumstances. The second commentary voices a similar dissatisfaction: Objectively, the royal batik motif of Yogyakarta is indeed not elaborate, certainly not when compared to archrival Solo, the neighbouring sultanate of Surakarta. In both cases, the guide is able to use the foreign tourists as a soundboard to voice his opinions, without risking accusations of trespassing culturally accepted levels of respect for established hierarchies and authorities. Y43 is one of those rare instances where higher authority (in this case a former president) is directly criticized. Again, the guide could afford to do this because he was among cultural outsiders. The power of the statement is evidenced by the fact that the guide quickly shifts the attention (and tension) to the tourists, knowing well that few visitors would be as rich as John D. Rockefeller, the US philanthropist whose fund substantially contributed to the restoration of Borobudur.

Guides may also use the expanded time they spend with foreign clients to present them with corrective interpretations of local heritage and history.

Plea to use Oldupai Gorge as the correct name for the famous archaeological site:
A19. I mention the two names, Olduvai and Oldupai Gorge. The word Oldupai, which is the correct name of this place, is the Maasai word for this plant here: wild sisal, sansevieria. But the sisal was mispronounced by Professor Kattwinkel from Germany in 1911, when he came to this place to study butterflies. When he came and asked the name of the site from the local people, and when he heard the name of the site is Oldupai, this professor unfortunately misheard and he wrote Olduvai, so that the word Olduvai remains written in history as an official name of this place, while Oldupai remains a local name. But time to time we're trying to correct this one day.

Ironic remark about the origins of the name Kilimanjaro:
A20. Of course, everyone knows that in truth the mountain was named after the legendary Tanzanian beer.

The museum guide in A19 is frustrated because so many foreigners wrongly talk about Olduvai, instead of the locally correct Oldupai (Figure 15). The same could be said for Ngorongoro (*Ikorongoro*), Serengeti (*Siringet*), and Kilimanjaro (*Kilemakyaro, Kilimangare*, or *Kilima Ngaro*), which are all misspellings or mispronunciations of the names used in various local languages. Guides inform tourists about this as a way of transculturally diffusing 'unofficial historical knowledge' (Schwenkel 2006: 18). Clearly, then, the power to define places can become a site of intense negotiation (reinforcing the local as a site of expertise over and above the officially accepted foreign expertise). While it makes sense from a cultural point of view to try to restore indigenous names (as massively happened in India), this is virtually impossible in the case of the Tanzanian places mentioned

FIGURE 15 • *Introducing Oldupai Gorge*

above because their 'wrong' names are circulating globally as markers for the country's most famous attractions. In A20, the guide implicitly acknowledges the impossibility of changing common misconceptions about Tanzania, so he instead decides to make fun of them.

## Sacrilege

Indonesia is the country with the largest Muslim population in the world, but this fact is largely absent in tourism imaginaries, which focus mainly on pre-Islamic heritage (the Hindu island of Bali and the Hindu and Buddhist temples on Java), non-Islamic minorities (in Sulawesi, Flores, Papua, etc.) and nature (e.g., Kalimantan and Sumatra). Once visitors have booked a trip to Java and come all the way, it is hard for them not to notice the presence of Islam, which has become more visible on the street in the last quarter of a century (e.g., more women are now wearing a veil). Right next to the entry gates of Borobudur and Prambanan, there is a *musholla*, a small building where Muslims perform their religious duties. When tourists visit the monuments around prayer time, they can hear the Islamic call to prayer all over the compound. As Ari, a standby guide at Borobudur, reminded me, 'most of the guides are Muslim ... Talking about a Buddhist temple, they don't understand the symbols. I mean, can you imagine if Catholics would show people around Mecca and Medina?'

Most of the local guides in Jogja are Muslims, but they have learned that their work in tourism requires pragmatism rather than dogmatism. The following anecdote is telling. When the group of transnationally networked guides I described in chapter 3 was hiring new staff, the senior guides invited me to participate in the interviews. They asked all candidates the following question: 'What would you do when you are guiding a group of tourists, and you hear the call to prayer?' Virtually all applicants answered as good Muslims: 'I would interrupt the tour and find a nearby mosque or musholla to pray'. The interviewing guides reacted strongly when they heard this, making it clear to the interviewees that this might be the right answer for a devout Muslim, but it is the wrong one for a professional guide. I later had a chance to observe the successful candidates during their first tours with tourists. None of them ever attempted to pray when it was prayer time. When I asked the senior guides why they had included this question in the interview, they told me they wanted to check if the candidates were able 'to think outside the box'. The guides know what the rules are to be a good Muslim, but they also realize that religious directives are not always compatible with a job in tourism.

Guides do talk about religion with their clients, but mostly in general and politically correct terms. This sometimes involves tweaking the truth a little.

Answering the question whether Borobudur is a temple or a monastery:

Y44. Eum [hesitating], it's a monument. The temple had its function, it's not a sacred place to pray or meditate, the temple functioned like a visual institute of Buddhism. Visitors don't come to meditate or pray but to study all the conceptions of life from the reliefs, and then apply this in real life.

The stance in Y44 is identical with the one the Indonesian government has officially taken since 1985. That year, the main structure was bombed by Muslim fundamentalists who viewed Borobudur as a symbol of Indonesia's pre-Islamic pagan past. The militants perceived the government's renovations of the site (largely for purposes of tourism) as emblematic of the state's refusal to embrace Islamic law. They therefore selected Borobudur as a target and, in response, the government made it clear that all temples on Java were to be considered as heritage monuments, not religious or sacred sites where ritual activities are held. Aware of the negative perception foreign visitors have about Islam, Muslim guides often omit the story about the bombing from their narratives. Guides resort to such 'politics of selection' (Trouillot 1995) to leave out or mask certain facts. While the guide in Y44 is simply repeating the officially sanctioned discourse, in reality Buddhists still use Borobudur for spiritual ceremonies, the largest of all being the annual celebration of *Waisak,* a national religious holiday commemorating the birth of the Buddha.

Whereas Javanese Muslims traditionally combine Islamic faith with their belief in the Javanese spirit world (Geertz 1960), Javanese Islam is currently undergoing a process of Arabization. This is not only visible in official discourse or female fashion; it also slips into guiding narratives. When talking about the arrival of Islam in Indonesia, for instance, guides stress the role of Arab traders, although Muslim merchants from India and Persia played historically an equally (if not more) important role.[5] In the Sultan's Palace, the traditional safeguard of Javanese culture, there is manifest resistance against this Arabization. Although most female Kraton guides are Muslim, not one of them wears a veil. As senior guide Dewi comments, 'One doesn't need to be an Arab to be Muslim'. Occasionally, criticism of the way Islam is heading in Java enters the guide-guest encounter.

While talking about the importance of scouting in Indonesian society:

Y45. Maybe this is the only place [in the world] where you can find young veiled scouts; scouts and veiled ... Because, scouting is not a religious thing.

This Kraton guide points to the fact that it is weird that in Indonesia scouting and Islam have been lumped together. In his opinion, none of the female scouts should be allowed to wear a veil because scouting is and should always remain religiously neutral.

While Javanese guides may have their opinions about Islam, they also have their ideas on traditional Javanese beliefs and cultural practices.

Interpreting elements of Javanese culture during a tour of the Prambanan temple complex:
Y46. The Javanese only come to visit the statue of Jonggrang and then, finished!
Y47. Can you see the birds here? [pointing to a wall relief] It's the cockatoo here. The cockatoo is a symbol both for Hindus and Buddhists. The same like you have the white dove in Christianity, the symbol of peace. But we have parrots, because parrots always say yes.

Talking about Javanese mythology in the Kraton:
Y48. The Javanese are incredible ... they are full of incredible beliefs ... and they do believe in the most incredible ones.

In Y46, the guide belittles his fellow Javanese for their perceived lack of appreciation of 'high culture', here translated as interest in the cultural history of Prambanan. The Javanese only want to visit and pat the statue of Loro Jonggrang, because local lore has it that touching the face of Durga's statue makes women prettier.[6] There is some self-interest of the guide involved in this comment, because this situation implies that Javanese do not want the service of a guide when visiting the complex. On the metadiscursive level, the guide is transmitting yet another message: By taking distance from the Javanese commoner, he is positioning himself on the side of the tourists, as another person with a broad cosmopolitan interest in other cultures (chapter 4). Y47 is an implicit criticism of Javanese culture. Because parrots are known for their ability to mimic sounds or speech, the guide is suggesting that the Javanese in general are uncritically parroting one another, and are certainly not contradicting the traditional holders of power (cf. Anderson 1972). With the third comment, the guide of the Sultan's Palace acknowledges the richness of Javanese mythology, while at the same time indexically distancing himself from it (using the deictic term 'they'). He is—he asserts—only sharing the legends and beliefs with the tourists to entertain them, provide them with some magic and show them his profound knowledge of the local culture. On the other hand, he himself, in sharp contrast, is to be considered a modern, rational man.

## Hiding Hardship

Travels to developing countries usually confront tourists with visible signs of destitution and inequality (Mowforth and Munt 2008). Guides prefer to avoid these too-direct confrontations with abject poverty—the 'touristic untold' (Bruner 2005: 22)—in order not to spoil the general atmosphere of relaxed leisure time and to reinforce the essentialized, mythologized and exoticized images upon which most (but not all) tourism imaginaries are drawing.[7] During a tour around Arusha's urban centre, for instance, city guide Joseph noticed some street children sniffing glue under the Uhuru Torch, a well-known landmark commemorating the independence of the country. Instead of bringing the group of tourists to the monument and giving a detailed explanation, as is usually done, Joseph instead drew their attention to a nearby shop. When one of the tourists spotted the kids and asked him about the problem of street children in Tanzania, Joseph was put on the spot and could no longer avoid the presence of the children. He skilfully combined his answer to the question with a more general commentary on the country's postindependence problems, using this as an opportunity to bring the monument back into the middle of his narrative.

Sometimes, guides unexpectedly draw the attention to their own economic situation, often in comparison to that of the tourists.

> Pointing to the luxurious Amanjiwo Hotel, which can be seen from Borobudur:
> Y49. For the Presidential Suite, $2,000 per night. Have you ever been there? I have only been there once: In my dreams! … OK, let's return to reality now.

> Small talk about beauty products from the Dead Sea, used in spas in Jakarta:
> Y50. It's very, very expensive, when I saw it on TV … I cannot afford to buy. If I have a lot of money, I'll not do such things … I can do spa in the rice fields.

In Y49, the guide can only dream about staying at an expensive place like the Amanjiwo Hotel (a hotel even the majority of his middle-class clients cannot afford). It seems equally hard for the guide as for the tourists to imagine the socioeconomic conditions in which the other is living. The second remark is similar in style, the small talk that takes place between guiding narratives in which guides have a chance to voice their opinion regarding the dire economic situation of their country (and their own hardship). I have heard guides on tour complain about how expensive schooling has become or how low official wages are. The nuisance of insistent itinerant traders at sites such as Borobudur, desperate to sell their low-quality souvenirs, is justified by the same arguments. Some guides are even proactive, and kindly inform their clients that hawkers will harass them at the end of the guided tour. In these situations, guides will again try to align themselves on the side of the tourists, by giving them good advice (and protect themselves against possible complaints).

> Advice before entering the Prambanan temple complex:
> Y51. If you want to buy water, you pay more here, because it's a tourist place.

Few guides use tours to deliver elaborate macroeconomic analyses of the problems of their country. However, if they notice their party is interested, they may share their visions on (economic) globalization gone wrong.

Macroeconomic analysis while driving past the Shoprite supermarket in Arusha:
A21. Multinational companies, like Shoprite here … You know, the advancements of the socioeconomy of the country had improvements just after the introduction of the multiparty system and hence, socioeconomic competitiveness. I can say, it started just almost 28–30 years ago. You understand, we were a socialist country and so the economy wasn't competitive … And now, because of the foreign investors and privatization of means of production and hence globalization again, it's shooting up very fast … Tanzania, now the economy is booming up and we have more improvement on social infrastructure than any other country in East Africa. But, on the other side of the coin, we are now creating two antagonistic classes of people that were not there. That's another effect.

While the statement above is a straightforward analysis of the current situation, other commentaries are more disguised.

Comment on the degrading quality of exported teak wood during a village tour nearby Jogja:
Y52. For the best quality it takes a long time. I have some information from the villagers. The best quality is 25 years. But you know, now it's less than 20 years, or just after 10 or 15 years they cut it. So it's only young teak. That's why sometimes there are insects on it, it's easier to collapse.

What remains unspoken here is the fact that unbridled capitalism drives the teak business, one of the Jogja's major export products. At stake is how to reconcile the interests of sustainable resource management with the needs of people dependent on the resources for their livelihood, but the guide is careful, providing her clients with only the basic facts, leaving it up to them to analyze the situation themselves.

## Blame Game

Above, I gave some examples of how criticism of local politics, religion and beliefs, or inequality surfaces in guiding narratives and practices. While guides usually express their opinions with care, such an attitude becomes even more imperative when talking about other people (including tourists).

### Scapegoats and Black Sheep

The grass is always greener on the other side of the fence, so the saying goes. Guides in Jogja and Arusha both have colleagues in allegedly better positions to look up to and begrudge. In Jogja, pretty much everything in local tourism is measured against Bali, Indonesia's success story (at least, until the Bali bombings of 2002 and 2005).[8] When I was interviewing local guides, I repeatedly heard one version or the other of the following account:

> Most tourists visiting Jogja come from Bali and never stay longer than two days on Java. This is due to the negative advertisement by Balinese. When there are pickpockets in Bali, guides there tell their clients those people are migrants from Java, warning tourists to be extra cautious when travelling to the neighbouring island. Some Balinese guides (many of whom have never been to Jogja) tell visitors that they should watch out when going to Jogja because it is full of pickpockets and that it is better to leave their money there. In Bali, there may be no pickpockets, but there are many liars! … On top of this, transit tourists often have the impression that Bali is much better because there is not enough time to establish a personal connection in Jogja, also not with the local guides.

Guides in Jogja also find it inconceivable when foreign tourists fail to realize that Bali is not a separate country but belongs to Indonesia, and they tend to blame this on the Balinese.

Thus, even though Jogja's own tourism service industry is greatly dependent on Bali (chapter 2), it is important for proud Javanese guides to inform their clients that Indonesia encompasses much more than one exoticized and eroticized island. A couple of guides told me they are upset every time it becomes evident that their clients from countries such as Russia or South Korea have only heard about Bali, never about Java. The Balinese in general are reprimanded publicly for having Westernized and self-commodified their culture and themselves (cf. Bunten 2008), whereas the Balinese guides in particular are accused of being far too shopping minded and money oriented, selling everything imaginable to foreign visitors. In their contacts with tourists, however, Javanese guides will camouflage this type of negative evaluation.

> Commenting on the Hindu rituals sporadically held at Prambanan temple:
> Y53. Here [in Prambanan], the flowers are taken away soon after the festival. In Bali, they leave them up to three weeks or a month. That is why temples in Bali are dirtier compared to here.

> After having told a story about a Hindu friend who lives on the island of Bali:
> Y54. All these offerings [they do in Bali] are expensive and take up a lot of time.

Javanese guides cannot afford to be more direct in their criticism because they know tourists generally love Bali, and by giving vague comments like the ones above, they leave the final interpretation and judgment up to their clients.[9]

If the Balinese are identified as scapegoats on Java, the Kenyans undergo a similar fate in Tanzania. One frustrated driver-guide in Arusha told me, 'Tourists ask me what Tanzania is, but they know Kenya and have heard about Serengeti and Swahili'. As discussed in chapter 2, this has much to do with Kenya historically being the tourism star of East Africa, tending to lure visitors with attractions that are actually Tanzanian: Mount Kilimanjaro and splendid wildlife. A widely spread story among guides in northern Tanzania is that Kenyan marketers use the slogan 'Come to Kenya and See Kilimanjaro' to attract foreign tourists. Tanzanians take offence at this shrewd but deceptive kind of advertising. You can 'see' Mt. Kilimanjaro from southern Kenya, but to visit it you have to cross the border. With regard to wildlife, guides in Arusha rely on scientific literature to argue that the Kenyan parks are like deserts these days, the habitat killed by off-road driving and too many tourists. The buzz goes that in some national parks in Kenya they put up stuffed animals in the distance and that safari lodges hang meat in nearby trees to attract leopards.[10]

Tanzanian guides are afraid that with the opening up of the EAC labour markets, Kenyans (and, to a lesser extent, Ugandans) will come to take their jobs. They consider Kenyans more confident, more aggressive and much better trained. The Tanzanian inferiority complex, sometimes more imagined than real, is overcome via denigrating comments: 'I noticed in Kenya that the guides are old fossils, old people that drive the car badly and just point at animals and say "zebra," "giraffe," "a goat that I just ran over"'. In fact, there are already a substantial number of Kenyans working in Tanzania's tourism service industries, both legally and illegally. In this context, many people in Arusha retold me the story of President Kikwete's visit to Serengeti at the end of 2006. Apparently, the Tanzanian head of state became upset when he realized that many of those serving him and the products being served were Kenyan, a distress that led to a serious crackdown on foreigners working (illegally) in the tourism business. As in Jogja, guides in Arusha utter these comments in public but are very careful regarding what they share of this with their foreign clients. In both destinations, guide liar and flycatchers (self-employed street guides) function as the respective black sheep. Regular guides identify them as troublemakers and they often warn tourists explicitly not to trust their services.

## You Stupid Tourist

During tours, local guides not only voice their opinions vis-à-vis their close and distant colleagues, but also regarding tourists. The most common (and safest) mode of doing this is by sharing anecdotes about the foolishness of previous clients:

Before having lunch at a picnic site in the Ngorongoro Crater:
A22. Baboon [pointing to the animal sitting next to the road], a big boy, waiting for our lunchbox! There will come stupid tourists who don't close their windows [of the car] and they [the baboons] will pick one [lunchbox].

Telling anecdotes while driving through Serengeti National Park:

A23. You know, last time, the last group I had were two ladies from the US, a mother with her daughter. Once they had seen something [referring to wildlife] they said 'Let's go, let's go'. You know, I drove about 1,600 kilometres for seven days. Normally, it is supposed to be like 1,300 maximum. Instead of watching the animals, they said: 'We can see them on TV, let's go.' Sure, this is true …

A24. When it's sun here, lions tend to come by the shade of the car. On the same spot here, four, five or eight years ago, I had people with me. Four ladies of your age in the car. There was a big male lion lying down and she [one woman] was taking a picture just like that [mimicking]. And I didn't see her actually. She was reaching out and the lion saw the shadow moving and this male lion jumped out and started roaring. And she was screaming like crazy and banging on the chair. It was somewhere here actually. I don't forget that because that lion was angry!

Telling tourists to mind their head while stepping out of an inner temple room at Prambanan:

Y55. Yesterday, there was a tourist who wanted to film the building over there, like this [imitating the tourist's pose] and, without seeing this [pointing to the low entry arch], oew … It's not the head that is the problem, but the broken stone. One has to pay $10 extra for restoration [tourists laughing]. If all tourists break stones, there will be no temple left.

Driver-guides in Arusha confirmed there are monkeys around the Ngorongoro picnic areas at all times, vervet monkeys or baboons, because the animals have learned that tourists carry delicious fruits inside their picnic boxes, and each day they are able to snatch some of it away. Instead of warning their clients on beforehand, some guides prefer to have a good laugh when the confrontation between tourists and animals takes place—a rather irresponsible way of showing their agency. By sharing A23 and A24 with his clients, the safari guide is positioning them on a higher level than the tourists he is talking about, yet the anecdotes also serve as an implicit warning not to commit the same stupidities (or they will be degrading themselves). Y55 functions in a similar way. In every case, the guides transmit the message that they encounter quite a number of brainless people.

Presenting contested opinions coming from unidentified others allows guides to give visitors their own version of the story in ways that are not threatening.

About female circumcision in Indonesia:

Y56. Some people think we still have circumcision for girls. Here we do it, but only as a ritual. We have a kind of ceremony, normally when she's still a baby.

Discussing poverty in Tanzania:

A25. Sometimes people say our country is poor. It's not poor. We have Tanzanite, we have diamonds here in Tanzania, we have gold, we have mountains, we have national parks, we have good ground. But if the government says we are poor, I don't know what to think about that. Don't say our country is poor, our country is rich.

In these examples, the guides do not accuse their clients of having wrong ideas about circumcision in Indonesia or poverty in Tanzania. However, just in case they would, the tourists are invited kindly to change those opinions. In other words, such comments serve as a corrective for imaginations that tourists may have about the destinations—imaginations that are not necessarily in harmony with the widely circulating tourism imaginaries. Guides will hardly ever criticize their clients in an open and direct manner, however, or only when the situation is exceedingly bad. After all, they would not want to risk losing their tip. But they may show their dissatisfaction in more hidden ways, by keeping their interpretative narratives extremely short, for instance, or by giving no commentaries at all—'Show it, move on', as one Tanzanian guide calls this.

## The Native's Viewpoint

Circulating tourism imaginaries project essentialized images of cultures, thereby acting as an instrument of exploitation that masks the lived reality. Tourates do not always agree with the stereotypical ways in which local guides and other tourism mediators represent them (Porter and Salazar 2005; Salazar and Porter 2004), which can lead to a vicious struggle between touristic imagery and self-imagery (Dann 2004) (Figure 16). As a rule, destination residents in developing countries have little say over how they are represented in tourism, and even less so when these representations are constructed by cultural outsiders. They may also decide to enact tourism fantasies because they understand the (economic) benefit of promoting themselves as isolated, pristine primitives (Sylvain 2005; Adams 2006). The long-term implication of 'playing the native' is that locals will maintain, or at least act out, traditions they are sure will satisfy and attract more tourists, a process MacCannell (1984) refers to as 'reconstructing ethnicity'. In other words, tourism has as much potential to restore old (often atavistic) values as it does to destroy them (Van den Berghe 1994).

In situations such as village or boma tours, where there is more contact between tourists and locals, guides skilfully orchestrate the encounter (chapter 4). Benefiting from the fact that residents and tourists usually have no common language in which they can communicate directly with one another, guides keep the contact to a minimum.

Before starting a village tour nearby Jogja:
Y57. For taking a picture, you have to ask first ... Do not give anything to the people! ... For questions: Anytime, anywhere, anything, ok?

**FIGURE 16** • *Local Perceptions of Tourists*

Explaining the operation of a deep-fried cracker home factory in a village:
Y58. Most of the labourers working here are from West Java. Not many are villagers; no people from the neighbourhood want to do this.

Commentary about a Javanese mother feeding a baby during an urban neighbourhood tour:
Y59. The baby receives breastfeeding from the mother. Sometimes a bit too long [laughing shyly].

In Y57, the guide is giving clear instructions to the tourists, making sure everything will be under her control when they visit the rural area. The other two comments include value judgments, made in the presence of the people talked about.

Because they do not understand English, the tourates do not know what is being said about them and, consequently, do not know how to react accordingly.

## Misrepresenting Maasai

So-called meet-the-people tourism can be totally staged, local guides willingly participating in the game of 'staging authenticity' (MacCannell 1973). The predicament of the Maasai in northern Tanzania is a good example (Bachmann 1988). At the Maasai museum in Meserani, for instance, a museum guide dressed as a Maasai warrior takes visitors through the exhibition (Figure 10). When asked to which ethnic group he himself belongs, the guide claims he is a Maasai. However, his looks and the way he indexically shifts in his narrative from 'we' to 'they' and back indicate he might be faking his identity. My Maasai research assistant, who accompanied me on this visit, was convinced the museum guide was not a Maasai but belonged to the Meru or Arusha people. The guide in question tries to amaze the visitors with fantastic stories about male and female circumcision, polygamy, hunting and the drinking of blood. In his stories, Maasai culture is represented as static (read: immobile).

> Vague explanation about traditional Maasai bush retreats:
> A26. Here [pointing to a reconstructed bush camp], they learn more about the culture. There, the men go to teach the young men about culture, immediately after circumcision.
>
> Commentary about female circumcision:
> A27. Here for women, they circumcise women too. Do you know circumcision? [question directed to a female tourist] ... But nowadays it's illegal for women to do. But they [the Maasai] still practice it in secret.

The guide cannot help but remain vague about what is being transmitted during a Maasai retreat because he has most likely never experienced one himself.[11] The comment about female circumcision contains an explicit criticism of the continued Maasai practice. By doing this, the guide knows he will score with the tourists because it would be quite rare to have visitors who are in favour of female genital mutilation.

On some occasions, tourates have a chance to communicate directly with the visitors, sometimes with unexpected consequences. On a cultural tourism tour to a village near Arusha, a group of tourists observed how a man belonging to the ethnic group of the Arusha (but whom they mistook for a Maasai) was sharpening his machete. A young villager who knew some English explained that under colonial rule, villagers used to buy knives imported from the United Kingdom.

Nowadays they purchase cheap knives coming from China. The blades of the imported Asian knives are sharpened and made smaller so that they fit locally crafted protective sheaths. The youngster went on to tell that used machetes are sold to visitors because 'tourists always like something historic'. The realism of stories like this one takes away some of the magic surrounding the (imagined) Maasai culture. Guides have little control over such situations (at least not over the very moment of their occurrence).

While ethnic groups like the *Waarusha* (Arusha people) will sometimes take advantage of the fact that they are related to the Maasai, others will do everything they can to distinguish themselves from the Maasai.

During a Meru cultural tourism tour:
A28. The Maasai are the ones that wear blankets. The *Wameru* don't wear blankets.
A29. Today we are more developed compared to the other tribes. We are more transitioned compared to the Maasai. The Maasai are more primitive compared to us. We adapted quicker.

The Meru cultural guide in A28 and A29 made it clear to the visitors that his ethnic group is not to be confused with the Maasai. His comments indicate he knows many foreigners think all Tanzanians are Maasai (chapter 2), but also serve to denigrate the latter by depicting them as backwards and primitive. Interestingly, in one Meru village, the guides indexically distinguish their ethnic group from the Maasai by never dressing in red (blankets or shirts) but often in blue, although this colour is not particularly associated with the Meru. Little do the visitors know there are growing tensions between Meru and Maasai people in the area because the land they share around Mt. Meru is becoming overcrowded and overstocked.

Sometimes, tourism imaginaries are not demystified by tourates or guides, but by other foreigners (cf. Salazar 2004). A group of US tourists, for example, happened to be visiting a beaded jewellery cooperative of Maasai women on the day an Italian NGO volunteer was there (Figure 1). The Italian girl briefly played the role of a guide, explaining to the group that good-quality beads these days are imported from the Czech Republic (bad-quality beads come from China). She went on to explain that Italian designers had changed the traditional designs to be suitable for the European market. Her task was to train the women in replicating the new designs. Tourists looking to buy 'authentic' Maasai jewellery were apparently at the wrong address. The US tourists continued their walking safari with a Meru tour guide who brought them to a Maasai boma next.

Brief explanation when entering the Maasai homestead:
A30. So this is the Maasai *boma*. They build houses in this area. This [pointing] is a place for the cattle. There are two entries. So maybe this [pointing] is the entrance and the other the exit … So you can walk around and take pictures.

Talking about Maasai medicine:
A31. Tourist: Have scientists already checked to see if this [pointing to the bark of a tree] has real healing value or is it just tradition?
Guide: Just tradition.

The Meru guide would seem to know very little about Maasai culture. He does not know how a boma is structurally organized or how important traditional Maasai knowledge has been for both conventional and alternative medicine. One of the tourists, a general practitioner, seriously doubted the response of the guide in A31. The next day, the same group went on a camel safari. At the start, the tour guide introduced all the camels by name. The accompanying Maasai men (one per camel) were neither mentioned nor properly introduced.[12]

For Tanzanian driver-guides, the high season is their 'harvesting' time. Apart from receiving considerably large commissions for bringing clients to souvenir and curio shops, they can earn good money by visiting Maasai bomas. It is in their own interest not to inform tourists of the fact that most of the home-steads along the main roads were specifically created for receiving visitors. Guides charge around US$50 to take tourists there, giving the boma people itself as little as TZS 10,000 (less than US$10).[13] The Maasai know about this malpractice, and some are extremely upset about it and angry with the drivers. As a result, the visit to a Maasai homestead is generally preceded by lengthy discussions about the price to be paid.

While driving through the Ngorongoro area:
A32. Do you want to visit a Maasai *boma*? The Maasai have been quarrelling with the conservation authority.

Remark while passing a group of Maasai standing along the road:
A33. Begging along the road is prohibited [disapprovingly] … There have been meet-ings with Maasai elders about this.

In A32, the driver-guide wants to discourage his clients from visiting a boma, in order to avoid the hassle of having to negotiate the fee. I recorded this com-mentary at the beginning of the 2007 high season, and the Ngorongoro Con-servation Area Authority, becoming aware of the problems between guides and Maasai, had just introduced a fixed price of TZS 20,000 (around US$17) for a visit to a boma within their area. Guides as well as resident Maasai, however, pretended not to know about the new arrangement. In the second comment, the guide shows little understanding for the dire socioeconomic circumstances in which many Maasai live.

Due to lack of cultural and linguistic understanding, tourists do not always realize that what they are presented with is not the genuine contact with local people that they were promised. The most flagrant case of deceit I encountered was when accompanying a group of international volunteers on their visit to the Barabaig, a herding people living in the volcanic highlands near Mt. Hanang. This community-based tour, widely praised in travel guidebooks such as *Lonely Planet* and *Rough Guide* and on the Responsible Travel website, was actually organized by an entrepreneur from a distant part of northwestern Tanzania. The accompanying guide, a young man from the Mt. Kilimanjaro region, did what he had been doing during the last seven years: pretending to be a 'local' Barabaig. But the trick did not work so well this time: Because the foreign volunteers had been in the country for a while and spoke fluent Swahili, they quickly noticed from the interactions the guide had with Barabaig people that he did not speak the local language. After insisting on obtaining information directly from the people, they discovered that much of what the guide had told them was simply fabricated. The volunteers were so upset that they later filed a formal complaint with the Tanzania Tourist Board.

## Local Imaginations

The above examples indicate that tourates have little agency in how they are represented by tour guides, especially if these guides are cultural outsiders. The power of residents mainly resides in metadiscursive commentaries that circulate within local communities about guides and their representational narratives. I wanted to find out more about these local imaginations in Jogja and Arusha but knew that it would be difficult for me as a foreigner to access them. I therefore trained my local research assistants to conduct short, semistructured interviews and sent them out to converse with people in the respective cities and the surrounding villages. Based on these interviews, we could compose the following composite image that locals in and around Jogja commonly have about local guides:

> Mainly because they have advanced foreign language and communication skills and are knowledgeable about many topics, local tour guides are able to meet people from many different countries, travel to beautiful places within Indonesia with them, tell them nice stories about how beautiful the places and how good and well-mannered the Javanese are, learn from them, and become friends with them. The job of a guide is considered to be paid very well (mainly because of the tipping), estimations starting around IDR 500,000 to over IDR 2 million per month (roughly from US$50 to over US$200 per month).[14]

The people of Jogja rank guides relatively high as far as economic status is concerned. This is not surprising, because the senior guides who worked during the golden years of tourism (1980s to the mid-1990s), did indeed earn good money then and today still live in nice houses. While the situation has dramatically changed since the economic crisis of 1997, such that many can no longer survive by guiding alone, the popular image remains the same. Some envy the guides for their perceived economic success, while others criticize them for destroying Javanese culture by bringing in immoral foreign elements (an implicit reference to sex tourism and drugs). Sexual activities and romantic affairs between guides and clients do exist in Jogja, but are primarily found in the street guide milieu (Dahles and Bras 1999). People who know little about licensed guides look down on guiding, because they associate the job with the more questionable practices of some of the guide liar operating around Malioboro Street and the Sultan's Palace.

Apart from some understandable cultural and contextual variation, a strikingly similar composite image emerged in Arusha:

> Local tour guides are rich, allowing them to send their kids to the best schools and lead an extravagant life, although the latter also brings them problems like debts (due to poor budget management skills), alcoholism, and diseases such as AIDS (linked to their contact with prostitutes). To be a guide you need to speak a foreign language, have a good reputation and good health, be educated, and know a lot about different subjects. Some guides are not qualified, tell tourists many lies, cheat on them, and beg them for money and tips. Others have gone to school, are trustworthy, and handle tourists with care. Depending on the company they work for, their monthly income probably ranges between TZS 50,000 and TZS 400,000 (roughly between US$40 and US$325).[15]

People seem to understand that guides come in many shapes and colours, from the aggressive, self-employed flycatchers hanging around the city centre to the much more reputable driver-guides who work for top safari companies. Guides may be envied for the cash they earn, but Tanzanians are clearly aware of the many dangers of the job as well. As in Jogja, I heard the cultural destruction argument in Arusha. On the Day of the Museum, the National Natural History Museum had organized a debate for secondary school students about heritage. Students took extreme positions, arguing that tourism was bad because it destroyed 'their' heritage. It was interesting to hear them give examples about the Maasai or Hadzabe people, while many of those speaking were actually of South Asian descent. Likewise, in the Arusha Guide School I frequently visited (chapter 3), discussions about which kind of tourism is *halisi* (authentic, genuine or real) always centred on the Maasai or other 'traditional' people.

In general, people in Jogja and Arusha seem to look up to guides, often because they have the idea that guides earn good money. They also envy the privileged contact guides have with foreigners, especially with Westerners, because these give them higher social status. People seem not to realize that the income of guides fluctuates, with dramatic differences between the high and low tourism season, and that guides often have to work long hours and can be away from their family for long periods. They fail to see that successful guides are like inventive artists or bricoleurs, 'on the watch for opportunities that must be "seized on the wing"' (de Certeau 1984: xix), carving imaginaries and a means of livelihood out of a hospitality industry dominated by considerations over which they often have little influence. Instead, the positive evaluation given to local guides is based on the perceived outcome of their jobs rather than on what they actually do while guiding. Many locals believe in the guide-as-ambassador model, primarily because they know little about how guides (re)present tourates in their discourses.

## Tragedy Strikes

Local guides or tourates are not the only ones demystifying tourism imaginaries and discourses. There are other threats that are far harder to control. In fact, the global tourism sector does everything it can to silence the hazards involved in international tourism, especially to developing countries. Many of these dangers are not imaginary but real. For example, illness (from common traveller's diarrhoea to much-dreaded malaria) and issues related to safety and security (from various kinds of traffic accidents to petty crime and even terrorism) can be severe. Tourism marketers can promise all the paradise they want, but people will seriously consider the probabilities of these risks before booking a trip. Of course, nobody can guarantee a trouble-free holiday and, in some cases, tourists can become enmeshed in situations that deal serious blows to rosy fantasies.

### *All-inclusive Catastrophe*

During the last decade, Jogja's tourism has suffered from a whole series of unfortunate events in Indonesia and the larger Southeast Asian region (chapter 2). However, 2006 dealt a fatal blow to Jogja's already ailing service industry. Between May and July of that year, the region had to endure numerous natural disasters. Mt. Merapi, one of the most active volcanoes in the world, erupted multiple times. While few people died, many were evacuated and the psychological coping with the almost constant threat of a major eruption was severe. A similar story can be told about the tsunami that hit the southern shores of the province on 17 July: While the damage and casualties were minor, the memory of the 2004 tsunami in Aceh was still fresh in everybody's mind and people's panic and fear caused many to overreact. And, on May 27, people had a valid reason to be afraid. On that infamous day, a major earthquake struck the province, killing around 6,000 people and leaving an estimated 1.5 million Javanese homeless. This chain of disasters affected tourism in multiple ways.[16] Not only did tourists cancel trips to Java on a massive scale, but the local service industry was crippled by the death, injury and displacement of its workers. Because of the quake, the

Royal Graveyard of Imogiri and parts of the Prambanan temple complex were extensively damaged and two pavilions in the Sultan's Palace collapsed. Borobudur, on the other hand, did not suffer from the earthquake but it was covered by dark grey ashes from Mt. Merapi's eruptions. The entire situation exposed the fragility of the local tourism sector but also brought to light the resilience of its workers.

The calamities did not spare the local guides. Some lost their relatives, others their houses, and most were deprived of their primary source of income. Yet, ironically, the dramatic events also opened a window of new opportunities, and some guides were able to turn the situation around and make use of it: only a few days after the catastrophe, earthquake tourism packages had been developed. Instead of the traditional heritage tours, this time around guides showed disaster tourists the surreal landscape of completely destroyed villages. Others found temporary work as scouts or translators for the multitude of journalists, international NGOs, medical teams and government delegations visiting the affected areas. In effect, these groups mainly replaced the regular tourists, using their free time to visit the sights of the area that normal tourists patronized. Kaliadem, a recreation site where people usually came to enjoy the cool mountain air, was virtually destroyed when massive clouds of hot ash from Mt. Merapi descended over it. The remaining huge piles of stones and volcanic ash and the destroyed infrastructure quickly became a popular new attraction as well.

These disasters also disclosed some of the local politics internal to tourism. The low position that guides occupy in the hierarchy, for example, became particularly clear in the case of the Prambanan temple complex. Although UNESCO rapidly sent experts to assess the damage, it took a long time before the people working at the site were informed about the recovery plans.[17] After the assessment, a newly built viewing platform (very similar to the ones erected after 11 September 2001 around Ground Zero in New York) allowed tourists to see the main temples from a safe distance, without being allowed to enter them (Figure 17). PT Taman Wisata, the state-owned enterprise managing the park, decided not to lower the entrance fees (US$10 for foreigners). Anticipating tourist complaints, many local travel agencies decided to suspend tours to Prambanan. The few tourists who still visited the temple complex did not want the service of a local guide (approximately US$5) because they knew that they could not get near the main temples anyway. This left the Prambanan guides in a very precarious situation. Some of the security guards in charge of protecting the site offered foreign tourists the opportunity to enter the damaged main complex anyway, in exchange for sizable amounts of cash. The on-site guides knew about these practices but preferred to keep quiet.

The disasters became breeding grounds for new narratives and tourist imaginations. Visually confronted by the damage caused by the quake, tourists tended to ask for much more information about it. In Prambanan, the on-site guides replaced the flashy 'Take a guide with you for a better visit' sign at the entrance by a

**FIGURE 17** • *Dealing with Disaster*

more sober message: 'Announcement: Please consider taking a guide. U help also the victims of the catastrophic earthquake. Thank for your attention. Head of the Prambanan Guide Association' (Figure 17). These new signs gave guides a chance to complain about the little aid the central government was giving to the affected families—a mere US$9 per month for 'living costs'. While walking around the closed main compound, guides did not always mention to tourists that the rubble they saw had not been caused by the earthquake but was simply the ruins of smaller temples that had never been restored. In addition, the large photographic panel 'Prambanan Temple before and after the "Gempa"' (I, quake), on display inside the temple park, made the imagined impact of the recent quake all the more dramatic. Inspired by folk disaster theories, guides were also given a good excuse to entertain their clients with endless tales about the legendary Queen of the South Sea, and her troubled relations with the current sultan. This kind of narrative circulates widely every time a disaster strikes in the area (Schlehe 1996). According to these stories, the earthquake was the result of an escalating conflict between the Queen of the South Sea and the sultan, in which the Queen's anger stemmed from the sultan's refusal to take her as his second wife (polygamy used to be common in the sultanate). A related hypothesis interpreted the quake as the Queen's protest against the proposed national antipornography legislation (which would prohibit some age-old Javanese rituals).[18] In such narratives, Mbah Marijan, the seventy-nine-year-old spiritual gatekeeper of Mt. Merapi, arose as a new hero and protector of Javanese tradition because he openly challenged the authority of the sultan regarding the evacuation of the villagers living on the mountain's slopes (Marshall 2008).

The tourists would have no way of knowing that some of these guiding narratives served as a criticism in disguise against the sultan and his agenda of rapid regional modernization. Over the last couple of years, the sultan (who is also the governor of the province) has endorsed the construction of shopping malls. He claims the malls, which he and his entourage co-own, will stimulate regional economic growth. Traditionalists, however, argue the malls obstruct the spiritual line between the sea (south) and the volcano (north), and they claim that while his divine mandate is to protect the cradle of Javanese culture, the sultan is actually destroying Jogja's heritage.[19] The northern and southern powers show their disagreement and the sultan does not have enough spiritual authority to negotiate a truce. Here again, guides were very careful in how they framed their opinions.

Postearthquake reflections at the Sultan's Palace:
Y60. G: The two buildings with six pillars came down.
    T: Will they [the sultan's family] rebuild it?
    G: Maybe … [silence]
    T: If they can pay five thousand servants, they can also reconstruct it!
    G: No, no, the servants are not being paid to work much, just to do the RATP [tourists laughing].[20] The servants haven't much to do around the palace. RATP means *reste assis, t'es payé* (F; remain seated, you are being paid).

In this comment, the guide expresses disapproval for the ways the palace is managing its budget. Many servants are paid to do virtually nothing, while the guides are paid less to work harder. The calamities facilitated this type of critical commentary, allowing for the business-as-usual guiding narratives and practices to take on new dimensions.

Commentary during a village tour at a brick maker industry (after the quake):
Y61. Brick makers, now, they have a good business he [laughing]. Ya, after the earthquake!

This comment served to entertain the clients but also relieved the guide from accumulated stress. The tourists did not know she too had lost her house and some of her relatives in the quake.

## Endangered Species

Whether it was a spate of bad luck or pure coincidence, during the period I was doing research in Arusha, there were volcanic eruptions of Ol Doinyo Lengai, the Maasai Mountain of God, and a long series of earth tremors (which are rare in Tanzania). Fortunately, the region is sparsely populated and there were almost no casualties. As in Indonesia, the spectacular damage caused by the eruptions became an attraction in and of itself and almost a standard item on the to-do list for people visiting Lake Natron. The more serious and growing danger in northern Tanzania is of a different kind, smaller in scale compared to the Indonesian natural disasters, but potentially more threatening to tourism because directly affecting tourists: the increasing number of violent and armed crimes in which tourists and their guides are victims. During my stay, I became aware of various cases of brutal violence.

In February 2007, armed bandits ambushed a safari car with five tourists, their driver-guide and a cook at a remote border of the Ngorongoro Conservation Area. The robbers, who were brandishing AK-47 assault rifles, forced the guide to park in the bush a few meters away from the main road before ordering everybody to lie down and then robbed them of money, bank documents, passports, mobile phones, cameras and other valuables. Park rangers and police officers later recovered most of the stolen items. Commentators were quick to identify the culprits as strife-torn Somalia bandits believed to have entered the country illegally, reminding locals of 1998, when bandits from Somalia terrorized tourists and villagers in the area's neighbouring wildlife parks, killing at least a dozen people. A similar confrontation occurred several weeks later in an adjacent district with a group of budget travellers who were looking for a safe place to camp.

In March 2007, armed bandits attacked one British and four US tourists and their tour guide near Lake Duluti during broad daylight. One tourist was shot in the stomach, another in the knee. They were then robbed of their money and personal belongings. The seriously wounded tourists were airlifted to a hospital in Nairobi, Kenya, where their condition stabilized after treatment (although one pregnant woman lost her foetus). The tour guide, who had been shot in the head and leg, died of his injuries in a hospital in the nearby city of Moshi. This horrible incident irked President Kikwete, who happened to be on an official tour of the Arusha region at the time. The regional police commander, who was accompanying the president on his tour, had to rush back to his office in order to supervise the operation, where, following an alleged tip-off, his team arrested six suspects within hours. According to the *Guardian* (a national newspaper published in Dar es Salaam), the police 'arrested six people at a witch doctor's house'. The six were 'undergoing some rituals at the home of alleged witch doctor Juma Shaban Juma … believed to be a specialist in dispensing "invulnerability charms" needed to protect armed robbers from being captured by law enforcers'. Because the incident involved two people from Manhattan, the story appeared in the *Daily News* (New York) and was also taken up by the Reuters news agency and distributed globally. Reliable local sources told me the whole story about the witch doctor was made up by the police, because they felt pressured by the president's presence to resolve the case quickly. In reality, the police had no idea who was behind the brutal attack and simply rounded up innocent youngsters. Desperate to obtain information, they also incarcerated and mistreated the surviving guide (who was already heavily traumatized by the death of the apprentice guide).

That same week, bandits dressed in traffic police uniforms put a false roadblock in the middle of the Arusha-Dodoma highway (near the entrance gate of Tarangire National Park), ambushing a number of cargo and small vehicles coming from either side. Each time, the robbers ordered all passengers to lie on the ground facing downwards. They then stripped them and stole whatever they had, ransacking the cars for more goods from their luggage—mobile phones, wristwatches, jewellery and money. Having accomplished their mission, they ordered the victims to proceed peacefully with their journey. The government announced a special joint operation between the army and additional security forces to hunt down the armed thugs, most of them believed to be (again) Somalis conspiring with locals. The president himself appealed to the Arusha residents to assist the security forces in identifying the well-connected and syndicated networks of criminals. He called on the people to stop immediately harbouring the Somali bandits.

These incidents happened during the low season. When similar things happen during the tourism high season, however, the tourism service industry and authorities do everything possible to prevent the bad news from spreading. In July 2007, bandits dressed as Maasai and armed with wooden clubs and machetes broke into a (Maasai-style) luxury lodge on the Manyara escarpment. Around midnight, they forced their way into two bungalows, stole money, cameras and passports. When some of the sleeping tourists did not react quickly enough, they were seriously beaten. The usual strategy of silencing worked well, however, and the conventional international news media did not report on this incident. However, one eyewitness posted the news on the TripAdvisor website and from there it was copied onto the Fodor's Travel Talk Forum and other travellers' websites. The lodge manager, understanding the power of the Internet and its globally sharing virtual communities, was quick to post a reply, detailing the security measures that had been taken since the assault. Other incidents include pedestrian mugging and robberies, sometimes accompanied by violence or the threat of violence, often on the street or in private bars in Arusha. Accidents involving wildlife, such as the case of the leopard attack mentioned earlier (note 10) or wild animals colliding with vehicles, do occur but are rare. Many of these incidents are mentioned in the Tanzania travel advisories of Western countries. Tanzanian tour guides frequently discuss the increased violence and the negative effects it may have on the booming tourism sector. For obvious reasons, the topic is silenced during the guide-guest encounter. Guides would rather not see tourists become an endangered species.

## Clash of Imaginaries

Tourism can be seen as an ideological framing of history, nature and tradition, a framing that has the power to shape culture and nature to its own needs. Tourism products are the result of several materializations, translations and displacements in which discourses or words are not the only agents. Yet, it would be oversimplistic to consider tourism merely to be an exogenous force, or to assess its effects as either good or bad. Glocal ethnographic research, like the one at hand, helps us to move beyond studies of the one-sided impact of global industries on people to more complex analyses of the ways in which cultures develop during the dynamic process of making use of tourism to define their own identities. Local factors and agents play an important role in mediating global processes. Instead of passively accepting their predicament, people can be proactive and resistant, as they constantly negotiate and contest the direction of tourism development (Figure 16).

Processes of meaning making in international tourism are thus deeply grounded in relations of power. Who represents what, whom and how are critical and often contested issues (Morgan and Pritchard 1998; Mowforth and Munt 2008). Tourism imaginaries and discourses are primary factors in the contest over power, recognition and survival in a world where the logic of unbridled economic globalization can only be fought with the tools it has helped create (Chatelard 2005). Any in-depth analysis of tourism reveals that power works in many directions and at many levels. The roles of all parties involved are highly complex and involve discursive power relations as well as performative resistance, that is an intricate micro-macro relationship of what Giddens (1984) calls 'structure and agency'. The examples discussed in this chapter show that all stakeholders generally hold and wield some kind of power through the encounters with other players. These power relations are enacted through micropractices and discursive structures. Tourism representations carry considerable ideological and political freight. As they cross borders, people remain relatively free to rework them and attach meaning to them. Whether guiding practices and local metadiscourses are hegemonic or strategies, or are tactics of resistance is a function of the confluence and conflicts between the many overlapping fields of power (Feldman 2007). And although the nature of their engagement may vary, such attempts to (re)produce tourism fantasies are not straightforward matters of 'telling and showing', but entail 'complex negotiation between guides' self-positioning, that of their organization, the particular genre of tourism involved, the audience and the site itself' (MacDonald 2006: 136).

The interactive service work that guides perform is shaped by a complex mixture of company-imposed mandates, customer demands, peer scrutiny and self-subordination. In this context, the tension between guides and local people is understandable. Guides were not democratically elected to act as unofficial ambassadors of a culture, city, region or country, just as (it is interesting to note) diplomats who officially represent their own country to a foreign sovereign, government or international organization are also not elected by their constituencies (and in some democracies, can be rather arbitrary). Few local guides express the wish to act as representatives of the public interest, but rather have more personal motivations (chapter 4). Some of these aspirations are shared by other people, who also dream of becoming 'modern' and cosmopolitan, two desirable characteristics that would demonstrate their success in the accumulation of symbolic capital and increase their social status.

A microanalysis of the encounter between tourists, mediators and tourates reveals that the tourism meeting ground is not only one between people, but also between their ideas and sociocultural imaginaries. Whereas this encounter in developing countries seems to provide tourists a possibility to rediscover an imagined (premodern) past, it also gives local people a means to generate aspirations and creative possibilities for the (modern) future. Thus, just as tourism imaginaries have a tendency to essentialize the Other, the people in Jogja and Arusha have a tendency to essentialize tourists and the mythical 'West' they come from.[21] And while the movement of ideas across space certainly provides opportunities for the imaginative construction of possible lives, this process is always shaped by local values and norms. The presence of affluent Western tourists prompts yearnings for change based on an illusionary imaginary of the Western good life, but it also produces tensions between local projects. Locals consider African tourists in Arusha or Asian tourists in Jogja, somewhat jealously, as sociocultural proxies who have (materially) made it in their lives and are able to realize their dreams of exploring Other worlds. The fact that these quickly expanding groups of new clients devotedly embrace their role of nouveau riche by being much more de-manding with respect to service personnel leads to a whole different set of power dynamics that falls outside the scope of this book (Salazar 2008a).

Weiss notes that 'lived worlds distinctly situated as they may be throughout the globalized world are increasingly constructed through fantasies and fabri-cations that must first be imagined in order to be realized' (2002: 96). On a day-to-day basis, people in Jogja and Arusha must negotiate the problem of de-velopment and modernity, and they often do so through imaginative engage-ments with global culture and tourism. Increased transnational mobilities and new means of communication enable them to desire the signs and styles of a global order, while facing ever-narrower means by which to satisfy them. Highly desired cultural goods may only be accessed within particular spaces, and that isolation often creates struggles over the right to imagine possible futures. This leads people to produce 'fantastic geographies' (Weiss 2002: 100), exhilarating possibilities for personal betterment that are unrealizable by the vast majority of people as anything but possibilities.

Imagination for people in Jogja and Arusha is an essentially creative act that facilitates their ability to move beyond structural imbalances of power and eco-nomic constraints. It is not simply that the encounter with affluent tourists cre-ates a false belief among locals, imaginatively bridging the gap between their desires and economic realities. The process of imagination also allows them to contemplate the gap between them and tourists in ways that do not necessarily imply success or failure. In sum, even as imaginaries and practices of modernity are developing in different sites around the globe and are in dialogue with one another, they do not always, as Ong (1999: 53) suggests, challenge Western hege-mony. Power on the microlevel does not automatically bring about change on the macrolevel. Remember the paradox I discussed in chapter 4. In Jogja and Arusha, people dependent on tourism can only create a distinctively modern and cosmo-politan habitus by not criticizing the global tourism system and its premodern representational fantasies all too openly.

# 7
# COMING HOME

$\sim$

I just want to tell you the story about me being a guide to Borobudur for the first
time. The first woman I drove, who also gave me a tip of 100,000 Rupiah, was Eve.
It was a good and surprising experience for me. To go to Borobudur, a far away
journey, made me a little bit afraid at first. Just me, only a girl, and that woman.
But that doesn't really matter. During the journey, I have a good talk with the
woman. She's so calm and I can discuss anything with her; it makes it a joyful
journey. It is not really a boring trip because along the way I make lots of new
friends. Even until now, I still maintain a good connection with them ... A very
exciting journey. We finish at Borobudur in the evening and suddenly Eve tells
me that she wants to buy some Indonesian videos for her friends. She lets me
drive her around until night. We go to Gramedia and Mirota Batik. And, the
surprising thing is, she gives me a 100,000 Rupiah tip. Of course, this is too
much for me. For driving, I also receive a tip. Phuf, how important tips are!

And, what surprises me most is that Eve later sends me a picture of our journey.
Surprising because I didn't expect too much from exchanging our addresses.
I thought, like Ningsih had told me before, that 'foreigners just like to exchange
e-mail addresses and home addresses but there's no action following after it. We
just collect e-mails, nothing more or less'. I simply adopted this assumption from
my seniors, Ningsih and Putri. But now, I must admit I'm wrong. I suddenly
received a letter from Europe. When I opened it, there were two photographs
inside. One is a nice picture of me and the other is Eve, in Telaga Warna I
think. This was very touching, really! Immediately, I searched for her address,
but could not find it. That's very bad of me, really, because I wanted to send her
an e-mail thanking her for the pictures. I was really, really wrong about that
assumption. They [foreign tourists] can be very nice actually ...
—Hawa (tour guide trainee, Yogyakarta)

Eve, like so many other tourists, had a fantastic holiday on Java. This was partly
thanks to the flexibility and kindness of Hawa, her driver and guide-to-be in and
around Jogja. Most likely, Eve is spreading the word among relatives and friends
that, despite the almost constant stream of negative Indonesian imagery in the
media, Java is truly a Garden of Eden. For Hawa, the encounter with Eve was
momentous in a number of ways: Apart from earning good money, it gave her

a unique chance to practice her intercultural communication, social networking and guiding skills.[1] To her surprise, it also created a personal connection, a link that became material when Hawa received pictures from Eve, making tangibly real her daydream of what she imagines to be paradise on earth, Europe. We can criticize the overcommercialised tourism system for a variety of reasons, but tourism does create cross-cultural bonds between people, often temporary, sometimes lasting.[2] Tourism creates relations in a world hitherto unconnected, creating a new expanding universe. Connections are made and unmade that reach beyond the specificity of time and place. It is a common story, one I was told repeatedly in Jogja and Arusha (Figure 19).

## Glocalization

> The study of tourism, and the management of it, demands that it be seen as an extended field of relationships, not readily disentangled from one another, not easily sorted … into clear-cut and exclusive, opposing categories: host and visitor, inside and outside, local and global, we and they, here and there.
> —Clifford Geertz (1997: 20)

In all its fluidity and multidimensionality, tourism not only embodies border-crossing physical mobilities but relates also to the imagination, to social contexts and to the process of making sense of practices (or performances) and places. There is a striking complicity and circularity in the relationship between international tourism and (neoliberal) globalization. They are inseparable from one another, as hybrid parts of the same set of processes. The set is 'hybrid because it is made up of an assemblage of technologies, texts, images, social practices and so on that *together* enable it to expand and to reproduce itself across the globe' (Urry 2002: 144). On the one hand, this leads to global integration and homogenization, which are given tangible form via the standardization of tourism training, service and hospitality standards. This book describes in detail how local tour guides in destinations as diverse as Jogja and Arusha are dealing with standardized planned curricula (chapter 3) and converging professional roles, rules and regulations (chapter 5).

At the same time, international tourism encourages tourists to believe that the very act of travel and the encounter with cultural Others guarantees both a broadened cosmopolitan horizon—itself a fashionable commodity—and greater intercultural understanding (Molz 2005; Swain 2009). While this stimulates local differentiation and the resurgence of (ethnic) identities within and between nation-states, it also leads to conflicting discourses of cultural and natural heritage (chapter 6). Tourism marketing shrewdly exaggerates difference while neglecting and obfuscating the power of commonality. For tourism to propagate itself, peoples and cultures must remain 'Othered'. Such othering helps distinguish between home and away, or known and unknown. What causes such boundary-creating imaginaries to move around the globe? Urban writes that 'whatever is in motion tends to remain in motion unless something else stops it' (2001: 15). This observation has been made implicitly by many other scholars, notably by the early diffusionists, for whom invention was understood as arduous, copying as easy. Reproduction processes, however, are rarely without negotiation and resig-nification (Schwenkel 2006: 9); more often, they are cases of (re)entextualization rather than mere replication.[3] The current circulation of tourism discourses and imaginaries is, in many respects, an ongoing translocal process involving vari-ously situated actors and their glocal engagements with tourism to (re)produce 'stereotypic images, discredited histories, and romantic fantasies' (Bruner 2005: 76). Rather than mere projections, these transactions are mediated in various ways and both restrict the lives of people and create new subject positions.

Analyzing the global circulation of images and ideas of tourism and seeking to determine the local dynamics of this process is a complicated matter. Imaginar-ies quickly become the symbolic objects of a significant contest over economic supremacy, territorial ownership and identity. In some destinations, tourism imaginaries are so firmly established and all-encompassing that they are difficult to escape. In other places, tourismifying images and ideas are much more diffuse and open to changes (Bruner 2005; Picard 1996). This book shows that imaginar-ies never travel spontaneously and independently but need agency.[4] Tourism 'in-volves networked orderings of people, natures, materials, mobilities and cultures; production as well as consumption of those different elements' (Jóhannesson 2005: 141). As actor-network theory stresses, everything circulating within such networks is continuously 'translated', deformed and modified (Latour 2005).

While tourism has torn down certain borders, it has also erected new boundar-ies (Salazar 2006b). Perhaps more than any other glocal practice, tourism demon-strates, in the absence of a clearly identifiable hegemonic power, the importance of multiple centres from which people, ideas and capital circulate across the globe and interact dialectically with local circumstances. The inequalities entrenched in in-ternational tourism between tourists, tourism intermediaries and tourates serve as a reminder that boundaries do not exist naturally but are made in social practices. Therefore, beyond merely acknowledging the fact that power relations in tourism operate on different levels (chapters 5 and 6), it is also necessary to theoretically link those levels. As I explained in the introductory chapter, there are serious ana-lytical weaknesses if we stress local, national, regional or global power dynamics separately, while an ethnographic approach combining vertical (local-to-global) and horizontal (multisited) scaling offers many possibilities in this respect.

Anthropologists are well placed to draw attention to the multiplicity, specific-ity and mobility of the tourism structures, discourses and imaginaries that sustain real communities and ways of life, put into place or emerging as part of the practices of everyday life. In the context of international tourism, such orientation recommends increased analytical attention to the role of brokers or mediators, of the guides, interpreters, travel agents, accommodation providers, government agencies at all levels and international organizations that are prominent in tourism development. This book exemplifies how a combination of discourse-centred and grounded ethnographic analysis allows us to go beyond mere description and unpack some of the mechanics behind these complex processes.

## Image the Local, Imagine the Global

A party of elderly Americans—from their conversation I gather they are day-trippers from Malindi—is sitting at a nearby table drinking Cinzano. They are accompanied by a 'guide' … She [one of the tourists] turned toward the guide, exuding goodwill and sympathy. 'Would you like to travel abroad one day and see how other people live?' … The guide stares wildly toward the sea. Everyone around the table is smiling relentlessly at him. 'Maybe, though, you wouldn't like it in our country. Where I come from, it's full of noise and busy people. Hurry, hurry, hurry. That's how it is in my country. You wouldn't like that, would you?' The guide, all too willing to please but not knowing precisely what is expected of him, alternately nods and shakes his head.
–Shiva Naipaul (1979: 179)

With studies like the one at hand, there is an inherent danger of moving from global questions to globalizing answers. A multisited approach, however, reveals that local tour guides working in international tourism operate under very dissimilar circumstances across sites, but also within a single destination. At the same time, the comparison between guides in Jogja and Arusha does reveal some striking commonalities (Salazar 2007). For one, their lives are entangled with local-to-global connections, connections that are not imaginary but tangibly real. A holistic analysis of tour guiding thus gives us an entry into some of the inner dynamics of border-crossing mobilities. This book reveals the Janus-faced role and liminal positionality of local guides. On the one hand, they act as mechanics of glocalization, performing partially as actors of hegemonic forces well beyond their reach. They are part of an expansive but loosely structured system of global tourism that represents peoples and places in predefined and scripted ways—ways that are rooted in discursive hegemonies of colonialism and orientalism as well as in the commoditization of the past. Tour guides are instrumental in tourism because they provide the system with not only a local but also a human face—giving them an advantage over technological competitors such as virtual, audio or mobile guides. I call them *mechanics of glocalization* because they are usually well skilled and have to labour hard to mirror fashionable tourism imaginaries while guiding, selling and telling a message that is not their own and performing under conditions they cannot completely determine. Their project is one of glocalization rather than globalization, because localizing the global and globalizing the local is what international tourism is all about.

Yet, guiding involves more than simply rehashing memorized seductive screenplays, learned through formal or informal 'seducation' (chapter 3). The interactive nature of the guide-guest encounter can lead to results unanticipated by those crafting tourism (marketers, governments, etc.). Various meanings are communicated and negotiated, and personal responses, commitments and rules have to be accepted. On tour, guides mediate not only cultural differences but also the interests and imaginations of a variety of stakeholders, and, like ethnographic fieldwork, guiding is always to some extent improvised, creative and spontaneous, in this way defying complete standardization. While guides perform scripted roles, having a variety of puppeteers manipulating their moves (e.g., tour operators, authorities at various levels and law enforcement), they are not like shadow puppets with little or no control over their own performances. Narrating and enacting tourism fantasies can be liberating because it offers a small window of opportunity to undermine the structures of tourism power while reifying them. And if guides sometimes have to act like puppets, they commonly choose the role of Semar, the Javanese wayang character acting like a clown, but who is in fact very wise (think of the example of pun-loving Pak Padmo in chapter 4, who uses humour to showcase his vast cosmopolitan knowledge).[5]

An ethnographic and discourse-centred analysis of guiding practices shows how the content (tourism imaginaries) can become detached from the container (the guide), illustrating that tour guiding is not just a joke perpetuated by ignorant locals, but possibly also a play on intercultural othering, with the tour guides othering the tourists, the tourates and sometimes themselves. This is most evident in the small talk that takes place in between stretches of guiding narrative and in the metadiscursive comments guides transmit while guiding (chapters 4 and 6). While tourism is often characterized by exoticized holiday package products, moving beyond an imaginary that is blind to whom the Other really is, is still a possibility that tourism offers for intercultural personal growth. The exchange taking place between local guides and tourists is an example of a face-to-face interpersonal relation that crosses territorial and cultural boundaries. Tourists can be transformed by these experiences, even though not all of them necessarily seek understanding (Bruner 1991).[6] In the end, the guides undergo long-term changes through the encounters, far more than the other way around. Whereas the role of mechanic of glocalization primarily serves the tourists, guides are able to use their privileged contact with foreigners to nourish their dreams of escape from the harsh local life and to enhance their imaginative cosmopolitan mobility or cosmobility. They do not physically travel abroad, giving the traditional idea of cosmopolitanism a new meaning (cf. Notar 2008). However, no matter how hard they try to be cosmopolitan, tourists continue seeing them as 'local', in part because their own need to represent the local creates a kind of economically driven denial of mobility.[7]

While from a tourist perspective, a local guide may be perceived as an effective figure of mediation—often a hybrid—he or she is likely to be seen quite differently by local people (chapter 6). Guides have to learn to make tours meaningful for tourists, for tourates and for themselves. They have to find a manageable equilibrium between spatial (local-to-global) as well as temporal (past-present-future) tensions. This involves not necessarily a hybrid social persona but rather the qualities of a chameleon, readily adapting roles to changing circumstances and interests. Various schemas of identity and identification are at work while guiding. These involve the construction of imaginations of not only the Other but also of oneself. The fact that guides are complicit in the (re)production of tourism imaginaries does not necessarily manufacture a resistive consciousness. Their practices are survival strategies rather than real weapons of resistance.[8] As guides realize, the most realistic chance of improving their quality of life is by becoming successful in their profession. Paradoxically, their dreams of moving forward and upward—becoming more cosmobile (and more modern and Western)—can only materialize if they represent to tourists the life world in which they live as developing little or not at all. In order to do so fruitfully, they need to constantly (mis)translate culture and (re)negotiate positions and imaginaries.

As this book has shown repeatedly, tour guides often function as a mirror through which we can learn something about anthropologists, too. The latter tend to have little insight into, or power over, the multiple ways that ethnographic knowledge is commoditized via the language of tourism (where it is thinly dressed up in discourses of cultural conservation and ecotourism) or in the creation of 'anthropological heritage' (Hitchcock 2004). More studies are necessary to explore not just the production of ethnographic representations, but the consumption and circulation of these representations beyond the academy. This has become all the more urgent in a time when technological advances allow for much speedier circulation, manipulation and contestation of ethnographic findings. Ethnographic subjects and others increasingly talk back, and rightly so. Moreover, with more people travelling wide and far, one could argue that local tour guides have taken over some of the culture brokering anthropologists did when much of their authority was derived from 'having been there'. What is the role and responsibility of anthropologists when nonanthropologists in the world out there (mis)apply their old and new theories?

## *Imagine All the People, Living for Today*

Indonesia, as part of the Far East, also conjures up images of the smell of incense, mysterious practices, dark back streets and something we may all be looking for

175

individually: our Shangri-La. Indonesia is all that and much more. You may find
your Shangri-La here (well, at least there are several five-star Shangri-La hotels),
the romance, the fiction, the dream. You may also find the mysticism and the
mystery that is associated with the Far East. But whatever you see and experience, Indonesia is a modernizing and developing country. We still have the
rice fields, fortunately, but almost half of the population now lives in urban
centres. We have our young democracy, but also our struggles. We have
mysticism, but also a huge debt burden to international creditors.
–Chris Soebroto (2004: 7)

This ethnography inscribes itself in a larger field of research that tries to come to
grips with how people imagine the world and how the world is imag(in)ed for
them, for instance through tourism. Anthropologists are well placed to examine
and comment on such complex issues. In several ways, anthropology is betwixt
and between—'between theory and practice, general and particular, global and
local, historical sweep and present fixation, academic understanding and activ-
ism or advocacy' (Knauft 2006: 425). It is the anthropologist's fate to be always
between things: countries, languages, cultures, even realities. As Rabinow writes,
'We live in-between … cosmopolitan insider's outsiders of a particular historical
and cultural world' (1986: 258). Yet this liminal positioning is attuned to understanding the fluid reality in which we live, more so than the boundary-driven
thinking that is so common in other disciplines. Boas and Malinowski already
showed how this in-betweenness, with constant methodological and theoretical
boundary crossings, is the most fruitful level of grounded and innovative ethnographic analysis. And such holistic ethnographies are always in the making, never
finished. These experiences transform us, changing our conceptions of who we
are, what we know and how we live in the world (Stoller 2008).

Anthropology helps us understand how phenomena grouped under the heading of globalization are often complex and paradoxical. We should not forget that
in between the local and global there are the important scales of nation-states and
regional blocs. At the same time, it is important not to conflate international or
interregional phenomena with transnational or transregional issues and events.
The national is certainly not disappearing in the context of tourism, although
its authority is challenged both from above and below (chapters 2 and 5). In the
international tourism market, dream destinations are still sold as countries.[9] Local tour guides are expected to play the role of unofficial ambassadors of national
ideologies, even if countries such as Indonesia or Tanzania have little means to
enforce and control how this is done (chapter 5). In any case, anthropologists
should pay more attention to the growing power of regional blocs over national
as well as global processes. Regional associations such as ASEAN or APEC and
EAC or SADC play increasingly important roles in the development of Indonesia
and Tanzania respectively. It remains to be seen whether regionalization indicates
the erosion of individual states or is a way by which nation-states may secure their

future by pooling sovereignty and resources. At any rate, the predicted growth of intraregional tourism—1.2 billion intraregional arrivals per year by 2020 (WTO 2001)—will seriously change the tourism landscape in Indonesia and, maybe to a lesser extent, in Tanzania.

Recognizing pluriversality, anthropology can track the ways cultural representations, once in circulation, recursively help to remediate unequal social conditions. Globally circulating imaginaries provide people with frames for imagining themselves in relation to larger national, regional or even global worlds (Figure 18). To glocalize imaginings requires attention to the agents and distinctive legacies that forge their distinctive differences. What people desire others (i.e., tourists) to think animates and defines them, how they want themselves to be seen and imagined. We need to retain a clear idea about the chief interest groups behind the image making in tourism and avoid the mistake of seeing imaginaries as just a range of possibilities. However, as Glover notes, 'distinguishing definitively between intermediaries and consumers in the present context is impossible' (2008: 113). Tourism imaginaries are the coproduct of tourates, mediators and tourists, and these different stakeholder groups are simultaneously intermediaries and consumers. Besides, 'the process of co-production … is no straight-forward affair. It is heteroglossic, and its (continuous) outcome is the result of the relationship between the different groups involved' (Glover 2008: 113).

Our failure to understand how imaginaries and mobilities are embedded within local, national, regional and global institutions of power restricts our ability to determine the underlying forces that restrict some mobile practices, and not others, some imaginings, and not others, and that make possible new hegemonies in new fields of power. Even if many imaginaries have a distinctively Western genealogy, we have to be careful not to exaggerate their co-

**FIGURE 18** • *Dreaming of Cosmopolitanism through Education and Tourism*

herence and consistency and to give more agency and autonomy to those represented, because the imaginative flow has certainly not been a one-way street. Multisited research shows how hard it is to come up with overarching theories because the ways global processes interact locally are always different. Besides, this book shows how people not only react to supralocal forces but how they also have a role in shaping them (though some more than others). With such agency comes responsibility (cf. Bunten 2008). At the same time, many people fail to fully grasp the supralocal factors that shape their lives, and the fragments they do grasp tend to be seen through localized lenses.

## Decapitalizing the "Other"

> So much of who we are is where we have been.
> –William Langewiesche (author; 1955– )

> Too often travel, instead of broadening the mind, merely lengthens the conversation.
> –Elizabeth Drew (journalist; 1935– )

Being a citizen of the world implies, so theory tells us, the possession of a cultural disposition, which is not limited to constraints of locality, but recognizes a certain global belonging, openness to the diversity of cultures, and a preparedness to understand and respect cultural perspectives of Others (Figure 19). While appeals to global citizenship are fundamental to the ideology of globalism and the mythology of neoliberal globalization, very few people give evidence of the intensification of their consciousness of the world as a whole (Kennedy 2007). The opportunities for such cross-cultural exposure, learning and practice present themselves today as never before (Vertovec and Cohen 2002). Can or does exposure to other cultures—through people, objects, images or ideas—make people more cosmopolitan?

The idea of cosmopolitanism is based on a desire for mutuality that, paradoxically, starts from the assumption that people(s) are different. As detailed in the scholarly literature, travel and tourism provide a stage upon which to act out the binaries by which we make sense of and order the world (Minca and Oakes 2006). However, a fine-grained analysis of local tour-guide discourses and practices reminds us that it is not the mere act of travelling or the geographical places visited that help people figure out whom they are and the Other is. Rather, it is what happens psychologically within the traveller or tourism worker and interactionally between them that deconstructs or reifies the neat binaries modernity presents us with (Salazar 2006b). In this sense, international tourism both thrives on the magnification of existing boundaries of 'Otherness' (diversity and difference) as it provides a small window of opportunities to tear down those same

FIGURE 19 • *We Are All Alike . . . or Not?*

divisions and to (re)discover the mutuality that unites every human being on this planet.

Many of the local guides I met in Jogja and Arusha have developed a personal repertoire of multicultural competence and experience. They substantiate the idea that cosmopolitanism is by no means a privilege of the rich and well connected (although, it may be true that the guides might be richer and more connected than many other people around them). Furthermore, they prove that physical or spatial mobility is not a necessary condition to become cosmopolitan. Their experiences confirm that travel signifies not only a physical movement across lands and cultures but also an imaginative journey in which wonderment about those who live differently makes it possible to see the world differently. Their 'glocalized cosmopolitanism' involves 'the capacity to live simultaneously in both the global and the local' (Urry 2003: 137) and the ability to think and feel concurrently beyond and within the local and the national. Close ties to the local are important not only for their personal and family lives, but also for their work as guides (in which they somehow need to keep local culture at a standstill). This goes against the common assumption that cosmopolitanism arises out of location (metropolitan coastal areas), travel and consumption (Notar 2008). Like Notar's ethnic minority café owners in borderland China, the guides I studied have developed cosmopolitan competences '*not* in making their way into other cultures and countries, but in catering to those who make their way to them' (2008: 642) and their cosmopolitanism 'has arisen not out of travel, consumption or metropolitan residence, but out of producing cosmopolitanism for transnational travellers, and increasingly, national tourists' (2008: 615). This production of cosmopolitanism has become their means for mobility, not necessarily spatial but both social and transcultural.

Attention to political economy and power relations, however, reveals that the guides' exposure to foreign people does not necessarily imply an easy blending of cultures. While local guides in developing countries certainly aspire for connections across the globe, their cosmopolitanism is not a universal but a qualified one. The Indonesian and Tanzanian guides who travelled together to Europe in 2002 have gradually lost contact with each other; I talked to most of them during my visits to Jogja and Arusha and immediately felt their nostalgia when they retold the story of their historic trip. They were curious to know how their colleagues in the other country were doing, but they did not feel the need to contact them. On the other hand, most guides were still in touch with Europeans they had met during their stay abroad. Apparently, such 'north-south' links were considered more attractive (because more different and more instrumental?). In other words, their 'dialogue trip' had created new transnational connections, reinforcing ties between old (colonial) centres and peripheries rather than creating new links between Indonesia and Tanzania. Cosmopolitan formations clearly imply constant remixes that reflect the influence of specific power structures in a specific setting at a particular period.

The idea that people worldwide are developing a consciousness, interest and identification with a global world might be on just too big a scale. In countries such as Indonesia or Tanzania, it is already difficult to imagine belonging to a shared region (Southeast Asia and East Africa respectively). International tourism, on the other hand, offers individuals unique opportunities to engage in a living space of transcultural encounter and exchange. While tourism often stands for the commoditization of a unidimensional culture, the exoticization (and, in the case of sex tourism, the eroticization) of contact with the Other along with cosmopolitanisms constructed on the foundation of colonialism and orientalism, it can also create interpersonal relationships that involve genuine intercultural exchanges. These cross-cultural connections 'may provide an important path into globality' (Kennedy 2007: 272), turning distant Others into close others and friends. As Kennedy (2007: 272) writes about such experiences,

> For those individuals involved, it may prove to be a more meaningful and therefore more effective and enduring one than the consciousness of belonging to a common humanity which comes from exposure to the increasing flows of techno, idea, finance, media scapes, consumer brands and images and the multiple visual mobilities which conjure many images of the world through technology and commerce.

However, such relationships are flexible, dynamic and hard to pin down. Studying them is a challenge for anthropologists but can also become the discipline's strength in the quest to unravel the complex dimensions of the current human condition.

## Tentative End of a Journey

> I love to travel, but hate to arrive.
> –Albert Einstein (physicist, 1879–1955)

This book is not a mere case study illustrating or developing theoretical points about globalization, transnationalism or cosmopolitanism in the context of tourism and tour guiding. Rather, it was the ethnographic approach itself, grounded in daily life, which allowed me to tack back and forth between data and theory, bringing them into dialogue. All ethnographies of global issues should be analytically glocal, paying attention to the circulation of people, objects or ideas as well as to the institutional and personal domains that standardize but also localize them. People and places are continually coproduced in 'the awkward, unequal, unstable, and creative qualities of interconnection across difference' (Tsing 2005:

4). Above all, what this book shows is 'how much more thinking, and how much more empirical social research, remains to be done before we can really understand a globalization that divides the planet as much as it unites it' (Ferguson 2006: 49). No, not everything is connected, and not everything changes ...

*    *    *

Since I have left Jogja and Arusha, life has continued unabated. In Jogja, there seems to be no end to the series of disasters. There are still regular tremors and occasional earthquakes, the region has not been spared from global health pandemics (e.g., avian influenza and swine flu), and a spectacular plane crash at Adisucipto International Airport in 2007 led EU authorities to ban all Indonesian airlines from entering European skies (a ban partially lifted in 2009). People in Jogja remain optimistic that they will be able to change the tides, however; and as part of the Visit Indonesia 2008 promotional campaign (extended into 2009), direct flights from Kuala Lumpur to Jogja were resumed. Unfortunately, the launch of the Visit Indonesia campaign was accompanied by howls of protest because its slogan—'Celebrating 100 Years of Nation's Awakening'—contained a grammatical error and its contents were deemed incomprehensible for international tourism markets and Indonesian citizens alike.[10] If tourism is to recover in Jogja, it will be a slow process. In Arusha, on the other hand, the tourism boom seems unstoppable. The political unrest in neighbouring Kenya after the general elections of December 2007, and the official visit of US president George Bush to the country in February 2008 (including Arusha) have given it an even bigger boost. Tourism is becoming the country's leading source of foreign exchange, with nearly triple the annual income accrued from agriculture. The main short-term challenge is to keep rising crime under control. In the long term, environmental degradation may seriously threaten wildlife tourism. The worldwide economic crisis has affected both Indonesia and Tanzania and has brought much uncertainty, especially to those in unstable jobs such as tour guiding.

In the end, this is a study about people, and I keep in touch with many of those I have met along my journey (Figure 20). My Indonesian contacts, spending countless hours in Internet cafés, are constantly pushing me to communicate via social networks such as Facebook and chat through Yahoo Messenger or Skype. Erlis, my Indonesian assistant, finished his master's degree in Regional Development at Gadjah Mada University. After returning from a visit to Hawaii, where his spouse was completing a master's degree at the University of Hawaii, he took up a junior lecturer position in the Faculty of Geography. Hawa, who helped me with street interviews in Jogja, has left her tour guide ambitions temporarily aside to fully concentrate on her Bachelor in Anthropology at Gadjah Mada University and her passion for documentary and ethnographic film. She was selected to participate in an exchange programme with German students and

**FIGURE 20 •** *Ethnographer and Assistant … On the Move*
[Photograph by Steven Demeyer. Used with permission.]

spent six weeks in Freiburg during the summer of 2007. Unfortunately, she had neither the time nor the resources to meet with Eve and thank her in person for the photographs she received. From my contacts in Arusha, I regularly receive e-mails with updates about their lives and work. Joseph, my Tanzanian assistant, finished his diploma in Professional Tour Guiding and Leadership. After taking driving lessons, he quickly found a job as a safari guide for one of Arusha's high-end safari companies.

When my fieldwork in Arusha was nearing its end, my spouse and I decided to invite my assistant Joseph to lunch. We chose Maasai Café, a fine Italian restaurant where a Maasai chef—nothing fake here—prepares the best pizzas in town. The place is extremely popular among the expatriates working for the UN Rwanda Tribunal, just across the street. Joseph felt slightly uncomfortable among the men in suits. He was startled when he heard the Maasai cook, who worked nine years in Italy, fluently speaking Italian to his mixed-blood toddler. Joseph's curious nature made him order a Maasai pizza, one with heaps of meat. By the time the food was served, he had drunk half of his Kilimanjaro beer (no tea or coffee this time) and felt more relaxed. We looked at him expectantly when he took a first bite. This was obviously a new taste experience for Joseph. He kept quiet at first. After having swallowed the food, he lifted up his head, and in his typical radiant smile, concluded: 'I like this'.

# ENDNOTES

## Chapter 1

1. The idea that everything is in constant movement is not new. It was already developed by the ancient Greek philosopher Heraclitus of Ephesus (ca. 540–480 BCE), who became known for his doctrine that change is central to the universe and that 'all things flow'. *Yi Jing* or *Zhouyi* (The Book of Changes), one of the oldest Chinese classic texts (dated ca. 475–403 BCE), conveys a similar notion of a continually changing cosmos.
2. According to the Oxford English Dictionary, *mobility* can mean different things: (1) the ability to move or to be moved; (2) the ease or freedom of movement; and (3) the tendency to change easily or quickly.
3. On mainland Africa, the phenotypic identity of Indonesian settlers quickly disappeared through intermarriage, but on the island of Madagascar, their Malayo-Polynesian language established itself to the point at which it absorbed the later arrivals of Bantu-speaking migrants.
4. Although I dislike the notion of 'developing country' because it has a negative connotation, I prefer this description above terms such as 'preindustrial' or 'underdeveloped' countries (having a clearer undertone of inferiority and backwardness), 'poorer', or 'lower income' countries (referring too much to economic factors alone), countries in 'the South' (geographically incorrect) or the 'Third World' (geopolitically outdated).
5. The imaginary has been conceptualized, for instance, as a culture's ethos or a society's shared, unifying core conceptions (Castoriadis 1987), a fantasy or illusion created in response to a psychological need (Lacan 1977) and a cultural model or widely shared implicit cognitive schema (Anderson 1991; Taylor 2004). For an account of the intellectual history and contemporary uses of the imaginary in anthropology, see Strauss (2006).
6. For comprehensive overviews of anthropologies of globalization, see Appadurai (2001), Eriksen (2003), Inda and Rosaldo (2002, 2007), Kearney (1995), Ong and Collier (2004), and Spindler and Stockard (2007).
7. Exceptions include Sassen (1998) and Tomlinson (1999).
8. It is not my intent to step into the endless conceptual discussion about whether there is a real division between 'global' and 'local' sociocultural phenomena or not. The fact is that many, academics and lay people alike, imagine the contemporary world to be functioning in a way that reifies the contested binary.

9. The glocalization concept is modelled on the Japanese notion *dochakuka* (becoming autochthonous), derived from *dochaku* (aboriginal, living on one's own land). This originally referred to the agricultural principle of adapting farming techniques to local conditions. In the 1980s, the term was adopted by Japanese businesspeople to express global localization or 'a global outlook adapted to local conditions' (Tulloch 1991: 134). The marketing technique of melding the global inside the local spread worldwide.

10. Related, but not identical, concepts used by anthropologists include acculturation, creolization, customization, hybridization, indigenization, mestizaje, mixing, mundialización, pidginization, transculturation and vernacularization.

11. Indonesians seem to be champions in glocalization. Other examples in Yogyakarta include Waroeng Steak and Shake (I, *warung makan,* casual restaurant) and Mr. Burger. These are copycat versions of respectively Steak 'n Shake and Burger King.

12. These official statistics include not only tourists but all international arrivals using tourist visas. This includes a sizable proportion of people (over 50 per cent) who travel for reasons other than leisure, recreation and holidays: business and other purposes such as visiting friends and relatives, religious reasons or pilgrimage and health treatment. Nevertheless, the figures are illustrative of the trend.

13. These industries include, but are not limited to, tour operators, travel agents, accommodation providers, carriers, tourism associations (both NGOs and market-oriented associations), destination organizations (e.g., tourism chambers of commerce) and consultancies.

14. For an overview of anthropologies of tourism, see Nash (1996), Santana (1997), Smith and Brent (2001), Stronza (2001), Graburn (2002), Wallace (2005), Leite and Graburn (2009) and Chambers (2010). Ethnographies of tourism in developing countries are a growing genre (Adams 2006; Bras 2000; Causey 2003; Cole 2008; Crick 1994; Dahles 2001; Ness 2003; Picard 1996; Van den Berghe 1994; Wynn 2007).

15. Urban (2001) makes a similar point about culture in general. According to him, 'culture is not just something that can be represented in metaculture, but something whose very nature—whose existence as thing in the world—is positively affected by that representation' (2001: 38). The circulation of metaculture provides a unique perspective on contemporary processes of globalization.

16. See, among others, Burawoy (2000), Marcus (1998), Merry (2000), Robbins and Bamford (1997) and Tsing (2000).

17. I have elaborated on the method of glocal ethnography and its usefulness for the study of tourism elsewhere (Salazar 2010b).

18. Interestingly, Marcus writes about multisited strategies as 'a research *imaginary* (provocations to alter or experiment with the orientations that govern existing practices) rather than a set of *methods* that are very specifically prescriptive for the conduct of fieldwork and writing' (1998: 6). He defines a research imaginary as 'a sense of the changing presuppositions, or sensibilities … that informs the way research ideas are formulated and actual fieldwork projects are conceived' (1998: 10).

# Chapter 2

1. The World Heritage List includes 890 sites forming part of the cultural and natural heritage that UNESCO considers as having outstanding universal value. The first twelve sites were inscribed in 1978. Thirty years later, the list includes 689 cultural, 176 natural, and 25 mixed sites in 148 countries (2009 data).

2. At Sangiran Early Man Site (a World Heritage Site nearby Solo), fifty fossils of *Meganthropus palaeo* and *Pithecanthropus erectus* ('Java Man', now reclassified as part of the species *Homo erectus*) were found.

3. The Javanese, speakers of the Austronesian language native to the central and eastern parts of the island of Java, are Indonesia's largest ethnic group. According to the 2000 population census, there are approximately 85 million Javanese (of a total Indonesian population numbering over 206 million).

4. During his short time as governor of Java, Raffles led an expedition in 1814 to (re)discover Borobudur and other ancient sites that lay forgotten under volcanic ashes and vegetation (Brown 1983). The Dutch continued the initial excavation work (1835) with a massive restoration project (1905–10). The Prambanan complex, which an officer of the Dutch East India Company had 'discovered' already in 1733, was only cleaned in 1885. Reconstruction work started in 1918 and continued from 1937 until 1953.

5. A *gamelan* is a musical ensemble typically featuring a variety of instruments such as metallophones, xylophones, drums and gongs; bamboo flutes, bowed and plucked strings; vocalists may be included too. *Wayang kulit* is an Indonesian (and especially Javanese) dramatic representation of mythological events in a shadow puppet play.

6. While most Javanese officially profess Islam as their religion, many are followers of Javanese mysticism, a metaphysical search for harmony within one's inner self, connection with the universe and with a supreme being (Geertz 1960; Mulder 2005).

7. Indonesia is home to the world's largest population of Overseas Chinese (nearly 8 million).

8. Two monuments located inside the province, the Yogyakarta Palace Complex (Kraton) and the Ratu Boko Temple Complex, have been on UNESCO's tentative list since 1995.

9. Returning tourism keywords are: ancient, *andong* (horse cart), art, (Southeast) Asian, batik, beautiful, *becak* (cycle rickshaw), Borobudur, civilization, culture, exotic, friendly, gamelan music, handicrafts, history, heritage, hospitable, (classical and contemporary) Javanese dance, Kraton or Sultan's Palace, Malioboro, market, Merapi volcano, old, oriental, Prambanan, Ramayana ballet, refined, rice paddies, ritual ceremonies, sculpture, shadow puppet show or wayang kulit, shopping, silverware, smile, sweet, (Hindu-Buddhist) temples, theatre, tradition, tropical, and *Tamansari* or Water Castle.

10. Said (1994) argued that historical travel practices to the Orient were an integral part of Western imperialist projects. His own 'Orient', though, does not extend much east of the Middle East.

11. The phrase 'Garden of Eden' is often used to describe any peaceful place or a state of perfect happiness or bliss. The genealogy of European representations of islands

has been rooted back to prebiblical descriptions of (happy) islands, descriptions that later merged with biblical visions of Adam and Eve's Garden of Eden and led to the belief in the earthly existence of paradisiacal islands (Delumeau 1995). Throughout European intellectual history, ideas of Eden-like places have been periodically recycled through artworks, literature, pleasure gardens, television series (e.g., *Lost*) and projections into specific geographical spaces. When, in 1891, the Dutch archaeologist Eugène Dubois discovered the first human fossil outside Europe in Trinil (East Java)—the *Pithecanthropus* (now *Homo*) *erectus* or 'Man from Java'—it led to speculation among scholars that Java had been the true Garden of Eden or birthplace of humankind.

12. Examples of these include Rush's *Java, A Traveller's Anthology* (1996), Vatikiotis's *Indonesia: Islands of the Imagination* (2006), Fischer's *Modern Indonesian Art* (1990), Choy's *Indonesia between Myth and Reality* (1976) and Koentjaraningrat's *Javanese Culture* (1985).

13. Garuda Indonesia, the country's national airline, started with regular direct flights to Singapore and Kuala Lumpur in 2004. However, due to low demand, it ceased these connections in 2006. In 2008, the Visit Indonesia Year, Malaysia Airlines and the low-cost company AirAsia started offering direct flights from Kuala Lumpur, while Garuda Indonesia resumed the Yogyakarta–Singapore route.

14. The slogan, based on the handwriting of Sultan Hamengku Buwono X, was developed and launched in 2001 by an Indonesian-based international management-consulting firm.

15. The current sultan, Hamengku Buwono X, was elected as governor of Yogyakarta in 1998. In 2008, his tenure was extended by three years, in a bid to prevent a vacuum of power in the province. The sultan also considered contending in the 2009 presidential race, but his candidacy did not gain wide support.

16. Indonesian is a normative form of Malay, an Austronesian lingua franca used in the archipelago for centuries. The language shows influences from trade and religion (Sanskrit, Mandarin, Arabic and Portuguese), colonization (Dutch) and media, technology and popular culture (mainly English).

17. *Ujamaa* stands for African socialism, the concept that formed the basis of President Nyerere's social and economic development policies in Tanzania after it gained independence from the United Kingdom.

18. The Maasai, speakers of the Eastern Nilotic Maa tonal language, are a widely dispersed group of seminomadic pastoralists and small-scale subsistence agriculturists who occupy arid and semiarid rangelands in southern Kenya and northern Tanzania—collectively known as Maasailand. In Tanzania, they are said to have lived in the Serengeti plains and Ngorongoro highlands for some two centuries. The Arusha people are originally from the foothills of Mt. Meru. Influenced by Maasai ancestry, they still use the Maasai age system and other elements of Maasai social organization. However, they have different clans and abandoned livestock herding in favour of settled cultivation (Spear and Waller 1993). The neighbouring Meru people, who have traditionally been farmers, also settled around the base of Mt. Meru.

19. Although Swahili is a Bantu language in structure and origin, its vocabulary draws on a variety of sources including Arabic, Persian, Portuguese, German and English.

It has become the lingua franca of central and eastern Africa, and one of the working languages of the African Union. In Tanzania, English is the official, primary language of commerce, administration and higher education.

20. Belgium possessed three African colonies between 1908 and 1962. The Belgian Congo had originated as the private property of King Leopold II (Congo Free State, 1885–1908) and was about 76 times larger than Belgium itself. After the First World War, Ruanda-Urundi became a Belgian protectorate by a League of Nations Mandate, later renewed as a UN Trust Territory.

21. In the United States, the tagline was changed into 'Tanzania: Land of Kilimanjaro, Zanzibar and the Serengeti' after the latter was chosen in 2006 as one of the seven New Wonders of the World by *USA Today* and ABC News's *Good Morning America,* an event that received wide attention in the Tanzanian media.

22. Representative examples of documentaries include *Serengeti Shall Not Die* (1959), *People of the Forest: The Chimps of Gombe* (1991) and *Wild Africa* (2001). Influential Hollywood productions are *Hatari!* (1962), *Tarzan* (1966), *The Lion King* (1994) and *George of the Jungle* (1997). *Born Free* (1966), *Out of Africa* (1985) and *Gorillas in the Mist* (1988) are some of the better-known autobiographic films based in East Africa. Books on the region are revealing too, with titles such as Johnson's *Four Years of Paradise* (1941), Ames's *A Glimpse of Eden* (1967), Ricciardi's *Vanishing Africa* (1971), Amin's *Cradle of Mankind* (1985) and Fay's *The Last Place on Earth* (2005).

23. Mbembe (2001) describes in detail how the African native as a prototype of the 'animal' was a creation and object of the colonizer's imagination.

24. Because too many people already know and have seen the Maasai, tour operators are now aggressively promoting visits to the small ethnic group of Hadzabe bushmen of Karatu District (Eastern Rift Valley), portrayed as the last true hunter-gatherers of East Africa.

25. *Safari* is a Swahili term, itself derived from the Arabic *safariya,* meaning overland journey (originally on foot). The British explorer-adventurer Sir Richard Burton (1821–1890) allegedly introduced the word into English. In tourism discourse, safari traditionally referred to a hunting expedition and, since mass tourism, more generally to wildlife tourism.

26. The Convention relative to the Preservation of Fauna and Flora in their Natural State was signed in London on 8 November 1933 by the governments of the Union of South Africa, Belgium, the United Kingdom, Egypt, Spain, France, Italy, Portugal and the Anglo-Egyptian Sudan. It entered into force in 1936.

27. These are all protected area management categories, as defined by the International Union for the Conservation of Nature and Natural Resources (now known as the World Conservation Union).

28. The East African Community had a special subcommittee on tourism. Among the successful ventures were a railway system and a common airline, East African Airways, both of which assisted in the movement of tourist traffic. For a more extensive account of Tanzania's tourism history, see Salazar (2009b).

29. *Tingatinga* is a popular tourist art form of painting in Tanzania (normally using bicycle paint), named after the painter Edward Tingatinga (1932–1972).

30. Whereas Bali is Jogja's tourism rival, the almost mythical islands of Zanzibar are Arusha's fiercest competitor. Moreover, while Malaysia and Singapore receive many more tourists than Indonesia does, the same is true for Kenya when compared to Tanzania. Arusha's largest safari operators actually act as intermediaries for Kenyan companies.

31. Common keywords in Arusha's marketing are: 4X4, adventure, Africa, animals, authentic, baobab tree, beautiful, Big Five, birds, breathtaking, colonial, exotic, extraordinary, fascinating, game drive, grassland, hunting, hut, Kilimanjaro, landscape, lodge, luxurious, Maasai, national park, nature, Ngorongoro (crater), Northern circuit, overland, primitive, pristine, rural, safari, savannah, Serengeti, spectacular, stunning, tented camp, traditional, tribe, tropical, ultimate, unforgettable, unknown, untouched, vast, village, wildebeest migration, wilderness, and wildlife.

32. Despite these commitments, however, the Bologonja gate, joining Masai Mara National Reserve in Kenya to Serengeti National Park in Tanzania, has remained closed since 1977.

33. Herzfeld calls such collective representations of an edenic order, a time before time in which the balanced perfection of social relations has not yet suffered the decay that affects everything human, 'structural nostalgia' (2005: 147).

34. It was Bourdieu (1990: 112–21) who famously argued that in addition to economic capital, people's social worth is determined by possession of various forms of 'symbolic capital' (linguistic, social and cultural), the ability to enact or display, through one's habitus, valued cultural forms.

35. See Aitchison (2001), Hall and Tucker (2004), Mellinger (1994), Morgan and Pritchard (1998), Mowforth and Munt (2008), Selwyn (1996) and Urry (2002).

36. Shangri-La is a fictional place described in James Hilton's novel *Lost Horizon* (1933). The term has become synonymous with any earthly paradise, but particularly a mythical Himalayan utopia, a permanently happy land, isolated from the outside world. Shangri-La also evokes the imagery of exoticism of the Orient.

37. Except for Japan (Matsuda 1989; Moeran 1983; Moon 1989; Yamashita 2000), the (translated) literature on non-Western tourist imaginations is sparse (and some would characterize Japan as a Western-type society). Fortunately, scholars are increasingly studying tourism of Asian origin (e.g., Winter, Teo and Chang 2008), Asia being marked by rapidly increasing numbers of outbound tourists.

# Chapter 3

1. Exemplary studies on the production and consumption of tourism discourse include Aitchison (2001), Dann (1996b), Hall and Tucker (2004), Hannam and Knox (2005) and Jaworski and Pritchard (2005).

2. This book does not deal with the imagineering of new spaces for tourism and leisure (e.g., theme parks), but rather focuses on how otherwise lived spaces are shaped by and shaping tourism practices and imaginaries.

3. As tourism fragments into special-interest niches, it becomes difficult to describe tour-guide skills in universal terms. Increased attention is being paid to guide train-

ing in the context of ecotourism (Weiler and Ham 2001; Ballantyne and Hughes 2001; Black, Ham and Weiler 2001). Another rapidly growing segment that is developing specific requirements for guiding is heritage tourism (UNESCO 2005).

4. Some common examples of tourism keywords are: adventure, authentic, beauty, discovery, dream, ecological, enchanting, escape, exotic, experience, fantasy, fascinating, fun, genuine, happy, historical, imagination, indigenous, interesting, lust, mysterious, mythical, native, natural, nostalgic, old, paradise, pleasure, precious, primitive, pristine, real, relaxed, romantic, sensual, thrilling, unique, unspoiled, untouched, virgin, wild, et cetera.

5. See Salazar, Bryon and Van Den Branden (2009), Feldman (2007), Fine and Speer (1985) and Katz (1985).

6. Once more, the similarities between tour guiding and cultural anthropology are striking. Anthropologists such as Geertz, Behar, or Bourgois can be seen as prototypes of theoretical storytellers, using narrative to organize their fieldwork experiences, make sense of a multiplicity of cultural worlds and develop theory. While anthropological narratives proceed from ethnographically validated facts or events, they necessarily require imaginative steps to place them in a coherent story. Taussig (2006), for instance, sees muted and defective storytelling as a form of cultural analysis. Such narrative knowledge is popular because, in contrast to scientific or paradigmatic knowledge, it seems to speak to something universally human.

7. At around the same time, the local chapter of the Association of Indonesian Tour and Travel Agencies (ASITA) proposed the creation in Jogja of an Institute of National Guides, Tour Managers, Public Relations and Convention Studies.

8. Many of these are written by experienced tour guides. Popular examples include Yoeti's *Guiding System: Suatu Pengantar Praktis* (2000), Purwanggono's *Pemandu Wisata: Teknik dan Mekanisme Kerja* (2002), Kesrul's *Panduan Praktis: Pramuwisata Professional* (2004) and Muhajir's *Menjadi Pemandu Wisata Pemula* (2005).

9. One eccentric manual, published in Jogja, has a whole section stereotyping tourists from different countries, tourist jokes, and short articles on brands such as Coca-Cola and Sharp, biosensors [*sic*], oral sex (referred to as 'lollysex'), twenty-five ways of kissing and three ways of committing suicide.

10. The traditional seven wonders of the ancient world also included the Mausoleum of Maussollos at Halicarnassus and the Statue of Zeus (not Athena) at Olympia (not the Acropolis). The temple in Ephesus was dedicated to Artemis (Diana being her Roman counterpart). The only wonder that has stood the test of time is the Great Pyramid of Giza.

11. The autodidactic formation of self-employed *guide liar* (street guides) working in the informal service sector has been described in detail elsewhere (Dahles 1994). Some of the licensed guides I met actually started their career and learned the tricks of the trade as street guides.

12. Although grammatically incorrect, many Tanzanians speak of *wazungu* (white people) in the singular (*mzungu*) when they are codeswitching with English.

13. The situation is quite different on Zanzibar, where a training programme for guides took place in 1994 under the auspices of UNDP and ILO. As a result, they do have local trainers there with the requisite skills. In this context, it is worth mentioning

that the Department of History of the University of Dar es Salaam offers a diploma in cultural heritage interpretation, though it is little known outside the university. Tanzania will experience a drastic rise in tourism management education at the graduate level once the planned World Tourism University for Africa in Bagamoyo (a coastal UNESCO World Heritage site) becomes operational.

14. The fact that students come from all regions should not be surprising because Arusha is Tanzania's most important tourism hub. Most arrive in the city looking for jobs in tourism, but soon realize they will not be able to find any without having undergone some training.

15. Locally produced tourism materials are almost nonexistent. Moreover, most of the nationally produced magazines have foreigners or expatriates on their editorial boards. Exemplary is the case of Steve Foreman, an adventurous Englishman who worked many years as a guide before starting to write articles for various Tanzanian travel magazines and even becoming the editor of *Tantravel*, the official Tanzania Tourist Board publication.

16. A fast-food restaurant might not be the first place tourists look for in Arusha (except for the occasional Western backpacker who spent too much time in the bush and hungers for food from home), but the teacher is confounding tourism imaginaries with his own imaginations of Westerners as 'modern' people, because fast-food restaurants, in his eyes, are an icon of development and progress.

17. Safari guides in Arusha proudly share wild stories about the sexual adventures they claim to have had with *wazungu* women. My assistant received such tales in graphically detailed accounts while interviewing and apprentice guides are certainly familiar with those narratives too.

18. Environmentalism is also promoted outside the circuit of schools and training programs. Environmental NGOs, for example, regularly organize sessions that tour guides attend. I was present at a two-day workshop on community-based tourism organized by the Tanzania Natural Resource Forum. Local hunting companies talked (rather convincingly) about sustainable tourism, while members of Ecotourism Kenya addressed the topic of their expertise.

19. It is noteworthy in the Javanese context that most of these guides are female. As a convinced feminist, Jenny considers employing and training young women an absolute priority.

20. Another way to become familiar with eco-discourse and practice is through the group's active involvement in a waste management project in various schools in the poor villages south of the city.

21. *Bule* is the Indonesian word to denote a white-skinned person (derived from *bulai*, which means "albino"). *Londo* is the equivalent concept in Javanese, derived from *belanda* (referring to people from the Netherlands during colonial time, but now used more generally).

22. It is interesting to note, in this context, that the term seduction is derived from the Latin *seducere*, which means not only to deceive but also to guide or to lead.

23. That does not mean that such knowledge is not to be found locally. Noteworthy in this respect are the efforts of *Yayasan Rumah Budaya Tembi* (House of Culture Foundation Tembi) in Jogja, a cultural centre that has an extensive library and organizes

many activities to promote Javanese culture and language. In Arusha, too, there is *Aang Serian* (M, House of Peace), an NGO that, among other activities, runs community projects focusing on the diffusion of indigenous knowledge (from Maasai and other ethnic groups).

24. Koentjaraningrat (1923–1999) was the founding father of postcolonial Indonesian anthropology. He was trained at Yale University but finished his doctorate at the University of Indonesia in Jakarta.

# Chapter 4

1. The consumption of globally circulating music and movies, arts and literature, fashion and lifestyle, food and drinks has been conceptualized as a form of 'banal cosmopolitanism' (Beck 2002) in which people (rather passively) experience themselves integrated into global processes and phenomena.

2. The term *cosmopolitanism* can be traced back to the fourth century BCE, when non-Athenian intellectuals began to use it to refer to an imagined community of intellectuals beyond the confines of their city-state. The Stoic Zeno, for instance, 'imagined an expanding circle of inclusion—from self, to family, to friends, to city, to humanity' (Fine and Cohen 2002: 137).

3. Anthropologists have argued that international travel is a fundamental aspect of cosmopolitanism, either mentioning it directly (Clifford 1997) or by describing the mobility that enables travel experiences (Ong 1999).

4. See Bærenholdt et al. (2004), Coleman and Crang (2002), Crang (1997) and Edensor (2001).

5. *Metapragmatics* refers to metacommunication and metanarration, by which the appropriate use of language and the negotiation of the relationship between reality and language are evoked within a certain interactional context (Lucy 1993; Urban 1991).

6. Linguistic anthropologists call this phenomenon *conversational codeswitching*, which is to say 'an individual's use of two or more language varieties in the same speech event or exchange' (Woolard 2004: 73–74).

7. This is a reggae tune written in the mid-1980s by the Kenyan band Them Mushrooms. The group first performed it in a hotel in Mombasa, where the melody became an instant hit among foreign tourists. The song was later recorded by Boney M (and others) and became an international success. It ends with the refrain *hakuna matata* (no worries), which was taken up by Elton John and converted into the title song for the 1994 Disney animation *The Lion King*.

8. To avoid confusion, all narrative examples from Arusha (Tanzania) start with an A, cases from Yogyakarta (Indonesia) with Y. I have underlined those words that lie at the core of the points I am trying to make. Words in languages other than the commentary language are in italics, in order to indicate codeswitching.

9. The guide's pun is inspired by a known French riddle: What is the name of a musician's house? Do mi si la do re = *domicile adoré* (F, treasured house).

10. The Ramayana is an ancient Sanskrit epic telling the story of Rama (an avatar of Vishnu in Hinduism or incarnation of Buddha in Buddhism), the legendary king

of Ayodhya whose wife Sita is abducted by a demon king. The Ramayana related in Indonesia differs slightly from the one preserved in India.

11. The conformity of guides to imaginaries and expectations of tourist groups is common to tourism workers in general (cf. Lanfant 1995; Crang 1997).

12. A *sarong* is a loose skirt that is made of a long strip of cloth (often batik) wrapped around the body and held in place by tucking or rolling at the waist, worn by both men and women.

13. A *linga* is a stylized phallic symbol connoting maleness, vitality and creative power, the emblem of the Hindu god Shiva. A *yoni* is a figure representing the vulva, serving as the formal symbol under which Shakti, the Hindu representation of the divine feminine, is worshiped.

14. In 2006, Islamist parties reintroduced the heavily contested Anti-Pornography Bill, a product of the late New Order government. The detailed bill includes provisions that regulate modes of expression in the media, films, dance, poetry, paintings and areas classified as 'lewd behaviour' (e.g., adults displaying sensual body parts or kissing in public places). Tourism workers feared such strict regulations would be dealing the already weakened sector yet another blow. The controversial legislation, offering heavy penalties for the listed violations of public morality, was tabled in October 2008.

15. A *keris* is a sacred double-bladed Indonesian heirloom dagger. Rolex, a globally distributed Swiss brand of luxury wristwatches, is a widely recognised status symbol.

16. TGV is a French acronym for *Train à Grande Vitesse,* France's well-known high-speed rail service, holding the world's fastest average speed for a regular passenger service.

17. The acronym RATP stands for *Régie Autonome des Transports Parisiens,* the major transit operator responsible for public transportation in Paris and its environs.

18. *La Marseillaise* is the name of the national anthem of France.

19. Garuda is a large bird-like creature that appears in both Hindu and Buddhist mythology. It is the vehicle of the Hindu god Vishnu, the national symbol of Indonesia and the name of the country's national airline. The origins of this eagle-like King of Birds go back to India, a detail the guide consciously leaves out of his narrative.

20. Spock is a humanoid character in the *Star Trek* television series and films, recognizable by his abnormal ears.

21. This is somewhat similar to Dann's (1996b: 183–85) 'languaging', a concept indicating a form of one-up-manship, a scoring over one's rivals using real or fictitious foreign or vernacular words.

22. The placing of such signs is actually part of UNESCO's Operational Guidelines for the Implementation of the World Heritage Convention. Article 268 of that policy document states: 'Properties inscribed on the World Heritage List should be marked with the emblem jointly with the UNESCO logo, which should, however, be placed in such a way that they do not visually impair the property in question' (UNESCO 2008: 69).

23. People around the globe seem to find this kind of ranking important, even if they are arbitrary. Many Russians, for example, were disappointed that there was no Russian monument among the 'New Seven Wonders of the World' (an initiative started by a Swiss corporation in 2001). Using the same Internet voting system, a number of

Russian media (including the travel magazine *The World Voyager*) organized a similar contest in 2008 for the Seven Wonders of Russia. Neighbouring Ukraine had already held its Seven Wonders contest in 2007, the same year in which Canada, Poland and Portugal held their respective competitions. The Czech Republic followed in 2009.

24. As Pratt notes in her book on the history of colonial travel, discovery claims often rely on documentation (by the foreign explorer, not by the local(s) who guided him or her): 'The "discovery" itself, even within the ideology of discovery, has no existence of its own. It only gets 'made' for real after the traveller (or other survivor) returns home, and brings it into being through texts' (1992: 240). In this case, the guide's statement is not historically correct. Missionaries working near Bukoba reported the existence of the paintings in 1908. The first published account, by a certain T. A. M. Nash, appeared in 1929 in the *Journal of the Royal Anthropological Institute*. Leakey only explored the site in the 1930s. His wife, however, brought the paintings to public attention through the publication of her book *Africa's Vanishing Art: The Rock Paintings of Tanzania* (1983).

25. According to Javanese mysticism, the Kraton possesses supernatural powers because it is located right in the middle of an imaginary mythical line that connects the South Sea with the northern Merapi volcano. The former is home to the Queen of the South Sea, while the latter is personified and addressed as *Si Mbah* (J, respected elderly man). The palace, led by the sultan, acts as the regulator of the relation between the male (Merapi) and the female (South Sea) realm.

26. According to local beliefs, the statue in the shrine does not represent the goddess Durga (an incarnation of Devi, the supreme Hindu goddess) but Loro Jonggrang. Legend has it she was a Javanese princess who agreed to marry a man she did not love if he could build her a temple ornamented with thousand statues between the setting and rising of the sun. When the man was about to succeed, she tried to trick him. He was so furious he petrified her and she became the last (and most beautiful) of the thousand statues.

27. The Makonde are an ethnic group living in southeast Tanzania and northern Mozambique. They are known for their woodcarvings (traditionally household objects, figures and masks).

28. Deixis is a particular kind of reference, depending crucially upon the time and place of utterance and upon the speaker's and the addressee's roles in the utterance-act itself. Deictic terms are typical examples of what linguistic anthropologists call 'indexicality' (Silverstein 1976).

29. Etymologically, the term *liminal* is derived from the Latin word for threshold, *limen*. On the threshold, one is not in, nor out, and the term *liminal* thus captures the in-between situation. The liminal positionality on the boundary between self and other is well captured in Spanish, where the word us (*nosotros*) contains the word others (*otros*).

30. The dynamics are very different with the rapidly growing group of Asian tourists because they generally want to visit globally renowned landmarks and sophisticated attractions such as theme parks and shopping malls. Instead of an escape from modernity, Asian tourists are immensely interested in evaluating the development levels of other places and searching for iconic representations of modernity (Salazar 2008a).

31. Despite the contested distinction Hannerz makes between cosmopolitans and locals, he does recognize the power of the media in making 'just about everybody a little more cosmopolitan' and ponders whether 'it is now even possible to become a cosmopolitan without going away at all' (1990: 249). In more recent work, Hannerz (2004) is much more nuanced but still expresses pessimism about the cosmopolitan potential of non-elites, arguing that 'bottom-up' cosmopolitans are unlikely to be recognized as such in their own environment.
32. Boon (1992), on the other hand, notes that anthropologists are sometimes seeking in the Others about whom they write a kind of (imagined) magic or enchantment marginalized in their own world.

# Chapter 5

1. Direct records about guides and guiding practices in other parts of the ancient world are difficult to find. For Asia, conjecture can be made by reviewing historical travel activities (Hu 2007: 14–15).
2. Wynn notes how, in contemporary Egypt, the term *turgoman*, sometimes pronounced *turkoman*, is used to denote 'a local who lacks formal training and is not employed as an official tour guide, but who befriends travellers and shows them around' (2007: 233n28).
3. In Philadelphia, for instance, the city council proposed a bill to institute a professional licensing process for tour guides only in 2008. This came amid growing concerns that some guides were telling the city's (patriotic) history inaccurately. However, a federal judge blocked the law from being enforced after three guides had challenged it arguing such a regulation would violate their free speech rights.
4. Although sometimes overlapping, a tour guide should be distinguished from a tour manager or tour leader (a person who manages and supervises an itinerary on behalf of a tour operator, ensuring the programme is carried out as described and sold, and who gives local practical information) and a tour escort (a representative of a tour operator providing basic assistance to tourists).
5. The notion of culture broker implies a model of discrete cultures, an assumption contemporary anthropology questions (e.g., Gupta and Ferguson 1997). Despite criticism (Sherlock 2001; Aramberri 2001), the concept is still widely used within tourism studies, where tour guides are conceived as intermediaries between dichotomized host and guest cultures.
6. In Guatemala, the term *Ladinos* refers to nonindigenous Guatemalans and to mestizos and Westernized Mayas who have attained some level of upward social mobility—related to material wealth and imitation of a North American lifestyle. According to some Maya, this is a betrayal to the traditional values of the indigenous community. Similar attitudes can be found among conservative Maasai in Arusha or Javanese in Jogja (chapter 6).
7. See Salazar (2008b) for a general overview of studies on tour guiding. Scholars with anthropological interests have focused their research on indigenous guides in developing countries, who do not merely provide services but often are an integral part

of the exotic spectacle (Howard, Thwaites and Smith 2001; Crick 1992; McGrath 2004; McKean 1976; Bras and Dahles 1999; Bras 2000; Dahles 1994; Dahles 2002; Gurung, Simmons and Devhir 1996; Cohen 1982; Adams 1997). Some anthropologists have examined the role of guides within their own society (Handler and Gable 1997; Eade 2002).

8. These include: Ambassador, animator, actor, buffer, catalyst, caretaker, communication link, companion, concierge, conduit, culture broker, demonstrator, director, disciplinarian, dragoman, educator, edutainer, entertainer, expert, facilitator, group integrator, host, informal educator, information-giver, infotainer, instructor, interactor, intermediary, interpreter, introducer, leader, manager, mediator, mentor, middleman, moderator, navigator, organiser, pathfinder, presenter, public relations representative, shaman, surrogate parent, teacher and translator.

9. See Cohen (1985), Holloway (1981), Jennings and Weiler (2006), MacDonald (2006), Werner (2003) and Yu, Weiler and Ham (2001).

10. Those who naively expect local tour guides to be (unofficial) ambassadors often uncritically assume that there exists a genius loci, a static and unchanging 'spirit' emanating from a place or from the people living there. However, as soon as one acknowledges that such a spirit does not exist a priori but is made real through everyday practices, including tour guiding, control of those practices becomes essential.

11. See Bras (2000), Bruner (2005), Eade (2002), Fine and Speer (1985) and Handler and Gable (1997).

12. During colonial times, locals commonly referred to game reserves as *shamba la bibi* (the woman's garden). Apart from being a derogatory term, it could also have been a way to indicate which kind of activities were allowed in these areas (growing crops, collecting firewood and cutting trees, predominantly work of the womenfolk) and which were not (hunting, the responsibility of men).

13. The flycatcher is a large group of small passerine or perching birds, who catch their insect prey on the wing, and fifty-eight species of flycatcher can be spotted in Tanzania. In tourism, however, the term is used metaphorically: Once tourists show interest in Arusha street touts, the latter catch their prey and are very reluctant to let the foreigners wander off without selling anything (including themselves).

14. The UNWTO Global Code of Ethics for Tourism is a comprehensive set of principles that guides stakeholders in tourism development. The UN General Assembly accepted it in 2001 (Resolution A/RES/56/212). Although it is not a legally binding document, its Article 10 provides for a voluntary implementation mechanism through the recognition of the World Committee on Tourism Ethics.

15. There are other efforts at creating labour unions, such as the Kilimanjaro Guides and Porters Limited, a union established in 2003 primarily for guides and porters on Mt. Kilimanjaro (but also Mt. Meru, Mt. Hanang, Ol Doinyo Lengai and the Usambara Mountains).

16. The Tourism Confederation of Tanzania (TCT) is the umbrella organization representing the private business sector involved in travel and tourism. Because it was launched only in 2001, the inclusion of the TTGA is a strategic move to make it a stronger apex body.

17. Given the rapid growth of EAC, the Uganda Safari Guides Association has been trying to convince its Kenyan and Tanzanian counterparts to set up an overarching East African Guide Association.

18. The *Pancasila,* literally 'five pillars', embodies the basic principles of the independent Indonesian state as set forth by Sukarno in 1945: (1) the belief in one Supreme Being; (2) a just and civilized humanitarianism; (3) the unity of Indonesia; (4) unanimous consensus or democracy led by wise policies; and (5) social justice for all Indonesians.

19. IDR is the international standard currency code for the Indonesian rupiah (Rp). In 2006, US$1 was worth about IDR 9,000.

20. It is not the first time that Indonesia has developed professional standards. During the golden years of tourism (1980s to the mid-1990s), the former Department of Tourism, Post and Telecommunications produced occupational skill standards in collaboration with the UNDP/ILO National Tourism Training Standards and Programs and the EC/ASEAN Regional Project on Tourism Human Resources.

21. The on-site guides of Prambanan are a separate branch of the large HPI Yogyakarta chapter, while those of Borobudur belong to HPI Magelang (Central Java).

22. When I left Indonesia in 2006, Pak Hardi demonstrated that he had perfectly understood the gist of my research. His symbolic farewell present for me was nothing typically local but his own worn WFTGA t-shirt.

23. The bird of paradise actually refers to several beautiful birds of the *Paradisea* family, common in western Indonesia, the males of which have brilliant colours, elegant plumes and often remarkable tail feathers. Under the New Order system, guides wore a coloured paradise wing badge to indicate the type of license they had: red for tour leaders, yellow for senior guides, green for junior guides, and white for on-site guides.

24. On-site guides working in the *Pagelaran* (the open front hall of the Kraton) and the *Tamansari* (Water Castle) are affiliated with Paguyuban Pemandu Wisata Kraton dan Tamansari, whose licenses are handed out by the city's Tourism Department. This is because different brothers of the sultan manage separate parts of the Kraton.

25. In this context, it is worth mentioning that the WFTGA came into being as a result of proposals put forward at the first International Convention of Tourist Guides in 1985, set up through the initiative of the Israel Tour Guides Association (Israel being the country where guides are probably most efficiently controlled by state authorities).

# Chapter 6

1. Resistance theory builds on the ideas of Marx and Gramsci, who saw the world divided into wealthy, powerful individuals who own the means of production, and poorer people who are dispossessed of the means of production and forced to labour for the wealthy. Scott's (1985, 1990) work on microprocesses of resistance is similar to that of de Certeau (1984), who also describes how individuals use strategies and tactics to carve out a semi-independent domain of practice within the constraints

placed on them by the powerful. See Castañeda (1996) for an in-depth application of de Certeau's concepts to the practices of tourism.

2. I draw here on the work of Ahearn, who defines agency as 'the socioculturally mediated capacity to act' (2001: 130), taking note of Adam's remark that such human action 'involves multiple, at times contradictory, motivations' (2006: 26).

3. An actor refers to 'a person whose action is rule-governed or rule-oriented'; an agent is 'a person engaged in the exercise of power in the sense of the ability to bring about effects and to (re)constitute the world' (Karp 1986: 137).

4. Myths are good examples of decontextualized or polycontextual discourse, not serving the specific local interests of any of the participants in the replication process and hence being more readily replicated by all. Not surprisingly, some scholars have pointed to the close similarity between myths and tourism imaginaries (Selwyn 1996).

5. On the role of Islam as a projection of Arabic culture or civilization into the culture or civilization of Indonesia, see Geertz (2001).

6. *Loro Jonggrang* (J, slender virgin) is the name the Javanese give to the statue of Durga in the Prambanan temple complex, referring to a legendary Javanese princess.

7. An exception to this rule is the phenomenon of poverty tourism or 'poorism', in which tourists are particularly interested in observing people living in poverty (often in very voyeuristic ways).

8. It once was the other way around. As Hitchcock and Darma Putra remark, 'in the early years of tourism development, Bali was little more than an appendage to much better known Java' (2007: 30).

9. While the guides in Jogja hold the Balinese accountable, also the advertisements of the central government play an important role. One of the latest branding slogans used by the authorities to promote tourism is 'Indonesia: Bali and Beyond'. Since the beginning of tourism, such marketing campaigns have focused on Bali. The latest catchphrase still acknowledges the dominance of Bali but also vaguely suggests there are other places worth visiting.

10. In 2005, though, a leopard killed a six-year-old French boy at a lodge inside Tarangire National Park. Some employees later claimed the leopard was a regular visitor, especially on Saturday night when the lodge organized its weekly barbecue. Rumour has it that Tanzanian service people actually threw chunks of meat at the leopard so that it would come closer and tourists could take better pictures of it.

11. Such a retreat, called *orpul* (M), is usually a weeks-long ritual isolation in the bush, in which elderly Maasai men teach warriors traditional ways, such as the proper treatment of animals and effective use of medicinal herbs (part of the transition from warrior status to that of elder).

12. The pattern of not treating Maasai as individuals is common practice among other ethnic groups in Tanzania. In one of the tour guide schools I frequented in Arusha, it came to a loaded discussion one day when a Maasai student formally requested to be called by his name instead of being addressed always as 'Maasai'.

13. TZS is the international standard currency code for the Tanzanian shilling. In 2007, US$1 was worth around TZS 1300.

14. Average salaries in Indonesia vary from around US$35 (farming jobs) to US$320 (management jobs) per month.

15. The average salary in Tanzania is estimated around US$30, but many people in the informal sector earn less than that.
16. Because the disasters also greatly affected my fieldwork, I wrote a public blog, entitled *Earthquake Disaster: An Anthropologist's Report from Yogyakarta, Indonesia,* with reflections as the events unfolded: http://web.archive.org/web/20080531123926/ http://www.museum.upenn.edu/new/research/blogs/earthquake_blog.shtml.
17. Although local people perceived it differently, UNESCO's Emergency Assessment Mission in June 2006 consisted of only one international expert (an Italian professor in the field of structural engineering), while the other people were Indonesian experts and representatives from the UNESCO office in Jakarta. An international meeting was organized in March 2007, bringing together Indian, Indonesian, Italian and Japanese experts from various fields (including archaeology, architecture, civil engineering, geodetic engineering, geology and history), representatives from UNESCO, ICOMOS Australia and the Global Heritage Fund, and government representatives from China, India, Italy, Japan and the Kingdom of Saudi Arabia.
18. In October 2006, the bill was revised to include articles that 'protected the sartorial preferences of people from indigenous cultures', allowing women to wear the tight-fitting Javanese *kebaya* (blouse). The controversial antiporn legislation was tabled in October 2008, under heavy protest from several civil society groups and organizations.
19. The Hindu and Buddhist temples in central Java, which are considered as the meeting points between gods and humans, were built on a spiritual line between Mt. Merapi and the South Sea (Dumarçay 1986: 88–91). The Kraton, where the sultan lives, is also organised around an axis of authority reflecting this mountain–sea polarity. The old fault from Merapi to Bantul, which was reactivated during the May 2006 earthquake, lies parallel to the sacred north–south axis in Javanese cosmology. Schlehe (1996) highlights a complex, often syncretic, amalgam of Islamic, Hindu, Christian and pre-Christian spiritualities and the important role these play in shaping reactions and responses to disasters. As is common throughout Southeast Asia, also in Java perturbations in the natural realm have long been interpreted as presaging perturbations in the social and political realm (Anderson 1972).
20. The acronym RATP stands for *Régie Autonome des Transports Parisiens,* the major transit operator responsible for public transportation in Paris and its environs. This joke is a variation of the one the same guide made while guiding another group of tourists (see Y14, chapter 4).
21. In this context, the 'West' refers to a widespread imaginary, not a specific geographic location with homogeneous cultural traits and historical background.

# Chapter 7

1. IDR 100,000 is a little over US$10. Knowing that cultural guides in Jogja are paid around IDR 10,000 per hour, this is a relatively large tip for an apprentice.
2. Already in 1963, a UN Conference on International Travel and Tourism in Rome highlighted the role of tourism in improving relations between nations. This idea has

been taken up by the Institute for Peace through Tourism, a nonprofit coalition of travel industry organizations founded in 1986 with the aim of fostering and facilitating tourism initiatives that contribute to international understanding and cooperation (Salazar 2006b).

3. The plethora of copycat enterprises I encountered in Jogja and Arusha are good examples of this: Debucks and Stiggbucks (Starbucks), McPitik and McMoody's (McDonald's), Kentukku Fried Chicken (KFC) or Plassa Hotel (Plaza Hotel) (Figure 2).

4. It is no coincidence that the travel concept is linguistically related to the French word *travail*, which means 'labour'. There is a long tradition of thought, from Marx and Weber to Bourdieu, that places human agency at the heart of social change. In this approach, people attempt to actively make and shape their destiny, engaging with evolving structures of power, knowledge and cultural meaning. Such analyses are best combined with complementary studies of the institutional locus of power over the domains that promote and constrain social change.

5. In Javanese wayang plays, Semar is the clown servant of the hero of the story, regardless of who that hero is.

6. Many people merely travel 'for the purpose of "home plus"—Spain is home plus sunshine, India is home plus servants, Africa is home plus elephants and lions' (Hannerz 1990: 241). Hannerz adds: 'Such travel is not for cosmopolitans, and does little to create cosmopolitans' (1990: 241).

7. Anthropologists can undergo an opposite fate. During fieldwork, some try to 'go native' but most realize it is virtually impossible to 'become native'. I will always remain neither a total insider nor a complete outsider: a *bule* in Jogja and a *mzungu* in Arusha (or even a tourist).

8. In the Marxian tradition, resistance must be a function of power, that is to say, it must entail the promise of change, for B to exert influence over A, rather than merely cope with an existing power dynamic.

9. Examples of such marketing campaigns: 'Amazing Thailand, dreams for all seasons', 'Croatia, the Mediterranean as it once was', 'Magical Kenya', 'Ireland, the island of memories', 'Colombia, the only risk is wanting to stay', 'The hidden charm: Vietnam', 'Live your myths in Greece', and so forth.

10. The slogan refers to the creation in 1908 of Boedi Oetomo (J, Noble Endeavour). This Javanese student movement is believed to have been instrumental for the later independence of the country, since it helped making people aware of a national Indonesian identity.

# BIBLIOGRAPHY

Adams, K. M. 1997. 'Touting touristic "primadonas": Tourism, ethnicity, and national integration in Sulawesi, Indonesia', in M. Picard and R. Wood (eds), *Tourism, ethnicity, and the state in Asian and Pacific societies*. Honolulu: University of Hawai'i Press, pp. 155–80.

———. 2004. 'The genesis of touristic imagery: Politics and poetics in the creation of a remote Indonesian island destination'. *Tourist Studies* 4: 115–35.

———. 2006. *Art as politics: Re-crafting identities, tourism, and power in Tana Toraja, Indonesia*. Honolulu: University of Hawai'i Press.

Agha, A. 2006. *Language and social relations*. Cambridge: Cambridge University Press.

Ahearn, L. M. 2001. 'Language and agency'. *Annual Review of Anthropology* 30: 109–37.

Aitchison, C. 2001. 'Theorizing Other discourses of tourism, gender and culture: Can the subaltern speak (in tourism)?' *Tourist Studies* 1: 133–47.

Allen, B. 2004. 'Revisiting the elephant hunters of Tanzania'. *National Geographic* 206: 1.

Almagor, U. 1985. 'A tourist's "vision quest" in an African game reserve'. *Annals of Tourism Research* 12: 31–47.

Amato, E. 1992. *Cultural tourism development Central Java—Yogyakarta. Activity report No. 3: Tourist guide review*. Jakarta: UNESCO/UNDP.

———. 2002. *Manual for guiding techniques*. Yogyakarta: Sanata Dharma University Press.

Amirou, R. 1995. *Imaginaire touristique et sociabilités du voyage*. Paris: Presses Universitaires de France.

Anderson, B. R. 1972. 'The idea of power in Javanese culture', in C. Holt (ed.), *Culture and Politics in Indonesia*. Ithaca, NY: Cornell University Press, pp. 1–69.

———. 1991. *Imagined communities: Reflections on the origin and spread of nationalism*, 2nd ed. New York: Verso.

Aposporos, D. 2004. 'Hunting for glory with the Barabaig of Tanzania'. *National Geographic* 206: 76–93.

Appadurai, A. 1996. *Modernity at large: Cultural dimensions of globalization*. Minneapolis: University of Minnesota Press.

———. (ed.). 2001. *Globalization*. Durham, NC: Duke University Press.

Aramberri, J. 2001. 'The host should get lost: Paradigms in the tourism theory'. *Annals of Tourism Research* 28: 738–61.

Arnould, E. J. and L. L. Price. 1993. 'River magic: Extraordinary experience and the extended service encounter'. *Journal of Consumer Research* 20: 24–45.

Ateljevic, I. 2000. 'Circuits of tourism: Stepping beyond the "production/consumption" dichotomy'. *Tourism Geographies* 2: 369–58.

Ateljevic, I., A. Pritchard and N. Morgan (eds). 2007. *The critical turn in tourism studies: Innovative research methodologies.* Amsterdam: Elsevier.

Århem, K. 1985. *Pastoral man in the Garden of Eden: The Maasai of the Ngorongoro conservation area, Tanzania.* Uppsala: University of Uppsala.

Bachmann, P. 1988. 'The Maasai—choice of East African tourists—admired and ridiculed', in P. Rossel (ed.), *Tourism: Manufacturing the exotic.* Copenhagen: International Work Group for Indigenous Affairs, pp. 47–64.

Ballantyne, R. and K. Hughes. 2001. 'Interpretation in ecotourism settings: Investigating tour guides' perceptions of their role, responsibilities and training needs'. *The Journal of Tourism Studies* 12: 2–9.

Barnes, S. T. 2005. 'Global flows: Terror, oil, and strategic philanthropy'. *African Studies Review* 48: 1–22.

Barron, P. and B. Prideaux 1998. 'Hospitality education in Tanzania: Is there a need to develop environmental awareness?' *Journal of Sustainable Tourism* 6: 224–37.

Bauman, R. and C. L. Briggs. 1990. 'Poetics and performance as critical perspectives on language and social life'. *Annual Review of Anthropology* 19: 59–88.

Bærenholdt, J. O., et al. (ed's). 2004. *Performing tourist places.* Aldershot: Ashgate.

Beck, U. 2002. 'The cosmopolitan society and its enemies'. *Theory, Culture & Society* 19: 17–44.

Beck, U. and N. Sznaider. 2006. 'A literature on cosmopolitanism: An overview'. *British Journal of Sociology* 57: 153–64.

Bendix, R. 2002. 'Capitalizing on memories past, present, and future: Observations on the intertwining of tourism and narration'. *Anthropological Theory* 2: 469–87.

Benjamin, W. 1969. 'The storyteller: Reflections on the work of Nikolai Leskov', in H. Arendt (ed.), *Illuminations.* New York: Schocken Books, pp. 83–109.

Bhabha, H. K. 1994. *The location of culture.* London: Routledge.

Bishop, R. and L. S. Robinson. 1999. 'Genealogies of exotic desire: The Thai night market in the Western imagination', in P. A. Jackson and N. M. Cook (eds), *Genders and sexualities in modern Thailand.* Chiang Mai: Silkworm, pp. 191–205.

Black, R., S. Ham and B. Weiler. 2001. 'Ecotour guide training in less developed countries: Some preliminary research findings'. *Journal of Sustainable Tourism* 9: 147–56.

Black, R. and B. Weiler. 2005. 'Quality assurance and regulatory mechanisms in the tour guiding industry: A systematic review'. *The Journal of Tourism Studies* 16: 24–37.

Blanton, D. 1981. 'Tourism training in developing countries: The social and cultural dimension'. *Annals of Tourism Research* 8: 116–33.

Boon, J. A. 1992. 'Cosmopolitan moments: Echoey confessions of an ethnographer-tourist', in D. Segal (ed.), *Crossing cultures: Essays in the displacement of Western civilization.* Tucson: University of Arizona Press.

Bourdieu, P. 1977. *Outline of a theory of practice,* trans. R. Nice. Cambridge, MA: Cambridge University Press.

———. 1984. *Distinction: A social critique of the judgement of taste,* trans. R. Nice. Cambridge, MA: Harvard University Press.

————. 1990. *The logic of practice*, trans. R. Nice. Stanford, CA: Stanford University Press.

Bowman, G. 1992. 'The politics of tour guiding: Israeli and Palestinian guides in Israel and the Occupied Territories', in D. Harrison (ed.), *Tourism and the less-developed countries*. London: Belhaven Press, pp. 121–34.

Bras, K. 2000. *Image-building and guiding on Lombok: The social construction of a tourist destination*. Amsterdam: ATLAS Publications.

Bras, K. and H. Dahles. 1999. 'Pathfinder, gigolo, and friend: Diverging entrepreneurial strategies of tourist guides on two Indonesian islands', in H. Dahles and K. Bras (eds), *Tourism and small entrepreneurs: Development, national policy and entrepreneurial culture—Indonesian cases*. New York: Cognizant Communication Corporation, pp. 128–45.

Breckenridge, C. A., et al. (eds). 2002. *Cosmopolitanism*. Durham, NC: Duke University Press.

Brennan, T. 2001. 'The cuts of language: The East/West of North/South'. *Public Culture* 13: 39–63.

Brown, M. W. 1983. 'Indonesia rescues ancient Borobudur'. *National Geographic* 163: 126–42.

Bruner, E. M. 1991. 'Transformation of self in tourism'. *Annals of Tourism Research* 18: 238–50.

————. 2005. *Culture on tour: Ethnographies of travel*. Chicago: University of Chicago Press.

Bunten, A. C. 2008. 'Sharing culture or selling out? Developing the commodified persona in the heritage industry'. *American Ethnologist* 35: 380–95.

Burawoy, M. (ed.). 2000. *Global ethnography: Forces, connections, and imaginations in a postmodern world*. Berkeley: University of California Press.

————. 2001. 'Manufacturing the global'. *Ethnography* 2: 147–59.

Cabaton, A. 1911. *Java, Sumatra and the other islands of the Dutch East Indies*, trans. B. Miall. London: T. Fischer Unwin.

Candea, M. 2007. 'Arbitrary locations: In defence of the bounded field-site'. *Journal of the Royal Anthropological Institute* 13: 167–84.

Carter, S. 1998. 'Tourists' and travellers' social construction of Africa and Asia as risky locations'. *Tourism Management* 19: 349–58.

Casson, L. 1974. *Travel in the ancient world*. London: Allen & Unwin.

Castañeda, Q. 1996. *In the museum of Maya culture: Touring Chichén Itzá*. Minneapolis: University of Minnesota Press.

Castoriadis, C. 1987. *The imaginary institution of society*, trans. K. Blamey. Cambridge, MA: MIT Press.

Causey, A. 2003. *Hard bargaining in Sumatra: Western travelers and Toba Bataks in the marketplace of souvenirs*. Honolulu: University of Hawai'i Press.

Chambers, E. 2010. *Native tours: The anthropology of travel and tourism*, 2nd ed. Prospect Heights, IL: Waveland Press.

Chatelard, G. 2005. 'Tourism and representations: Of social change and power relations in Wadi Ramm, Southern Jordan', in S. L. Abdallah (ed.), *Images aux frontières:*

*Représentations et constructions sociales et politiques, Palestine, Jordanie 1948–2000.* Amman: Institut Français du Proche-Orient, pp. 193–252.

Cheong, S.-M. and M. L. Miller. 2000. 'Power and tourism: A Foucauldian observation'. *Annals of Tourism Research* 27: 371–90.

Christie, M. F. and P. A. Mason 2003. 'Transformative tour guiding: Training tour guides to be critically reflective practitioners'. *Journal of Ecotourism* 2: 1–16.

Clifford, J. 1997. *Routes: Travel and translation in the late twentieth century.* Cambridge, MA: Harvard University Press.

Cohen, E. 1982. 'Jungle guides in Northern Thailand: The dynamics of a marginal occupational role'. *Sociological Review* 30: 236–66.

———. 1985. 'The tourist guide: The origins, structure and dynamics of a role'. *Annals of Tourism Research* 12: 5–29.

Cohen, E. and R. L. Cooper 1986. 'Language and tourism'. *Annals of Tourism Research* 13: 533–63.

Cole, S. 2008. *Tourism, culture and development: Hopes, dreams and realities in East Indonesia.* Clevedon: Channel View Publications.

Coleman, S. and M. Crang (eds). 2002. *Tourism: Between place and performance.* New York: Berghahn.

Comaroff, J. and J. L. Comaroff (eds). 2001. *Millennial capitalism and the culture of neoliberalism.* Durham, NC: Duke University Press.

———. 2003. 'Ethnography on an awkward scale: Postcolonial anthropology and the violence of abstraction'. *Ethnography* 4: 147–79.

Comaroff, J. L. and J. Comaroff 1992. *Ethnography and the historical imagination.* Boulder, CO: Westview.

Conklin, B. A. and L. R. Graham. 1995. 'The shifting middle ground: Amazonian Indians and eco-politics'. *American Anthropologist* 97: 695–710.

Cooper, F. 2001. 'What is the concept of globalization good for? An African historian's perspective'. *African Affairs* 100: 189–213.

Costa, J. A. 1998. 'Paradisal discourse: A critical analysis of marketing and consuming Hawaii'. *Consumption, Markets and Culture* 1: 303–46.

Crang, M. 2006. 'Circulation and emplacement: The hollowed out performance of tourism', in C. Minca and T. Oakes (eds), *Travels in paradox: Remapping tourism.* Boulder, CO: Rowman & Littlefield, pp. 47–64.

Crang, P. 1997. 'Performing the tourist product', in C. Rojek and J. Urry (eds), *Touring cultures: Transformations of travel and theory.* London: Routledge, pp. 137–54.

Cresswell, T. 2006. *On the move: Mobility in the modern Western world.* New York: Routledge.

Crick, M. 1989. 'Representations of international tourism in the social sciences: Sun, sex, sights, savings, and servility'. *Annual Review of Anthropology* 18: 307–44

———. 1992. 'Life in the informal sector: Street guides in Kandy, Sri Lanka', in D. Harrison (ed.), *Tourism and the less developed countries.* London: Belhaven Press, pp. 140–53.

———. 1994. *Resplendent sites, discordant voices: Sri Lankans and international tourism.* Langhorne: Harwood Academic Publishers.

Crouch, D., R. Jackson and F. Thompson (eds). 2005. *The media and the tourist imagination: Converging cultures.* London: Routledge.

Cunningham, H. and J. Heyman. 2004. 'Introduction: Mobilities and enclosures at borders'. *Identities: Global Studies in Culture and Power* 11: 289–302.

Dahles, H. 1994. *Ticket to a better life: The unlicensed tourist guides of Yogyakarta.* Tilburg, NL: Tilburg University Press.

———. 2001. *Tourism, heritage and national culture in Java: Dilemmas of a local community.* Richmond: Curzon Press.

———. 2002. 'The politics of tour guiding: Image management in Indonesia'. *Annals of Tourism Research* 29: 783–800.

Dahles, H. and K. Bras. 1999. 'Entrepreneurs in romance tourism in Indonesia'. *Annals of Tourism Research* 26: 267–93.

Dann, G. M. S. 1976. 'The holiday was simply fantastic'. *Revue de Tourisme* 3: 19–23.

———. 1996a. 'Greenspeak: An analysis of the language of eco-tourism'. *Progress in Tourism and Hospitality Research* 2: 247–59.

———. 1996b. *The language of tourism: A sociolinguistic perspective.* Wallingford: CABI.

———. 2001. 'The self-admitted use of cliché in the language of tourism'. *Tourism, Culture & Communication* 3: 1–14.

———. 2004. '(Mis)Representing the "Other" in the language of tourism'. *Journal of Eastern Caribbean Studies* 29: 76–94.

de Certeau, M. 1984. *The practice of everyday life,* trans. S. Rendall. Berkeley: University of California Press.

Delumeau, J. 1995. *History of paradise: The Garden of Eden in myth and tradition,* trans. M. O'Connell. New York: Continuum.

Desmond, J. 1999. *Staging tourism: Bodies on display from Waikiki to Sea World.* Chicago: University of Chicago Press.

Dumarçay, J. 1986. *The temples of Java,* trans. M. Smithies. Singapore: Oxford University Press.

Durand, G. 1999. *The anthropological structures of the imaginary,* trans. M. Sankey and J. Hatten. Brisbane: Boombana Publications.

Dwyer, L. K. 2000. 'Spectacular sexuality: Nationalism, development and the politics of family planning in Indonesia', in T. Mayer (ed.), *Gender ironies of nationalism: Sexing the nation.* New York: Routledge, pp. 25–52.

Eade, J. 2002. 'Adventure tourists and locals in a global city: Resisting tourist performances in London's "East End"', in S. Coleman and M. Crang (eds), *Tourism: Between place and performance.* Oxford: Berghahn, pp. 128–39.

Eastman, C. M. 1995. 'Tourism in Kenya and the marginalization of Swahili'. *Annals of Tourism Research* 22: 172–85.

Echtner, C. M. and P. Prasad 2003. 'The context of third world tourism marketing'. *Annals of Tourism Research* 30: 660–82.

Edensor, T. 1998. *Tourists at the Taj: Performance and meaning at a symbolic site.* London: Routledge.

———. 2001. 'Performing tourism, staging tourism: (Re)producing tourist space and practice'. *Tourist Studies* 1: 59–81.

Elliott, C. 2001. 'Consuming caffeine: The discourse of Starbucks and coffee'. *Consumption, Markets and Culture* 4: 345–437.

Erb, M. 2000. 'Understanding tourists: Interpretations from Indonesia'. *Annals of Tourism Research* 27: 709–36.

Eriksen, T. H. (ed.). 2003. *Globalisation: Studies in anthropology.* London: Pluto Press.

Fabian, J. 2002. *Time and the other: How anthropology makes its object,* 2nd ed. New York: Columbia University Press.

Favero, P. 2003. 'Phantasms in a "starry" place: Space and identification in a central New Delhi market'. *Cultural Anthropology* 18: 551–84.

Featherstone, M. 2006. 'Genealogies of the global'. *Theory, Culture & Society* 23: 387–92.

Feldman, G. 2005. 'Estranged states: Diplomacy and the containment of national minorities in Europe'. *Anthropological Theory* 5: 219–45.

Feldman, J. 2007. 'Constructing a shared Bible Land: Jewish Israeli guiding performances for Protestant pilgrims'. *American Ethnologist* 34: 351–74.

Ferguson, J. 2006. *Global shadows: Africa in the neoliberal world order.* Durham, NC: Duke University Press.

Fine, E. C. and J. H. Speer. 1985. 'Tour guide performances as sight sacralization'. *Annals of Tourism Research* 12: 73–95.

Fine, R. and R. Cohen 2002. 'Four cosmopolitan moments', in S. Vertovec and R. Cohen (eds), *Conceiving cosmopolitanism: Theory, context and practice.* Oxford: Oxford University Press, pp. 137–62.

Foucault, M. 1980. *Power/knowledge: Selected interviews and other writings, 1972–1977,* trans. C. Gordon. New York: Pantheon Books.

Friedman, J. 2002. 'From roots to routes: Tropes for trippers'. *Anthropological Theory* 2: 21–36.

Gaonkar, D. P. 2002. 'Toward new imaginaries: An introduction'. *Public Culture* 14: 1–19.

Gaonkar, D. P. and E. A. Povinelli. 2003. 'Technologies of public forms: Circulation, transfiguration, recognition'. *Public Culture* 15: 385–97.

Geertz, C. 1960. *The religion of Java.* Glencoe, IL: Free Press.

———. 1973. *The interpretation of cultures: Selected essays.* New York: Basic Books.

———. 1983. *Local knowledge: Further essays in interpretive anthropology.* New York: Basic Books.

———. 1997. 'Cultural tourism: Tradition, identity and heritage construction', in W. Nuryanti (ed.), *Tourism and heritage management.* Yogyakarta: Gadjah Mada University Press, pp. 14–24.

———. 2001. 'The Near East in the Far East: On Islam in Indonesia', *Occasional Paper No. 12.* Princeton, NJ: Institute of Advanced Studies.

Giddens, A. 1984. *The constitution of society: Outline of the theory of structuration.* Cambridge: Polity Press.

Glover, N. 2008. 'Co-produced histories: Mapping the uses and narratives of history in the tourist age'. *The Public Historian* 30: 105–24.

Goffman, E. 1959. *The presentation of self in everyday life.* New York: Doubleday.

———. 1974. *Frame analysis: An essay on the organization of experience.* Harmondsworth: Penguin.

————. 1981. *Forms of talk*. Philadelphia: University of Pennsylvania Press.

Gogia, N. 2006. 'Unpacking corporeal mobilities: The global voyages of labour and leisure'. *Environment and Planning A* 38: 359–75.

Graburn, N. H. H. 2002. 'The ethnographic tourist', in G. M. S. Dann (ed.), *The tourist as a metaphor of the social world*. Wallingford: CABI, pp. 19–39.

Graeber, D. 2002. 'The anthropology of globalization (with notes on neomedievalism, and the end of the Chinese model of the nation-state)'. *American Anthropologist* 104: 1222–27.

Gronroos, C. 1978. 'A service oriented approach to marketing of services'. *European Journal of Marketing* 12: 588–601.

Guldin, G. E. 1989. 'The anthropological study tour in China: A call for cultural guides'. *Human Organization* 48: 126–34.

Gupta, A. and J. Ferguson (eds). 1997. *Anthropological locations: Boundaries and grounds of a field science*. Berkeley: University of California Press.

Gurung, J. D., D. G. Simmons and P. J. Devhir. 1996. 'The evolving role of tourist guides: The Nepali experience', in R. Butler and T. Hinch (eds), *Tourism and indigenous peoples*. London: Thompson International Business Press, pp. 107–28.

Hage, G. 2005. 'A not so multi-sited ethnography of a not so imagined community'. *Anthropological Theory* 5: 463–75.

Hall, C. M. 2005. *Tourism: Rethinking the social science of mobility*. Harlow: Prentice Hall.

Hall, C. M. and H. Tucker (eds). 2004. *Tourism and postcolonialism: Contested discourses, identities and representations*. London: Routledge.

Hall, S. 1995. 'New cultures for old', in D. B. Massey and P. Jess (eds), *A place in the world? Places, cultures, and globalization*. New York: Oxford University Press, pp. 175–213.

Handler, R. and E. Gable. 1997. *The new history in an old museum: Creating the past at Colonial Williamsburg*. Durham, NC: Duke University Press.

Hannam, K. and D. Knox. 2005. 'Discourse analysis in tourism research: A critical perspective'. *Tourism Recreation Research* 30: 23–30.

Hannam, K., M. Sheller and J. Urry. 2006. 'Editorial: Mobilities, immobilities and moorings'. *Mobilities* 1: 1–22.

Hannerz, U. 1990. 'Cosmopolitans and locals in world culture'. *Theory, Culture, and Society* 7: 237–52.

————. 2003. 'Several sites in one', in T. H. Eriksen (ed.), *Globalisation: Studies in anthropology*. London: Pluto Press, pp. 18–38.

————. 2004 'Cosmopolitanism', in D. Nugent and J. Vincent (eds), *A companion to the anthropology of politics*. Oxford: Blackwell, pp. 69–85.

Hardt, M. and A. Negri. 2000. *Empire*. Cambridge, MA: Harvard University Press.

Harvey, D. 1989. *The condition of postmodernity: An enquiry into the origins of cultural change*. Oxford: Blackwell.

Haugerud, A., M. P. Stone and P. D. Little (eds). 2000. *Commodities and globalization: Anthropological perspectives*. Lanham, MD: Rowman & Littlefield.

Henderson, C. E. and M. K. Weisgrau (eds). 2007. *Raj rhapsodies: Tourism, heritage and the seduction of history*. Aldershot: Ashgate.

Hennig, C. 2002. 'Tourism: Enacting modern myths', in G. M. S. Dann (ed.), *The tourist as a metaphor of the social world.* Wallingford: CABI, pp. 169–87.

Herzfeld, M. 2005. *Cultural intimacy: Social poetics in the nation-state,* 2nd ed. New York: Routledge.

Hitchcock, M. 2004. 'Margaret Mead and tourism: Anthropological heritage in the aftermath of the Bali bombings'. *Anthropology Today* 20: 9–14.

Hitchcock, M. and I. N. Darma Putra. 2007. *Tourism, development and terrorism in Bali.* Aldershot: Ashgate.

Hobsbawm, E. and T. Ranger. 1992. *The invention of tradition.* Cambridge: Cambridge University Press.

Hollinshead, K. 1998. 'Tourism, hybridity, and ambiguity: The relevance of Bhabha's "third space" cultures'. *Journal of Leisure Research* 30: 121–56.

———. 1999. 'Surveillance of the worlds of tourism: Foucault and the eye-of-power'. *Tourism Management* 20: 7–23.

Holloway, J. C. 1981. 'The guided tour: A sociological approach'. *Annals of Tourism Research* 8: 377–402.

Holmes, D. R. and G. E. Marcus. 2004. 'Cultures of expertise and the management of globalization: Toward the re-functioning of ethnography', in A. Ong and S. J. Collier (eds), *Global assemblages: Technology, politics, and ethics as anthropological problems.* New York: Blackwell, pp. 235–52.

Honey, M. 1999. *Ecotourism and sustainable development: Who owns paradise?* Washington, DC: Island Press.

Howard, J., R. Thwaites and B. Smith. 2001. 'Investigating the roles of the indigenous tour guide'. *The Journal of Tourism Studies* 12: 32–39.

Hu, W. 2007. 'Tour guides and sustainable development: The case of Hainan, China', Ph.D. dissertation. Waterloo, ON: University of Waterloo.

Hughes, L. 2006. '"Beautiful beasts" and brave warriors: The longevity of a Maasai stereotype', in L. Romanucci-Ross, G. A. de Vos and T. Tsuda (eds), *Ethnic identity: Problems and prospects for the twenty-first century.* Lanham, MD: Altamira Press, pp. 246–94.

Hutnyk, J. 1996. *The rumour of Calcutta: Tourism, charity, and the poverty of representation.* London: Zed Books.

Inda, J. X. and R. Rosaldo (eds). 2002. *The anthropology of globalization: A reader.* Malden, MA: Blackwell.

———. (eds). 2007. *The anthropology of globalization: A reader,* 2nd ed. Malden, MA: Blackwell.

Jafari, J. 2007. 'Entry into a new field of study: Leaving a footprint', in D. Nash (ed.), *The study of tourism: Anthropological and sociological beginnings.* Amsterdam: Elsevier, pp. 108–21.

Jaworski, A. and A. Pritchard (eds). 2005. *Discourse, communication, and tourism.* Clevedon: Channel View Publications.

Jaworski, A. and C. Thurlow. 2004. 'Language, tourism and globalization: Mapping new international identities', in S. H. Ng, C. N. Candlin and C. Y. Chiu (eds), *Language matters: Communication, identity, and culture.* Hong Kong: City University of Hong Kong Press, pp. 297–321.

Jaworski, A., et al. 2003. 'The uses and representations of local languages in tourist destinations: A view from British TV holiday programmes'. *Language Awareness* 12: 5–29.

Jennings, G. and B. Weiler. 2006. 'Mediating meaning: Perspectives on brokering quality tourist experiences', in G. Jennings and N. P. Nickerson (eds), *Quality tourism experiences*. Oxford: Butterworth-Heinemann, pp. 57–78.

Jóhannesson, G. T. 2005. 'Tourism translations: Actor-Network Theory and tourism research'. *Tourist Studies* 5: 133–50.

Jones, A. M. 1971. *Africa and Indonesia: The evidence of the xylophone and other musical and cultural factors,* 2nd ed. Leiden: E. J. Brill.

Kahn, J. S. 2003. 'Anthropology as cosmopolitan practice?' *Anthropological Theory* 3: 403–15.

Karp, I. 1986. 'Agency and social theory: A review of Anthony Giddens'. *American Ethnologist* 13: 131–37.

Kaspin, D. 1997. 'On ethnographic authority and the tourist trade: Anthropology in the house of mirrors'. *Anthropological Quarterly* 70: 53–57.

Katz, S. 1985. 'The Israeli teacher-guide: The emergence and perpetuation of a role'. *Annals of Tourism Research* 12: 49–72.

Kearney, M. 1986. 'From the invisible hand to visible feet: Anthropological studies of migration and development'. *Annual Review of Anthropology* 15: 331–61.

———. 1995. 'The local and the global: The anthropology of globalization and transnationalism'. *Annual Review of Anthropology* 24: 547–65.

———. 2004. *Changing fields of anthropology: From local to global.* Lanham, MD: Rowman & Littlefield.

Kennedy, P. 2007. 'Global transformations but local, "bubble" lives: Taking a reality check on some globalization concepts'. *Globalizations* 4: 267–82.

Knauft, B. M. 2006. 'Anthropology in the middle'. *Anthropological Theory* 6: 407–30.

Koentjaraningrat, R. M. 1985. *Javanese culture.* Singapore: Oxford University Press.

Kuper, A. 1994. 'Culture, identity and the project of a cosmopolitan anthropology'. *Man* 29: 537–54.

LaBianca, Ø. S. and S. A. Scham (eds). 2004. *Connectivity in antiquity: Globalization as a long-term historical process.* London: Equinox.

Lacan, J. 1977. 'The mirror stage as formative of the function of the I', in J. Lacan (ed.), *Écrits: A selection.* New York: W.W. Norton, pp. 1–7.

Lanfant, M.-F. 1995. 'International tourism, internationalization and the challenge to identity', in M.-F. Lanfant, J. B. Allcock and E. M. Bruner (eds), *International tourism: Identity and change.* London: Sage, pp. 24–40.

Latour, B. 1993. *We have never been modern,* trans. C. Porter. Cambridge, MA: Harvard University Press.

———. 2005. *Reassembling the social: An introduction to actor-network theory.* Oxford: Oxford University Press.

Lee, B. and E. LiPuma. 2002. 'Cultures of circulation: The imaginations of modernity'. *Public Culture* 14: 191–213.

Leite, N. and N. H. H. Graburn. 2009. 'Anthropological interventions in tourism studies', in T. Jamal and M. Robinson (eds), *The Sage handbook of tourism studies.* London: Sage, pp. 35–64.

Lengkeek, J. 2001. 'Leisure experience and imagination: Rethinking Cohen's modes of tourist experience'. *International Sociology* 16: 173–84.

Lewellen, T. C. 2002. *The anthropology of globalization: Cultural anthropology enters the 21st century.* Westport, CT: Bergin & Garvey.

Little, K. 1991. 'On safari: The visual politics of a tourist representation', in D. Howes (ed.), *The variety of sensory experience: A sourcebook in the anthropology of the senses.* Toronto: University of Toronto Press, pp. 148–63.

Little, W. E. 2004. *Mayas in the marketplace: Tourism, globalization, and cultural identity.* Austin: University of Texas Press.

Lombard, D. (ed.). 1993. *Rêver l'Asie: Exotisme et littérature coloniale aux Indes, en Indochine et en Insulinde.* Paris: École des Hautes Études en Sciences Sociales.

Lucy, J. A. (ed.). 1993. *Reflexive language: Reported speech and metapragmatics.* Cambridge: Cambridge University Press.

Lutz, C. and J. Collins 1993. *Reading National Geographic.* Chicago: University of Chicago Press.

MacCannell, D. 1973. 'Staged authenticity: Arrangements of social space in tourist settings'. *American Journal of Sociology* 79: 589–603.

———. 1984. 'Reconstructed ethnicity: Tourism and cultural identity in Third World communities'. *Annals of Tourism Research* 11: 375–91.

———. 1992. *Empty meeting grounds: The tourist papers.* London: Routledge.

———. 1999. *The tourist: A new theory of the leisure class,* Revised ed. Berkeley: University of California Press.

MacDonald, S. 2006. 'Mediating heritage: Tour guides at the former Nazi party rally grounds, Nuremberg'. *Tourist Studies* 6: 119–38.

Malcomson, S. L. 1998. 'The varieties of cosmopolitan experience', in P. Cheah and B. Robbins (eds), *Cosmopolitics: Thinking and feeling beyond the nation.* Minneapolis: University of Minnesota Press, pp. 233–45.

Marcus, G. E. 1998. *Ethnography through thick and thin.* Princeton, NJ: Princeton University Press.

Marshall, A. 2008. 'The gods must be restless: Living in the shadow of Indonesia's volcanoes'. *National Geographic* 213: 34–57.

Matsuda, M. 1989. 'Japanese tourists and Indonesia: Images of self and other in the age of Kokusaika (Internationalization)', MA thesis. Canberra: Australian National University.

Mazzarella, W. 2004. 'Culture, globalization, mediation'. *Annual Review of Anthropology* 33: 345–67.

Mbembe, A. 2001. *On the postcolony.* Berkeley: University of California Press.

McCrummen, S. 2007. 'Enticing tourists is an art for Tanzania's safari guides', *Washington Post,* 21 May, AO7.

McGrath, G. 2004. 'Including the outsiders: The contribution of guides to integrated heritage tourism management in Cusco, southern Peru'. *Current Issues in Tourism* 7: 426–32.

McKean, P. F. 1976. 'An anthropological analysis of the culture-brokers of Bali: Guides, tourists and Balinese'. Paper presented at the Joint UNESCO/BRD Seminar on the Social and Cultural Impacts of Tourism, Washington, DC, December 8-10.

Mellinger, W. M. 1994. 'Toward a critical analysis of tourism representations'. *Annals of Tourism Research* 21: 756–79.

Mengara, D. M. (ed.). 2001. *Images of Africa: Stereotypes and realities.* Trenton, NJ: Africa World Press.

Mercille, J. 2005. 'Media effects on image: The case of Tibet'. *Annals of Tourism Research* 32: 1039–55.

Merrington, P. 2001. 'A staggered orientalism: The Cape-to-Cairo imaginary'. *Poetics Today* 22: 323–64.

Merry, S. E. 2000. 'Crossing boundaries: Methodological challenges for ethnography in the twenty-first century'. *Political and Legal Anthropology Review* 23: 127–34.

Michel, F. 2001. *En route pour l'Asie: Le rêve oriental chez les colonisateurs, les aventuriers et les touristes occidentaux,* 2nd ed. Paris: L'Harmattan.

Minca, C. and T. Oakes (eds). 2006. *Travels in paradox: Remapping tourism.* Lanham, MD: Rowman & Littlefield.

Mintz, S. W. 1998. 'The localization of anthropological practice: From area studies to transnationalism'. *Critique of Anthropology* 18: 117–33.

Moeran, B. 1983. 'The language of Japanese tourism'. *Annals of Tourism Research* 10: 93–108.

Molz, J. G. 2005. 'Getting a "flexible eye": Round-the-world travel and scales of cosmopolitan citizenship'. *Citizenship Studies* 9: 517–31.

Moon, O. 1989. *From paddy field to ski slope: The revitalisation of tradition in Japanese village life.* Manchester: Manchester University Press.

Moore, H. L. 2004. 'Global anxieties: Concept-metaphors and pre-theoretical commitments in anthropology'. *Anthropological Theory* 4: 71–88.

Morgan, N. and A. Pritchard. 1998. *Tourism promotion and power: Creating images, creating identities.* Chichester: John Wiley.

Morgan, N., A. Pritchard and R. Pride (eds). 2002. *Destination branding: Creating the unique destination proposition.* Oxford: Butterworth-Heinemann.

Mowforth, M. and I. Munt. 2008. *Tourism and sustainability: Development, globalisation and new tourism in the Third World,* 3rd ed. London: Routledge.

Mulder, N. 1994. *Inside Indonesian society: Cultural change in Java.* Bangkok: Editions Duang Kamol.

———. 2005. *Mysticism in Java: Ideology in Indonesia.* Yogyakarta: Kanisius.

Naipaul, S. 1979. *North of south: An African journey.* New York: Simon and Schuster.

Nash, D. 1996. *Anthropology of tourism.* Tarrytown, NY: Pergamon.

Nava, M. 2002. 'Cosmopolitan modernity: Everyday imaginaries and the register of difference'. *Theory, Culture and Society* 19: 81–99.

Nederveen Pieterse, J. and B. C. Parekh (eds). 1995. *The decolonization of imagination: Culture, knowledge and power.* London: Zed Books.

Ness, S. A. 2003. *Where Asia smiles: An ethnography of Philippine tourism.* Philadelphia: University of Pennsylvania Press.

Neumann, R. P. 1998. *Imposing wilderness: Struggles over livelihood and nature preservation in Africa.* Berkeley: University of California Press.

Norton, A. 1996. 'Experiencing nature: The reproduction of environmental discourse through safari tourism in East Africa'. *Geoforum* 27: 355–73.

Notar, B. E. 2008. 'Producing cosmopolitanism at the borderlands: Lonely planeteers and "local" cosmopolitans in southwest China'. *Anthropological Quarterly* 81: 615–50.

Nurcahya, J. 2006. *English for special purposes: Tour guides.* Jakarta: Kesaint Blanc.

Ong, A. 1999. *Flexible citizenship: The cultural logics of transnationality.* Durham, NC: Duke University Press.

Ong, A. and S. J. Collier (eds). 2004. *Global assemblages: Technology, politics, and ethics as anthropological problems.* New York: Blackwell.

Pajo, E. 2007. *International migration, social demotion, and imagined advancement: An ethnography of socioglobal mobility.* New York: Springer Verlag.

Palmberg, M. (ed.). 2001. *Encounter images in the meetings between Africa and Europe.* Uppsala: The Nordic Africa Institute.

Picard, M. 1996. *Bali: Cultural tourism and touristic culture.* Singapore: Archipelago Press.

Pond, K. L. 1993. *The professional guide: Dynamics of tour guiding.* New York: Van Nostrand Reinhold.

Popovic, V. 1972. *Tourism in Eastern Africa.* München: Weltforum Verlag.

Porter, B. W. and N. B. Salazar (eds). 2005. 'Heritage tourism, conflict, and the public interest'. Theme Issue, *International Journal of Heritage Studies* 11(5).

Prasso, S. 2005. *The Asian mystique: Dragon ladies, geisha girls, and our fantasies of the exotic Orient.* New York: Public Affairs.

Pratt, M. L. 1992. *Imperial eyes: Travel writing and transculturation.* London: Routledge.

Rabinow, P. 1986. 'Representations are social facts: Modernity and post-modernity in anthropology', in J. Clifford and G. E. Marcus (eds), *Writing culture: The poetics and politics of ethnography.* Berkeley: University of California Press, pp. 234–61.

Rapport, N. 2006. 'Anthropology as cosmopolitan study'. *Anthropology Today* 22: 23–24.

Rees, M. W. and J. Smart (eds). 2001. *Plural globalities in multiple localities: New world borders.* Lanham, MD: University Press of America.

Reilly, R. T. 1991. *Handbook of professional tour management,* 2nd ed. New York: Delmar.

Reisinger, Y. and C. J. Steiner. 2006. 'Reconceptualising interpretation: The role of tour guides in authentic tourism'. *Current Issues in Tourism* 9: 481–98.

Rekdal, O. B. 1998. 'When hypothesis becomes myth: The Iraqi origin of the Iraqw'. *Ethnology* 37: 17–38.

Robbins, J. and S. Bamford (eds). 1997. 'Fieldwork revisited: Changing contexts of ethnographic practice in the era of globalization'. Theme issue, *Anthropology and Humanism* 22(1).

Robertson, R. 1992. *Globalization: Social theory and global culture.* London: Sage.

———. 1995. 'Glocalization: Time-space and homogeneity-heterogeneity', in M. Featherstone, S. Lash and R. Robertson (eds), *Global modernities.* London: Sage, pp. 25–44.

Robinson, M. and H. C. Andersen (eds). 2002. *Literature and tourism.* London: Continuum.

Rodman, M. C. 1992. 'Empowering place: Multilocality and multivocality'. *American Anthropologist* 94: 640–56.

Rofé, H. 1980. 'Early cultural contacts between China, Indonesia and East Africa'. *Eastern Horizon* 19: 21–24.

Rosaldo, R. 1993. *Culture and truth: The remaking of social analysis,* 2nd ed. Boston: Beacon.

Rossel, P. (ed.). 1988. *Tourism: Manufacturing the exotic.* Copenhagen: International Work Group for Indigenous Affairs.

Said, E. W. 1994. *Orientalism,* revised ed. New York: Vintage Books.

Saitoti, O. T. 1988. *The worlds of a Maasai warrior: An autobiography of Tepilit Ole Saitoti.* Berkeley: University of California Press.

Salazar, N. B. 2004. 'Developmental tourists vs. development tourism: A case study', in A. Raj (ed.), *Tourist behaviour: A psychological perspective.* New Delhi: Kanishka Publishers, pp. 85–107.

———. 2005. 'Tourism and glocalization: "Local" tour guiding'. *Annals of Tourism Research* 32: 628–46.

———. 2006a. 'Antropología del turismo en países en desarrollo: Análisis crítico de las culturas, poderes e identidades generados por el turismo'. *Tabula Rasa: Revista de Humanidades* 5: 99–128.

———. 2006b. 'Building a "culture of peace" through tourism: Reflexive and analytical notes and queries'. *Universitas Humanística* 62: 319–33.

———. 2006c. 'Touristifying Tanzania: Global discourse, local guides'. *Annals of Tourism Research* 33: 833–52.

———. 2007. 'Towards a global culture of heritage interpretation? Evidence from Indonesia and Tanzania'. *Tourism Recreation Research* 32: 23–30.

———. 2008a. '"Enough stories!" Asian tourism redefining the roles of Asian tour guides'. *Civilisations* 57: 207–22.

———. 2008b. 'Envisioning Eden: A glocal ethnography of tour guiding', PhD dissertation. Philadelphia: University of Pennsylvania.

———. 2009a. 'Imaged or imagined? Cultural representations and the "tourismification" of peoples and places'. *Cahiers d'Études Africaines* 193–194: 49–71.

———. 2009b. 'A troubled past, a challenging present, and a promising future? Tanzania's tourism development in perspective'. *Tourism Review International* 12: 259–73.

———. 2010a. 'Towards an anthropology of cultural mobilities'. *Crossings: Journal of Migration and Culture* 1: 53–68.

———. 2010b. 'From local to global (and back): Towards glocal ethnographies of cultural tourism', in G. Richards and W. Munsters (eds), *Cultural tourism research methods.* Wallingford: CABI, pp. 188–98.

Salazar, N. B., J. Bryon and E. Van Den Branden 2009. *Cultural tourism storytelling in 'Flanders': The story behind the stories.* Leuven: Steunpunt Toerisme.

Salazar, N. B. and B. W. Porter (eds). 2004. 'Heritage and tourism, PIA and global interests'. Theme issue, *Anthropology in Action* 11(2/3).

Santana, A. 1997. *Antropología y turismo ¿Nuevas hordas, viejas culturas?* Barcelona: Ariel.

Sassen, S. 1998. *Globalization and its discontents.* New York: New Press.

———. 2000. 'Spatialities and temporalities of the global: Elements for a theorization'. *Public Culture* 12: 215–32.

Schellhorn, M. and H. C. Perkins. 2004. 'The stuff of which dreams are made: Representations of the South Sea in German-language tourist brochures'. *Current Issues in Tourism* 7: 95–133.

Schlehe, J. 1996. 'Reinterpretations of mystical traditions: Explanations of a volcanic eruption in Java'. *Anthropos* 91: 391–409.

Schwenkel, C. 2006. 'Recombinant history: Transnational practices of memory and knowledge production in contemporary Vietnam'. *Cultural Anthropology* 21: 3–30.

Scott, J. C. 1985. *Weapons of the weak: Everyday forms of peasant resistance.* New Haven, CT: Yale University Press.

———. 1990. *Domination and the arts of resistance: Hidden transcripts.* New Haven, CT: Yale University Press.

Selwyn, T. (ed.). 1996. *The tourist image: Myths and myth making in tourism.* Chichester: John Wiley.

Sheller, M. and J. Urry (eds). 2004. *Tourism mobilities: Places to play, places in play.* London: Routledge.

Sherlock, K. 2001. 'Revisiting the concept of hosts and guests'. *Tourist Studies* 1: 271–95.

Shetler, J. B. 2007. *Imagining Serengeti: A history of landscape memory in Tanzania from earliest times to the present.* Athens: Ohio University Press.

Silverstein, M. 1976. 'Shifters, verbal categories and cultural description', in K. H. Basso and H. A. Selby (eds), *Meaning in anthropology.* Albuquerque: School of American Research, pp. 11–55.

Silverstein, M. and G. Urban (eds). 1996. *Natural histories of discourse.* Chicago: University of Chicago Press.

Smith, V. L. (ed.). 1977. *Hosts and guests: The anthropology of tourism.* Philadelphia: University of Pennsylvania Press.

———. (ed.). 1989. *Hosts and guests: The anthropology of tourism,* 2nd ed. Philadelphia: University of Pennsylvania Press.

Smith, V. L. and M. A. Brent (eds). 2001. *Hosts and guests revisited: Tourism issues of the 21st century.* New York: Cognizant Communication Corporation.

Smithies, M. 1986. *Yogyakarta, cultural heart of Indonesia.* New York: Oxford University Press.

Soebroto, C. 2004. *Indonesia OK!! The guide with a gentle twist.* Yogyakarta: Galang Press.

Spear, T. T. and R. Waller (eds). 1993. *Being Maasai: Ethnicity and identity in East Africa.* London: James Currey.

Spindler, G. D. and J. E. Stockard (eds). 2007. *Globalization and change in fifteen cultures: Born in one world, living in another.* Belmont, CA: Thomson Wadsworth.

Staples, A. J. 2006. 'Safari adventure: Forgotten cinematic journeys in Africa'. *Film History* 18: 392–411.

Stocking, G. W. 1992. *The ethnographer's magic and other essays in the history of anthropology.* Madison: University of Wisconsin Press.

Stoller, P. 2008. *The power of the between: An anthropological odyssey.* Chicago: University of Chicago Press.

Strathern, M. 1991. *Partial connections.* Savage: Rowman & Littlefield.

———. (ed.). 1995. *Shifting contexts: Transformations in anthropological knowledge.* London: Routledge.

Strauss, C. 2006. 'The imaginary'. *Anthropological Theory* 6: 322–44.

Stronza, A. 2001. 'Anthropology of tourism: Forging new ground for ecotourism and other alternatives'. *Annual Review of Anthropology* 30: 261–83.

Sturma, M. 2002. *South Sea maidens: Western fantasy and sexual politics in the South Pacific*. Westport, CT: Greenwood Press.

Sukanta, P. O. 2000. 'Luh Galuh', in J. H. McGlynn (ed.), *Menagerie: Indonesian fiction, poetry, photographs, essays*. Jakarta: The Lontar Foundation, pp. 23–31.

Suntoro, N. 2002. *Conversations on tourism objects*. Jakarta: Kesaint Blanc.

Swain, M. B. 2009. 'The cosmopolitan hope of tourism: Critical action and worldmaking vistas'. *Tourism Geographies* 11: 505–25.

Sylvain, R. 2005. 'Disorderly development: Globalization and the idea of culture in the Kalahari'. *American Ethnologist* 32: 354–70.

Taussig, M. T. 1993. *Mimesis and alterity: A particular history of the senses*. New York: Routledge.

———. 2006. *Walter Benjamin's grave*. Chicago: University of Chicago Press.

Taylor, C. 2004. *Modern social imaginaries*. Durham, NC: Duke University Press.

Thoden van Velzen, H. U. E. 1985. 'The Gaan Gadu cult: Material forces and the social production of fantasy'. *Social Compass* 22: 93–109.

———. 1995. 'Revenants that cannot be shaken: Collective fantasies in a Maroon society'. *American Anthropologist* 97: 722–32.

Thornton, W. H. 2000. 'Mapping the "glocal" village: The political limits of "glocalization"'. *Continuum: Journal of Media & Cultural Studies* 14: 79–89.

Tierney, J. 1992. 'The search for Adam and Eve'. *Newsweek* 111, 46–52.

Tilden, F. 1957. *Interpreting our heritage*. Chapel Hill: University of North Carolina Press.

Tomlinson, J. 1999. *Globalization and culture*. Chicago: University of Chicago Press.

Torgovnick, M. 1990. *Gone primitive: Savage intellects, modern lives*. Chicago: University of Chicago Press.

Traweek, S. 1988. *Beamtimes and lifetimes: The world of high energy physicists*. Cambridge, MA: Harvard University Press.

Trouillot, M.-R. 1995. *Silencing the past: Power and the production of history*. Boston: Beacon Press.

———. 2003. *Global transformations: Anthropology and the modern world*. New York: Palgrave Macmillan.

Tsing, A. L. 2000. 'The global situation'. *Cultural Anthropology* 15: 327–60.

———. 2005. *Friction: An ethnography of global connection*. Princeton, NJ: Princeton University Press.

Tulloch, S. (ed.). 1991. *The Oxford dictionary of new words: A popular guide to words in the news*. Oxford: Oxford University Press.

UNESCO 2005. *Heritage tour guide training and certification for UNESCO World Heritage Sites*. Bangkok: UNESCO Bangkok Office.

———. 2008. *The operational guidelines for the implementation of the World Heritage Convention*. Paris: UNESCO World Heritage Centre

UNWTO 2006. *Tourism highlights. 2006 edition*. Madrid: United Nations World Tourism Organization.

———. 2008. *Tourism highlights. 2008 edition*. Madrid: United Nations World Tourism Organization.

Urbain, J.-D. 1994. *L'idiot du voyage: Histoires de touristes*. Paris: Éditions Payot & Rivages.

Urban, G. 1991. *A discourse-centered approach to culture.* Austin: University of Texas Press.
———. 1996. 'Entextualization, replication, and power', in M. Silverstein and G. Urban (eds), *Natural histories of discourse.* Chicago: The University of Chicago Press, pp. 21–44.
———. 2001. *Metaculture: How culture moves through the world.* Minneapolis: University of Minnesota Press.
Urry, J. 2002. *The tourist gaze,* 2nd ed. London: Sage.
———. 2003. *Global complexity.* Cambridge: Polity Press.
———. 2007. *Mobilities.* Cambridge: Polity Press.
Van den Berghe, P. L. 1994. *The quest for the Other: Ethnic tourism in San Cristóbal, Mexico.* Seattle: University of Washington Press.
Vertovec, S. and R. Cohen (eds). 2002. *Conceiving cosmopolitanism: Theory, context and practice.* Oxford: Oxford University Press.
Vogler, C. 2002. 'Social imaginary, ethics, and methodological individualism'. *Public Culture* 14: 625–27.
Wallace, T. (ed.). 2005. 'Tourism and applied anthropologists: Linking theory and practice'. Theme issue, *NAPA Bulletin* 23.
Weaver, A. 2005. 'Interactive service work and performative metaphors: The case of the cruise industry'. *Tourist Studies* 5: 5–27.
Weiler, B. and S. Ham. 2001. 'Tour guides and interpretation', in D. Weaver (ed.), *The encyclopedia of ecotourism.* Wallingford: CABI, pp. 549–63.
Weiss, B. 2002. 'Thug realism: Inhabiting fantasy in urban Tanzania'. *Cultural Anthropology* 17: 1–32.
Wels, H. 2002. 'A critical reflection on cultural tourism in Africa: The power of European imagery', in J. S. Akama and P. Sterry (eds), *Cultural tourism in Africa: Strategies for the new millennium.* Arnhem: Association for Tourism and Leisure Education, pp. 55–66.
Werbner, P. (ed.). 2008. *Anthropology and the new cosmopolitanism: Rooted, feminist and vernacular perspectives.* Oxford: Berg.
Werner, C. 2003. 'The new Silk Road: Mediators and tourism development in Central Asia'. *Ethnology* 42: 141–61.
Wilding, R. 2007. 'Transnational ethnographies and anthropological imaginings of migrancy'. *Journal of Ethnic and Migration Studies* 33: 331–48.
Winter, T., P. Teo and T. C. Chang (eds). 2008. *Asia on tour: Exploring the rise of Asian tourism.* London: Routledge.
Woolard, K. A. 2004. 'Codeswitching', in A. Duranti (ed.), *A companion to linguistic anthropology.* Malden, MA: Blackwell, pp. 73–92.
WTO 2001. *Tourism 2020 vision.* Madrid: World Tourism Organization.
———. 2002. *Sustainable development of ecotourism: A compilation of good practices.* Madrid: World Tourism Organization.
WTTC 2007. *The 2007 travel and tourism economic research.* London: World Travel & Tourism Council.
Wynn, L. L. 2007. *Pyramids and nightclubs: A travel ethnography of Arab and Western imaginations of Egypt.* Austin: University of Texas Press.

Yamashita, S. 2000. 'The Japanese encounter with the South: Japanese tourists in Palau'. *Contemporary Pacific* 12: 437–63.

———. 2003. *Bali and beyond: Explorations in the anthropology of tourism,* trans. J. S. Eades. New York: Berghahn.

Young, K. G. 1987. *Taleworlds and storyrealms: The phenomenology of narrative.* Dordrecht: Nijhoff.

Yu, X., B. Weiler and S. Ham 2001. 'Intercultural communication and mediation: A framework for analysing intercultural competence of Chinese tour guides'. *Journal of Vacation Marketing* 8: 75–87.

———. 2004. 'Cultural mediation in guided tour experiences: A case study of Australian guides of Chinese tour groups', *Working Paper 44/04.* Berwick: Monash University, Department of Management.

# Index

# New Directions in Anthropology